MICHAEL N

THE
PHOTOGRAPHY
BIBLE

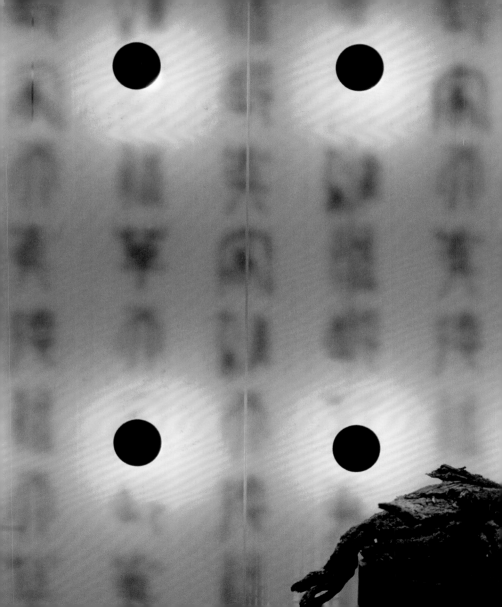

MICHAEL FREEMAN

THE
PHOTOGRAPHY
BIBLE

ALL YOU NEED TO KNOW TO TAKE PERFECT PHOTOS

ilex

An Hachette UK Company

www.hachette.co.uk

First published in Great Britain in 2018
by ILEX, an imprint of
Octopus Publishing Group Ltd

Octopus Publishing Group
Carmelite House
50 Victoria Embankment
London EC4Y 0DZ

www.octopusbooks.co.uk
www.octopusbooksusa.com

Design, layout and text copyright
© Octopus Publishing Group Ltd 2018

All photography © Michael Freeman
unless otherwise indicated.

Distributed in the US
by Hachette Book Group
1290 Avenue of the Americas,
4th and 5th Floors,
New York NY 10104

Distributed in Canada
by Canadian Manda Group
664 Annette St.,
Toronto, Ontario,
Canada M6S 2C8

Publisher, Photography: Adam Juniper
Managing Editor: Frank Gallaugher
Publishing Assistant:
  Stephanie Hetherington
Art Director: Julie Weir
Designer: Ellie Wilson
Senior Production Manager:
  Pete Hunt

ISBN 978-1-78157-623-6

A CIP catalogue record for this book
is available from the British Library.

Printed and bound in China

10 9 8 7 6 5 4 3 2 1

Contents

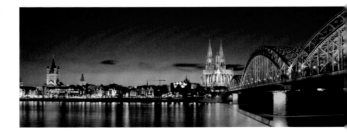

Introduction

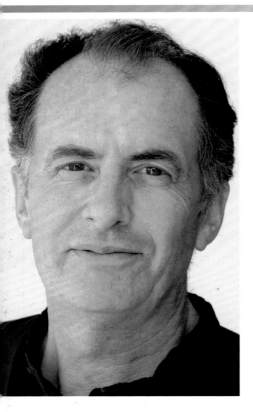

Where this book differs from the many others on basic photography is that we've designed it as a learning course in which I'm inviting you to participate, in much the same way that you would if you were attending an actual, physical course or an online one. The structure goes as follows. There are four sections that cover what I believe to be the essentials in learning photography: Exposure, Composition, Light & Lighting, and Processing. Each of these is divided into learning units, at the end of which is a Challenge. To get the most out of this book, I strongly recommend that you follow it in the order it's presented, rather than just dipping in here and there. Exposure will teach you not just how to get the camera settings to work, but how to think independently, more than following some idea of correctness. Composition is fundamental, and in the process of learning how to organize things in the frame, will encourage you to think about what and why you are shooting. Light & Lighting comes next, because this is the commodity with which we all work. Finally, Processing makes the most of your original inspiration, always purposeful, serving the image rather than playing with it. Most of all, I urge you to actually take up the Challenges that follow each unit, and put what you learn into practice.

~ *Michael Freeman*

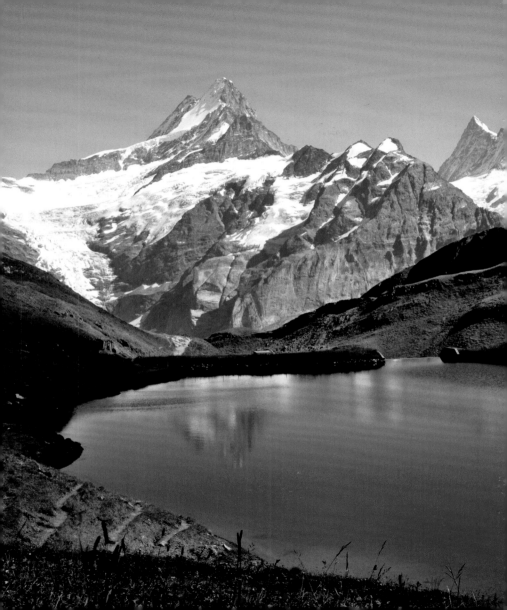

CHAPTER 1 | Exposure

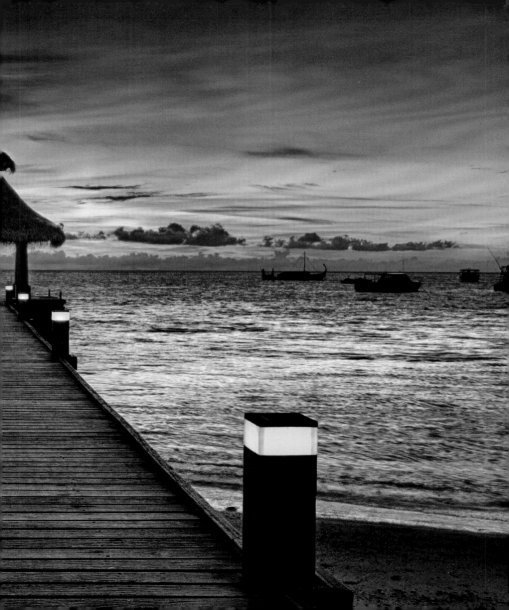

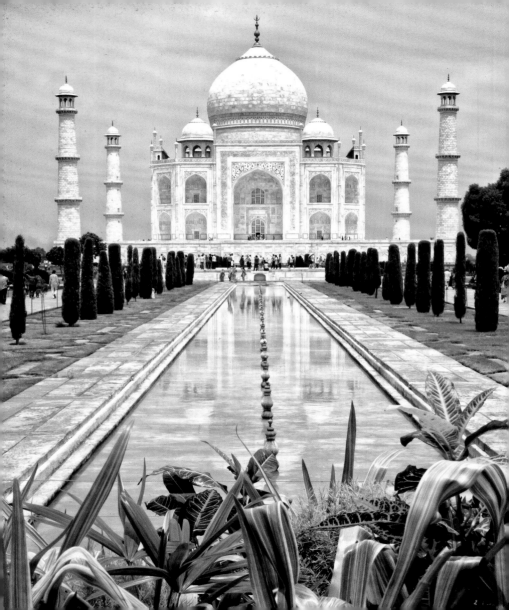

Introduction: Exposure

It has become easy to take exposure for granted. The automatic exposure functions on today's cameras are impressive pieces of technology, capable of producing excellent images all on their own (hence the Auto setting). There is something to be said for this, as it makes photography considerably more inviting and approachable, and is in no small part responsible for the democratization of photography that we've been enjoying for several decades (aided by autofocus, always-with-you cell-phone cameras, advanced processing tools, and the ease of sharing and displaying digital images online).

Yet, there is a significant drawback to automation. It encourages exposure to be rigidly understood as something that is either right or wrong—a problem to be solved. There is an element of truth in this, insofar as there is, in the end, just one dosage of light, manipulated by shutter speed, aperture, and ISO (or film speed), just as there has been for over a century. While some wax philosophical about how to interpret exposure, the final decision is a combination of just three simple factors. The problem is that viewing exposure in such a clinical way robs you, as a creative artist, of a significant and, frankly, enjoyable component of your art. There is another open-ended, highly subjective side to exposure. Two people can view the same scene and choose to represent it in entirely different ways. How you choose to capture a scene depends on your receptiveness to the subtle interplays of light and shadow, what you consider significant versus peripheral, the mood you want to impart to the viewer, and so on. Over time, these exposure decisions will form your personal aesthetic style. Some like it bright, some like it dark. Some need everything tack-sharp, others don't mind soft edges and a bit of blur. Photography is big enough to accommodate all these approaches, and exposure is the means by which you can achieve them.

And that's the purpose of this chapter: to give you an understanding of the exposure tools available, so that when the moment calls for it, you can not only determine the optimal settings for the best exposure, but also what that "best" exposure is, and what other options and interpretations exist. We also emphasize the moment of capture over processing, with the goal being to capture optimal data in-camera. Doing so will give you the most leeway during processing when you work on your Raw image files; but more importantly, this approach will reinforce the significance of your exposure decisions each step of the way, so you can work knowledgeably and effectively.

A Record of Tonalities

At its most basic, exposure is about one thing: getting the ideal amount of light to the camera's digital sensor so that the scene is captured as closely as possible to the way that it looked to you at the time. Record too much light and the image is overexposed and too bright—shadows are bland and highlights are completely without detail. Capture too little light and your image is underexposed—shadows are cast into dark blobs void of detail, and highlights and middle tones are muddled. In most cases, the ideal exposure lies somewhere between those two extremes.

Technically, your goal (and the camera's function) is to record the values in a scene in a way that looks similar to what your eyes saw. In a winter landscape, for instance, you want the snow to look white, the dark tree trunks to be nearly black, and most of the rest of the scene to fall between the two. Using just a light meter and few exposure controls, capturing such an exposure can be reduced to a very predictable process. A lot of clever engineering has gone into making the process quite painless, giving you time to concentrate on the creative side.

As you start out in photography, knowing how to carefully combine the settings of those exposure controls is an essential skill to master in order to create a good technical exposure. And as with any new skill, learning these fundamentals is at the core of creative growth. Great jazz musicians can't fly off into an inspired improvisation, can't twist and explore and return to a melody until they have mastered the basic skills of playing that melody first. Photography is very similar: You must know how a camera captures and records light before you can alter the camera's response.

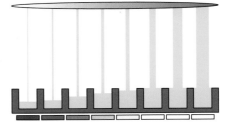

↑ **Filling the photosites**
Once the camera's shutter opens, the photosites (pixels) on the sensor's surface begin to fill with light. The more light, the fuller the well and the lighter the tone will be. But when completely full, the result is featureless white.

→ **Simple settings, complex solutions**
Understanding how basic camera settings control the amount and duration of light that reaches your camera's sensor is at the root of all exposures. Master this knowledge and no subject is beyond your control.

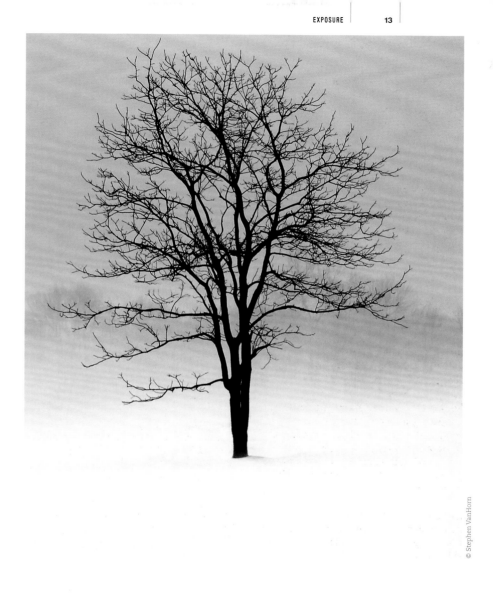

HUMAN VERSUS DIGITAL DYNAMIC RANGE

Unfortunately (or perhaps fortunately, depending on your point of view), the way your camera sees the world and the way it appears to your eyes and brain are two radically different things. For one, your eyes have an astounding and rapid ability to see an extraordinary contrast range. It's nothing for your eyes to see detail in the darkest shadow of a rock at midday and then, in a flicker, find detail in the white petals of a sunlit flower. Your eyes and brain together are constantly adjusting to the brightness range or "dynamic range" of your surroundings. Focus on a shadow and your pupils open to accept more light. Glance into a sunlight patch, your pupils close down instantly to control the burst of light. Given time to adjust to the changing conditions, your eyes can see across a dynamic range that is equal to more than 24 "stops" in camera terms.

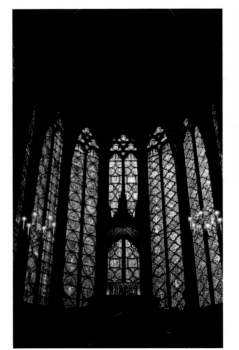

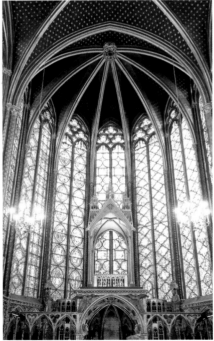

Your camera, on the other hand, is limited to capturing the finite dynamic range of its sensor—with contemporary sensors capturing a range of 10–14 stops of light, depending on the particular camera model. If you exceed that range at either end by trying to include too broad a range of darks and lights, something has to give: you will lose one end of the dynamic range or the other. There are methods, such as high-dynamic-range imaging, for extending that range and we'll discuss those later in this book. The challenge of a good exposure is to work within the fixed limitations of a camera's technology while at the same time exploiting the maximum emotional content from your subjects. And that is essentially what this chapter is about.

CONTROLLING EXPOSURE

Given the creative range that exposure can produce in a photograph, it's interesting that exposure is entirely a product of just three camera controls: ISO setting, lens aperture, and shutter speed. Every exposure, every creative

effect, and every manipulation or exaggeration of the light is created by the careful and clever combination of those three settings. ISO numbers are a relatively recent invention, but throughout the history of photography, the sensitivity of emulsions has been a factor, and these three controls haven't changed fundamentally since the earliest days. We can calculate exposure times in thousandths of seconds or use standardized apertures and ISOs, but the basic concepts remain the same.

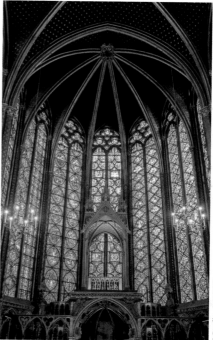

© Fotolia—IMAGINE

← ← → Tough decisions
This bracket of three exposures shows how delicate a process it can be to fit all the tones of an image in a single shot. A little too dark (the underexposed far-left shot), and the detail in the windows is there, but the architectural interior is lost to shadow. A little too bright (left) and the interior is there, but the windows are washed out. A middle exposure (right) balances these too extremes (helped with a bit of Raw processing—see page 260).

The Optimum Exposure for You

It's important to eliminate, or at least try to suppress, the idea that for every photo there is such a thing as a right or wrong exposure. While you certainly want to understand how to capture the tonalities in a scene so that you aren't sacrificing essential detail, you don't need to adhere to anyone else's definition of what a correct exposure should look like.

For example, there is nothing wrong with grossly underexposing a colorful sunset to saturated the colors. Nor is there anything wrong with providing too much exposure and creating a high-key interpretation (see page 96). Most great strides in art have been achieved by those who pierced through conventional barriers and expanded the territory of what is correct—Picasso, Van Gogh, Monet. (Though you can be certain that all knew the standard techniques well before shattering them.)

Were the entire world and all its scenery colored a consistent middle-toned gray, there would be no need for this chapter in the book, as your camera would never struggle to determine its exposure. Quite fortunately, the world is a bit more varied than that. Subjects present themselves in hues, saturation, and brightness, illuminated by a wide variety of lighting conditions (which themselves have their own subtle colors—see page 66), struck at angles that reveal contours and textures that can be highlighted or hidden at your discretion.

ʞ Underexposed for drama
One photographer's underexposure is another's idyllic sunset. As you become comfortable with the nuances of exposure, its technical accuracy will take on a more subjective outlook.

↓ Overexposed for vibrancy
This shot required a creative override of the camera's metering system, which typically fights against letting massive areas of the frame blow out to pure white.

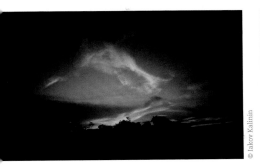

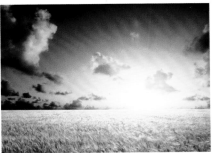

© Iakov Kalinin

© Iakov Kalinin

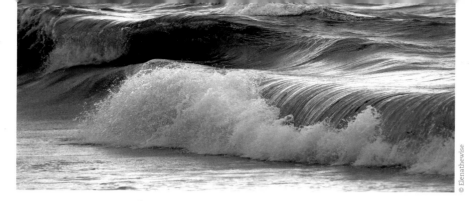

That discretion over how you choose to capture any given scene is your most powerful tool. While your camera can compute the exposure, it is up to you to take control and learn when to override your camera's decisions and assert your own vision for your photography. Some of that creative vision will deviate from your camera's suggested exposure—recognizing that, in fact, you prefer this scene with heavy, blocked-up shadows and a resulting sense of foreboding, or another with so much pure bright white you can barely make out your subject emerging from an ethereal cloud.

Other times, you will depend on a precise reading from your camera, but you will still need to ensure it is reading the specific area of the scene you want to base your exposure on. There is never a place in this photographic journey in which you should not be asserting yourself as the ultimate decider of proper, ideal, or "right" exposure.

↑ **Countless possibilities**
There are countless ways to capture this wave —a high shutter speed to freeze each drop, or a slower one for a more painterly effect; cold white balance to keep the blues of the water intact, or warm to infuse the image with a golden hue.

↓ **Not always shooting for a catalog**
If the goal was to accurately represent the shape of an apple, this photo would be a failure. But the apple itself isn't what was important; rather, it was the interplay of light and shadow.

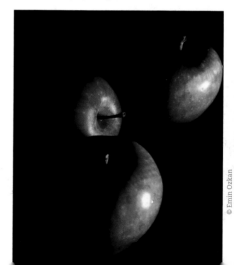

Underexposure & Overexposure

UNDEREXPOSURE

Images that are underexposed, either intentionally or by poor exposure choices, are those that appear darker than they did to the eye because they haven't received enough light. Often, scenes can be underexposed by design to give them drama or mood. In the Venezuelan Andes scene below, for example, intentional underexposure was used to contrast the brilliance of the white buildings against the dark mountain shapes. A slight amount of underexposure can be a good tool for saturating colors and bringing highlights under control—a good technique when shooting landscapes where you want to stress the intense colors of the sky without letting them overflow into pure white. Too much underexposure, however, tends to hide details and textures in shadow areas, and bunches up darker tonalities rather than revealing nuances in the dark areas of a scene.

Generally speaking, even when you are underexposing for dramatic effect, it's rare that you want to lose all details in darker areas of a scene, partly because such an exposure will also drag highlights down—though again, this is subjective. There's nothing wrong, for instance, with exposing for the delicate light tones of a clump of tulips so that the highlights become closer to middle tones and the shadows become a field of black around them. The tulips would fall into a more neutral palette, but this can create an unexpectedly dark mood. Often just the surprise factor of such extreme under-exposure is enough to draw attention.

↙ **Through a glass, darkly**
Intentional underexposure is a powerful tool for exaggerating or even fabricating mood. What the meter thinks is too little may be just enough.

↓ **The riches of saturation**
Correct exposure is fine for family snapshots, but art comes from having the courage to depart from reality. Just a few stops of underexposure turn tulips from ordinary to elegant.

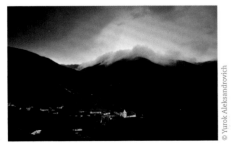

© Yurok Aleksandrovich

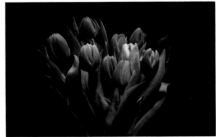

© Yurok Aleksandrovich

OVEREXPOSURE

Overexposure happens when a scene gets more light than is required for a "normal" exposure, and tones are recorded as lighter than they appear to the eye or to expectations. The danger of overexposing scenes is that, even when slight, detail may be completely lost in the lightest tones. There is a fine line between capturing the delicacy of a white swan feather, for example, and losing detail completely. Digital sensors are more prone to overexposure errors than film, and for that reason you'll often hear the advice "expose for the highlights" when shooting digitally. By exposing so that highlight areas retain fine detail you avoid having "blank" areas in the lighter tones where there is simply no discernible detail or surface texture.

Creative use of overexposure can produce interesting visual effects and often establishes a light, cheerful interpretation, particularly with light-toned and pastel-colored subjects. If you're photographing a field of tall yellow grasses in brilliant sunshine, for example, a small amount of extra exposure will exaggerate the dreamy, romantic quality of the scene. The danger of too much exposure, however, is that you'll lose so much detail in brighter-toned areas that the image will cross into the realm of abstraction or impressionism. That's not a problem if it's your intention, but such scenes can look like they were made with sloppy exposure technique—it's a fine creative line. In general, the rule in digital exposure is to expose for the highlights and correct for the shadows in processing.

↙ **Bright window light**
Too much light? Depends on the mood you're trying to establish. A bit of overexposure adds lightness to the atmosphere of a photo, as well as the tonalities.

↓ **Clipped wings**
"Clipping" is a term used to describe highlights that have received too much exposure and lost all detail as a result. It's unavoidable in some situations, but should always be carefully monitored.

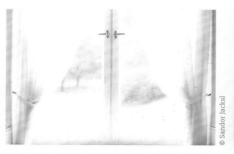
© Sandor Jackal

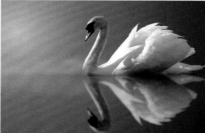
© Joss

Creative Use of Over- Or Underexposure

Challenge

"Correct" exposure renders the world the way that most people perceive it, but as you now know, with intentional underexposure or overexposure, you can radically transform not only the look of a scene, but its emotional climate as well. By making a shift toward lighter tones, for example, you can transform a morning meadow into a lifting, high-key melody; by subtracting exposure from a dim scene of an industrial block, you drag it into a gloomy low-key dirge. And that is your challenge: to use the extremes of exposure to value mood and expression above reality.

↓ **Overexposure as a choice**
The dynamic range of the frame required a creative exposure decision one way or the other, and having the sledder emerging from a bloom of pure white on the right is more expressive.

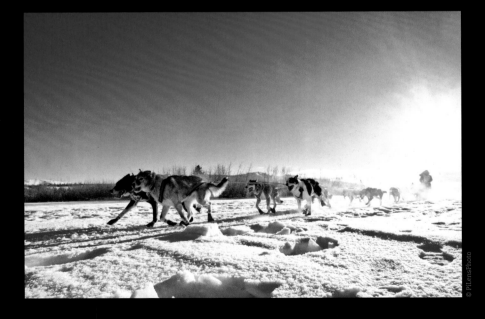

© PiLensPhoto

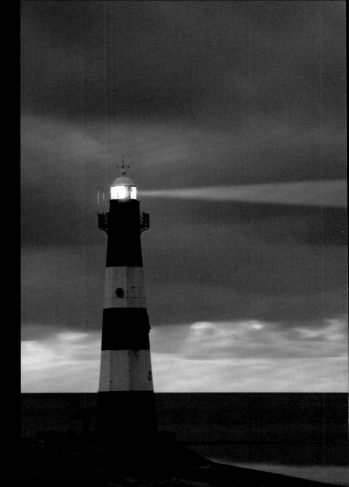

Capturing twilight

While your camera's metering system will happily boost dropping light levels to maintain a consistent, bright exposure, we tend to expect an underexposed rendering of twilight shots, as that is how we perceive such scenes—lighter than night, but darker than day.

Challenge Checklist

→ Ignore the boundaries implied by the histogram and intentionally push tones past the brink.

→ Use your exposure compensation control to add or subtract exposure, or shoot in the manual mode to override meter suggestions.

→ Be sure to match your exaggerated moods to your choice of subject.

→ Shoot in Raw and experiment with radical exposure changes after the fact.

ISO Speeds

The ISO setting on your digital camera enables you to adjust the light sensitivity of the image sensor. As with film, the higher the ISO number, the more responsive the sensor is to light; and the lower the setting, the less sensitive it is. In bright light you can use a lower ISO number and get a good, clean response; but if you find yourself shooting in a dim lighting situation (indoors by existing light, for example), you can raise the setting to increase the sensitivity of the sensor's response. So why not always use a high ISO? Because it comes with the price of noise, and so the highest image quality goes hand in hand with the lowest ISO.

Most digital cameras have both an automatic ISO mode and a manual setting. In auto mode, the camera will evaluate the amount of ambient light and set the ISO speed for you. The auto setting is useful if the ambient light is changing quickly—ducking in and out of historic buildings, for example—and you don't want to have to change the setting every few minutes. In manual mode, you have to assess the light and then set the

→ **A more sensitive response**
By raising the ISO speed, your camera responds better to low-light situations and avoids the necessity of turning on flash. But there's no such thing as a free lunch, and the price for the extra sensitivity is digital noise.

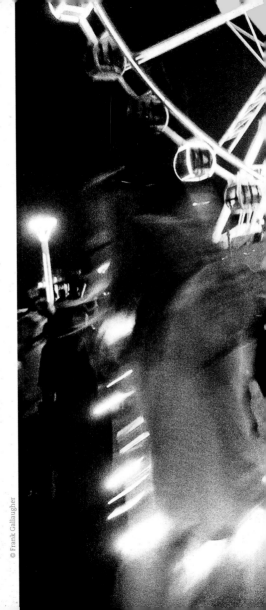

© Frank Gallaugher

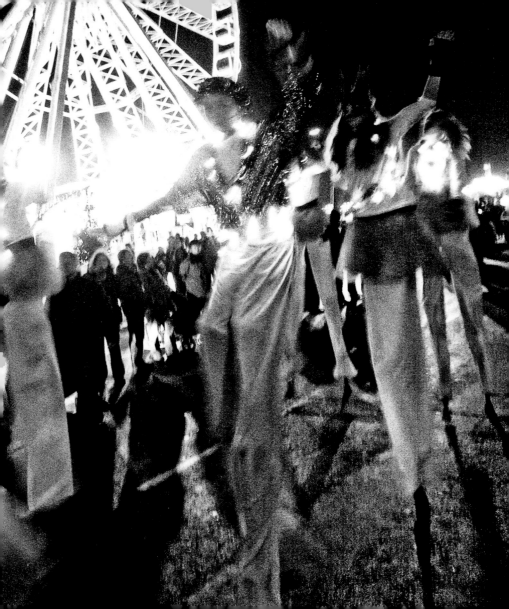

ISO setting using your judgement. All cameras have a default setting (typically ISO 100 or 200) that provides highest image quality when there is an abundance of existing light.

The beauty of having a variable ISO setting is that you can change it shot to shot. In the film days, changing the ISO meant changing an entire roll of film. With a digital camera, however, you can be shooting at a low ISO setting in bright sunlight one moment and then switch to a faster setting when you head indoors.

One important fact to keep in mind is that the sensitivity response of your sensor doubles each time you double the ISO. If you switch from the default setting of ISO 200 to a setting of ISO 400, for example, you double the sensor's response to light. Similarly, each time that you halve the ISO number you cut the sensitivity in half. Doubling (or halving) the camera's sensitivity can have significant technical and creative effects in terms of exposure.

ISO settings typically range from ISO 100 to ISO 6400 and above in most consumer cameras, with much higher settings in professional cameras. Top-end professional models now boast a maximum setting in excess of ISO 200,000—presumably for photographing fast-moving black panthers in the jungle on a moonless night.

ISO AND IMAGE NOISE

Being able to adjust the ISO does not come without a price—namely that of noise. Noise is a random textured pattern that occurs when you use an excessively high ISO speed. The amount of noise depends on several factors including the size and design of the sensor, and whether you've tried to pull up shadow detail in processing. In general, the higher the ISO and/or the smaller the sensor, the more likely you are to see noise.

Technically, noise is the result of electrical interference ("cross talk") between the photosites (pixels) on a sensor, and the more photosites there are, the greater the noise. That is why smaller sensors that have more pixels produce more noise. Larger sensors enable the pixels to be spaced farther apart and allow for greater isolation of their signals. Noise increases at higher ISO speeds because the analog-to-digital converter in-camera magnifies the signal from each photosite that in turn magnifies the interference that results in noise.

In general, you are better off using the lowest ISO that will provide the aperture and shutter speed combinations you require. Manufacturers continue to make great strides in reducing noise and increasing available ISO speeds, and the ability to shoot pictures in extremely low-light settings far outweighs the distraction of a small amount of noise.

↓ Into the night

It is important to keep perspective when evaluating your image for noise levels. What looks like a grainy mess at 100% magnification, may be perfectly fine at a reasonable viewing distance. Additionally, noise reduction is a powerful processing tool that can often salvage shots, provided you have the time.

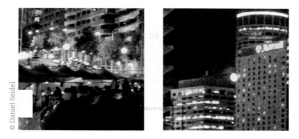

© Daniel Seidel

↓ The price of speed

The price of increased sensor speed is an increase in image noise. It's a price worth paying if it means getting a shot you would otherwise lose.

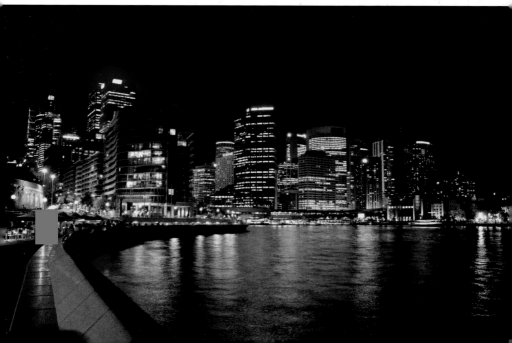

Get the Shot with a High ISO

Challenge

With ISO speeds of 3200 and 6400 common and with some cameras boasting speeds up to the 200,000 range, you can pretty much always find a way to expose even the dimmest of subjects. And so for this challenge, take a look into the nighttime world or into the realm of dim interior spaces and use your highest ISO settings to wrest properly exposed images from them. Try most of all to bring back images of subjects that you thought were beyond capturing: city streets at midnight, the unlit interior of a cathedral, or your favorite band in the local basement pub.

↓ **Not quite pure black**
Concerts in dark venues are a classic high-ISO scenario. Fortunately, the subject is often rather accommodating of a grittier, noisier rendering, as it suits the visceral feeling of such scenes.

© Konstantin Tavrov

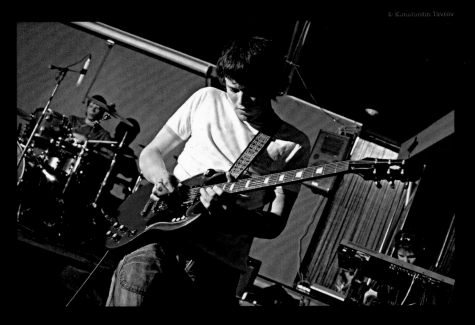

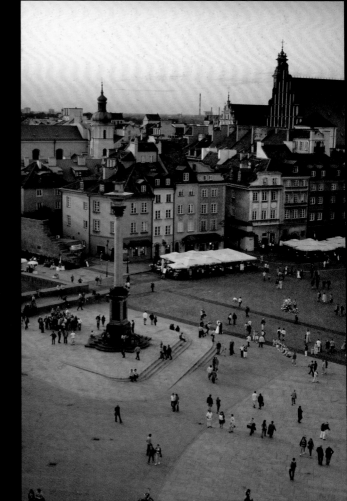

→ ISO as a failsafe

This required a fast shutter speed for a sharp shot (considering the moving subjects and the long focal length) and also a small aperture for the depth of field to stretch all the way to the horizon. Add in the dropping light levels of dusk, and a high ISO (1600) was the only way to adequately capture the shot.

Challenge Checklist

→ Each time you double the ISO, you are doubling the amount of light that reaches your camera's sensor. Doubling the ISO has the same effect as opening the lens a full stop or slowing the shutter a full stop.

→ Often metering is less reliable than just raising the ISO incrementally and viewing your results. Find an ISO speed that will record adequately without image noise becoming oppressive.

→ Using a wide-aperture will help get more light to the sensor. If noise is a distraction, try shooting at a more moderate ISO with a wider aperture.

Lens Apertures

Whether you are using a simple compact or a sophisticated mirrorless or DSLR, the purpose of the lens aperture is exactly the same—to regulate the amount of light that is allowed to pass through the lens to the camera's sensor. The size of the aperture is referred to as the f-stop and is controlled either electronically or, on older lenses, by a mechanical ring on the lens known as the aperture ring. In simplest terms, the larger the aperture opening is, the more light gets into the camera and onto the sensor; and the smaller the opening, the less light reaches the sensor. If you were to close the lens aperture entirely, of course, no light would reach the sensor at all; and at the other end, there is a limit as to how wide a lens can open (its "maximum aperture"). That maximum aperture is different depending on each lens, and with many zoom lenses, the maximum aperture is variable, meaning that it will narrow as you zoom in closer and reach into longer focal lengths.

In order to be able to use lens aperture to control either exposure or focus, it's important to understand how the f-stops are numbered and why. In fact, the more that you understand about the f-stop numbering system, the simpler the concepts become. The available number of full and partial f-stops on a given lens (or the electronic options for those settings provided by the camera) will vary by lens brand/model and by the camera's exposure system, but all lenses use the exact same sequence of full f-stops, illustrated below.

The concept is far simpler to understand if you think of the aperture numbers as multiples of each other. Each f-stop in the sequence allows double the exposure of its neighbor on one side, and half the exposure of its neighbor on the other. This is why the numerical sequence looks a little strange at first—because it's a logarithmic sequence, with bigger

↓ Larger numbers = smaller openings
If there's owne concept you should take away from these pages it's that the larger the f-number is, the smaller the opening is, and vice versa. If you want to let in more light, switch to a larger opening.

$f/16$	$f/11$	$f/8$	$f/5.6$	$f/4$	$f/2.8$	$f/2$	$f/1.4$

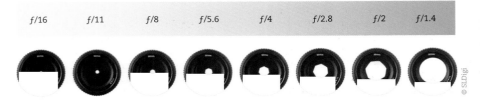

© SLDigi

apparent leaps between numbers the higher up you go. So, while the difference between 1.4 and 2 may look smaller than that between 11 and 16, in fact both steps are the same—halving the amount of light allowed through the lens. That sounds complicated only because you shouldn't think of f-numbers as a normal, numerical sequence. All you need to do is acquaint yourself with the standard f-stop sequence and you'll be ready to shoot with any camera.

CONTROLING DEPTH OF FIELD

In addition to its purely exposure-driven purpose of regulating the amount of light that reaches the sensor, the aperture also controls how much of the scene is in focus. When you focus your lens, you are moving a single, two-dimensional plane of ideal sharpness closer to and farther away from the sensor. However, the vast majority of subjects are three-dimensional, extending in front of and behind that ideal plane of focus, and in order to capture them sharply, you likewise need to expand that plane into a three-dimensional zone of sharp focus.

The name for that zone is the depth of field, and it is directly controlled by the aperture: the wider the aperture (the lower the f-number), the shallower the depth of field; and the smaller the aperture (the higher the f-number), the deeper the depth of field. Use a small enough aperture, and you can fit most of what is in front of you in focus, from the

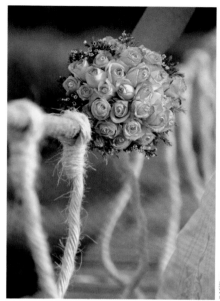

© Villiers

↑ **Pick your plane of focus**
In this shot, you can see that the bouquet of roses, situated midway into the scene, is sharp and in-focus, while the ropes extending in front of and behind the bouquet gradually fall out of focus in either direction. That is because a wide aperture ($f/2$) was used to create a shallow depth of field, and the lens was then focused to position the bouquet precisely within this depth of field, allowing the peripheral elements of the scene to fall off into the out-of-focus areas.

foreground all the way to the horizon line. Use a wide enough aperture, and you can sharply isolate a portrait subject against a soft, blurred out-of-focus background, concentrating attention only on what is important.

The Math Behind the Numbers

Let's look in more detail at the size of the aperture. The f-stop numbers represent the ratio of the physical aperture diameter to the focal length of the lens. For example, if you're using a 120mm lens and you're using an aperture of $f/4$, then the physical size of the aperture is 30mm or a quarter of 120. If you moved to a larger aperture (again, a smaller f-number) such as $f/2$, the size of the lens aperture would be 60mm (because 60mm is one-half of 120mm).

↓ Know when to take your time
With static landscape shots, time is often on your side, and you will be able to experiment with a variety of different exposure settings.

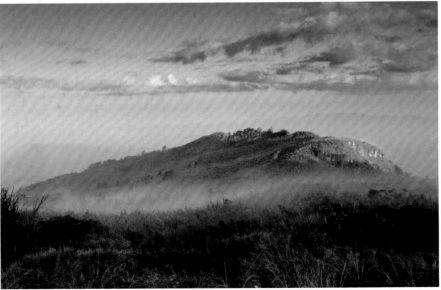

© lkunl

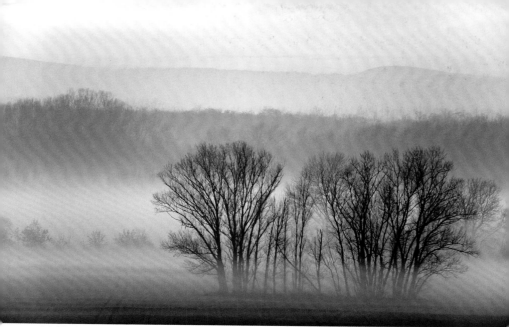

© Gudellaphoto

STOPS VERSUS F-STOPS

Before we continue with our discussions of exposure, it's important to clarify that while f-stops refer to apertures specifically, "stops" is often used to refer to exposure more generally, and relate equally to ISO, aperture, or—as you'll see on page 36—shutter speed. So, when you hear that exposure is decreased "by three stops," this can mean a narrow aperture was set, but it can also mean a lower ISO or a faster shutter speed was used. In terms of the final exposure, there is no difference.

↑ **Consider the side effects of aperture**
The light was low, but the aperture had to remain small in order to capture both the trees and the distant mountains sharply. So either the ISO needed to be boosted, or a slower shutter speed used (fortunately, a tripod made the latter the easy choice).

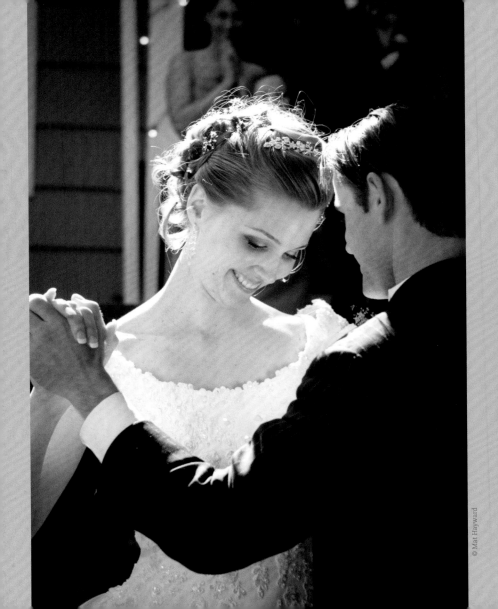

APERTURE CHANGES
& EXPOSURE CHANGES

One very significant bit of aperture math that it's important to understand is that each time you shift from one f-stop to another f-stop that is either a whole-stop larger or a whole-stop smaller, you either double or halve the amount of light that reaches the sensor. Suppose, for example, when you shift from a setting of $f/8$ to $f/5.6$ (an opening that is one whole-stop larger), you are doubling the amount of light that reaches the sensor. If you were to "close" the aperture by one stop and change from $f/8$ to $f/11$ (again, that's a change of one full stop), you would cut the mount of light reaching the sensor in half.

As you may remember from our discussion of ISO speeds, the exact same relationship exists when you change between apertures. If you set twice as big an aperture, you double the amount of light reaching the sensor. If you halve the aperture, you halve the amount of light. So, for example, if you change from a setting of $f/2.8$ to a setting of $f/2$, you double the light reaching the sensor. But if you cut the $f/2.8$ aperture down to $f/4$, you cut the amount of light being gathered in half.

The doubling and halving of exposures occurs with each of the three exposure controls, including shutter speed—as you are about to learn—and is of course deliberate, making it easier and more practical to juggle the three settings.

In other words, the relationship between the three controls is reciprocal. Though it may take some getting used to at the start, once you understand it you will rejoice in its simplicity, and exploit it for consistent, accurate exposures.

© Narcis Parfenti

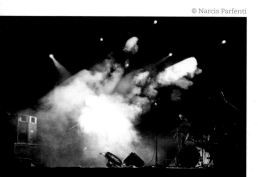

← An elegant relationship
Aperture and the amount of light reaching the lens have a profound relationship that is both simple and elegant: open the lens by one stop, the light doubles, close it by one stop, the light drops by a half. In order to maintain a consistent exposure, you must compensate for the f-stop changes with either an ISO or shutter-speed adjustment.

← Making radical changes
One of the things that an adjustable aperture allows is a rapid response to changes in the quantity of light. If you're working with an autoexposure mode (see pages 46–47), those changes will take place instantaneously.

Demonstrate Depth-of-Field Control

Challenge

Once you understand the forces that control depth of field—aperture, focal length, and subject distance—you have control over what is or isn't in a scene. A wide-angle lens and a small aperture can create images that are in sharp focus from your toes to the horizon. A long-focal-length lens and a wide aperture can restrict depth of field to as little as a few inches. For this challenge, demonstrate you understand how to control depth of field, and match it to an appropriate subject: selective focus in a portrait, for example, or boundless sharpness in a rural landscape.

↓ **Fitting it all in**
When looking for maximum depth of field, focus about a third of the way into the scene, as the depth of field extends disproportionately in either direction away from the plane of focus (except for extreme close-ups): 1/3 of the total depth of field extends in front of the focused plane, while 2/3 of it extends beyond.

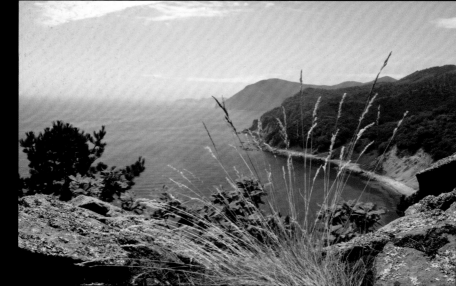

→ **Blurred but visible**
With careful composition, you can make out-of-focus subjects a meaningful part of your shot.

Challenge Checklist

→ The higher the aperture, the smaller the lens opening and the more extensive the depth of field. If your shutter speeds get too slow, put the camera on a tripod.

→ Restricting depth of field in bright light isn't always possible because you may not have a shutter speed fast enough to allow wide aperture. But you can add a neutral density filter to reduce the light entering the lens.

→ When using shallow depth of field, be sure to focus carefully on the part of the subject you want in sharpest focus— the eyes in a portrait, for instance.

→ Be aware that a DSLR's viewfinder shows the scene at your lens' maximum aperture, whereas a mirrorless camera's LCD may only show your shooting aperture—depending on how it is set up.

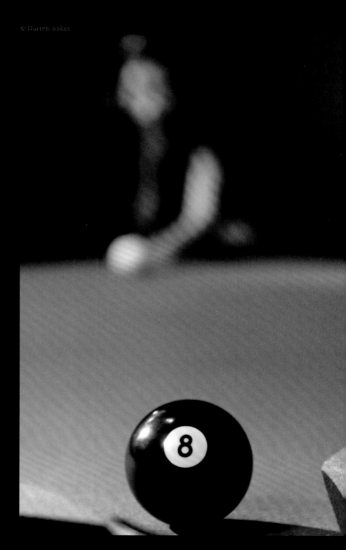
© Darren Baker

Shutter Speed

The third element in the exposure triangle is shutter speed. While aperture controls the amount of light that reaches the sensor, the shutter speed controls the duration of time that the sensor is exposed. The longer the shutter is kept open, the more light that reaches the image sensor to build up the exposure. Leaving your shutter open is like leaving your garden hose running into your sink—the longer the tap remains "open" the more water that fills the basin. Similarly, the shorter the duration of the exposure, the less light that hits the sensor (or water that fills your sink).

THE SHUTTER SPEED SEQUENCE

The shutter-speed settings on your camera represent either fractions of a second (1/60, 1/4, 1/2 second, etc.) or whole seconds (1, 4, 8 seconds, and so forth). Some cameras also have shutter speeds that represent full minutes, as well. Your camera manual will list the full shutter-speed range and progression that your camera offers.

Because these shutter speed settings represent the actual amount of time that the shutter remains open, most of us find the concept of shutter speeds far simpler to understand than aperture designations. If you set the shutter at 1/125 second, for example, that's precisely how long the shutter remains open: 1/125 of a second. While most of us can't necessarily comprehend just how long such a brief exposure is, we can understand that it's certainly much more brief than an exposure of, say, 10 seconds. Unlike ISOs, with numbers reaching into the hundreds of thousands, and apertures with their logarithmic f-stops, shutter speeds work in the straightforward measurements of time that we use every day.

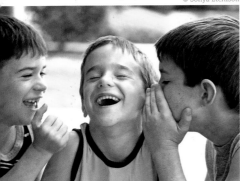
© Sonya Etchison

← Frozen in time
Candid moments like this shared laughter require a fast shutter speed (and a keen compositional eye).

→ Easy choices
With an unmoving subject, choosing a shutter speed is easy: you just need it fast enough to prevent camera shake; if a longer speed is unavoidable, use a tripod to steady your camera.

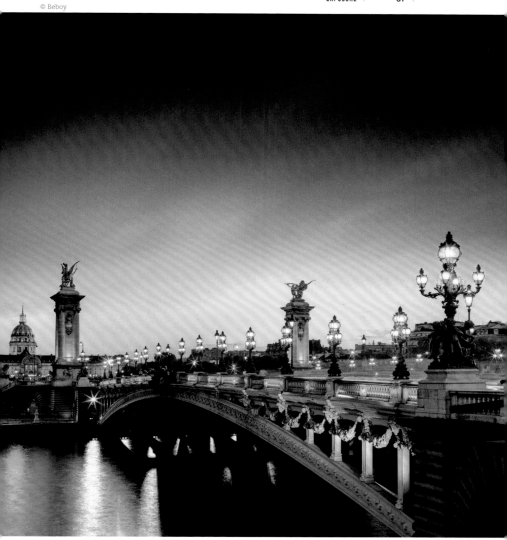

THE WHOLE-STOP SEQUENCE

All cameras use a standard selection of shutter speeds that typically ranges from, say, 30 seconds or 60 seconds at one extreme to speeds as brief as 1/2000 or 1/4000 second at the other. Again, obviously, a shutter speed of 30 seconds is a much longer duration than one of 1/4000 second. In fact, one of the interesting things about the difference in shutter speeds is that you can actually hear the shutter opening and closing on most cameras, so detecting a long exposure from a short one is relatively easy. Try it.

Before electronics entered the world of camera design all cameras used a series of "whole" shutter speed increments that followed a standard progression such that typically included the group of shutter speeds shown below.

These shutter speeds are referred to as "whole" stops because as you progress from one shutter speed to the next, you either double or halve the amount of time the light has to enter the camera. As you move from an exposure of 1/60 second to one of 1/30 second, for example, you double the amount of time that the sensor is exposed to light.

Conversely, as you move from 1/250 second to 1/500 second, you halve the amount of time that the shutter remains open. You should begin to see a pattern here of either halving or doubling exposure—and we'll discuss that very special reciprocal relationship (that is the basis of all exposure settings) in the coming pages.

Since cameras became more electronic and less mechanical, this absolute progression of whole shutter speed stops has been tinkered with, because fractional stops have been introduced. Some cameras, for instance, have a shutter speed of 1/320 second that falls (roughly) midway between 1/250 second and 1/500 second. While these new intermediary stops can be useful in fine-tuning shutter-speed response, to understand the mathematical theory of exposure, you will probably find it simpler to concentrate on the whole-stop sequence.

You might also find that some cameras also feature a shutter speed designated as "Bulb" and that setting allows you to keep the shutter open for as long as you like (shutters in old cameras were

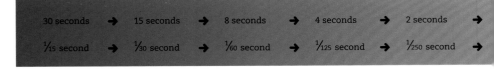

30 seconds ➜ 15 seconds ➜ 8 seconds ➜ 4 seconds ➜ 2 seconds ➜

1/15 second ➜ 1/30 second ➜ 1/60 second ➜ 1/125 second ➜ 1/250 second ➜

activated hydraulically, by squeezing a rubber bulb). Once you press the shutter release button in the Bulb position, the camera's shutter will remain open until you press it again. This setting is useful for long time exposures—taking night scenes of traffic, or capturing the light trails of stars, for example.

↓ **The shutter sequence**
Though you're unlikely to see such a shutter speed dial on your modern camera, their presence on old film cameras was a testament to their significance in every shot.

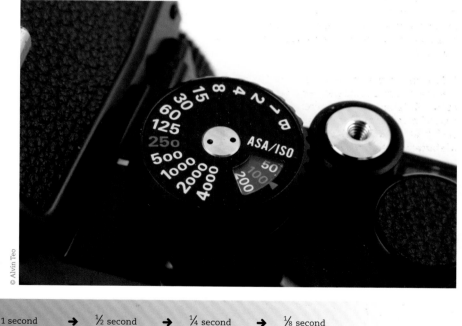

© Alvin Teo

| 1 second | ➜ | ½ second | ➜ | ¼ second | ➜ | ⅛ second |
| $\frac{1}{500}$ second | ➜ | $\frac{1}{1000}$ second | ➜ | $\frac{1}{2000}$ second | ➜ | $\frac{1}{4000}$ second |

Freeze the Action with a Fast Shutter Speed

Challenge

One of the best aspects of shutter speed is being able to use very brief shutter speeds to completely stop even the fastest subject motion. You'll need to remember that subjects coming toward or going away from the lens are easiest to stop with moderate shutter speeds and those moving parallel to your sensor require faster shutter speeds. Experiment with various subject and shutter-speed combinations to see what the minimum speed is for stopping action completely.

↓ **Catching the moment**
Fast-moving subjects are going to push your autofocus system to its limits, but with sufficient light, you can reduce the aperture to increase the chance that the subject will fall within the depth of field.

© Proma

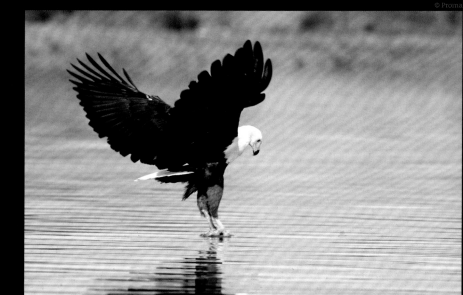

→ Make them come to you
The climactic moments that make the best action shots can often be predicted, giving you time to move into an ideal position and test a few exposures while waiting for the action to come to you.

Challenge Checklist

→ Find a subject that repeats the same motion over and over again and test several shutter speeds to determine which is the slowest speed that will still freeze the action.

→ The larger the image is on the sensor the faster the shutter speed you will need to get a sharp image, so as you zoom to a longer focal length you'll need to increase shutter speed.

→ Approach your subject from several angles to see how the direction of the action changes your ability to freeze motion.

→ If you need to boost the shutter speed by one stop, just double the ISO. If you want to go two stops faster, double it again.

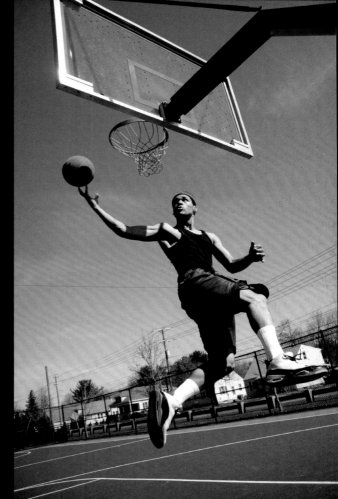

The Reciprocal Relationship

As we noted, the "whole" stops up or down in both aperture and shutter speed have a similar effect on the exposure. If you make a change in one direction by a full stop in either shutter speed or aperture, you can maintain exactly the same levels of light being recorded on the sensor if you make an equal but opposite change in the other setting. This reciprocal relationship is the basis for all changes in exposure settings.

Let's assume, for example, that you meter a scene and the camera tells you that the ideal exposure setting is 1/125 second at f/8. But what if you want to use a faster shutter speed of 1/500 second to stop fast action? That's an increase in shutter speed of two full stops. If you were to leave the aperture at the same f/8 setting, the image would be underexposed by two stops. But if you were to open the lens by two stops to f/4 (to allow in more light) you would get the exact same exposure. (Look at the sequence on page 28 and you'll see that f/8 to f/5.6 to f4 is two stops.)

This relationship works in the opposite direction too, naturally. If you were given a meter reading of 1/125 second at f/4, but wanted to shoot at an aperture setting three stops smaller (f/11), to get more depth of field, you could simply set that aperture and slow the shutter by three stops. The equivalent setting

would be 1/15 second at f/11. Again, the full-stop sequence for slowing down shutter speeds would be: 1/125 to 1/60 to 1/30 to 1/15 second, or three stops.

This perfect reciprocal relationship lies at the heart of not just exposure, but photography in general. Metering a scene is one thing, but recognizing the full range of possible ways to interpret your exposure, through shutter speed, aperture, and even ISO, cuts straight to the creative side of taking pictures.

BEWARE THE CONSEQUENCES

As you make shifts in either aperture or shutter speed you must remain aware that such changes can create significant visual changes. As you switch to a faster shutter speed and increase aperture size, for example, you are not only letting more light through the lens but you are changing the depth of field. If depth of field is important for the shot, this must be taken into account. If you were to use a smaller aperture and had to slow the shutter speed to get an equivalent amount of light into the camera, you might have to take into account changes in how subject motion is recorded.

→ **You control the focus**
Here the photographer opted for a wide aperture to limit depth of field—an option that suits the subject by making her stand out in relief against a blurred background.

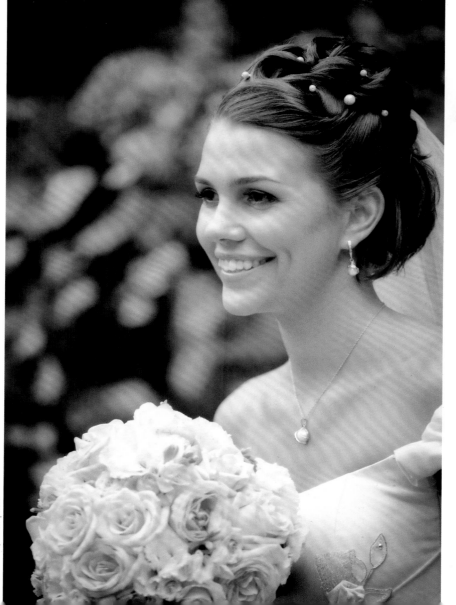
© Julia Shepeleva

LAST RESORT: CHANGE THE ISO

What happens if you want to increase the shutter speed by, say, two full stops but don't want to open the lens because you want to maintain the same depth of field? The only solution in this case would be to raise the ISO setting by two stops. By raising the ISO two full stops (for example: 200 to 400 to 800) you could maintain the same aperture and still raise the shutter speed by two stops.

→ **Cause and effect**
As you scroll through various combinations of shutter speed and aperture, be aware that certain aspects of a scene will change with each pairing. In a scene like this seascape, either the depth of field or the motion of the water will be affected by exposure changes—or both.

↓ **Extending your depth of field**
By choosing a small lens aperture and adjusting the ISO accordingly (i.e., up), the photographer was able to exploit almost infinite depth of field in showcasing the foreground of the Taj Mahal.

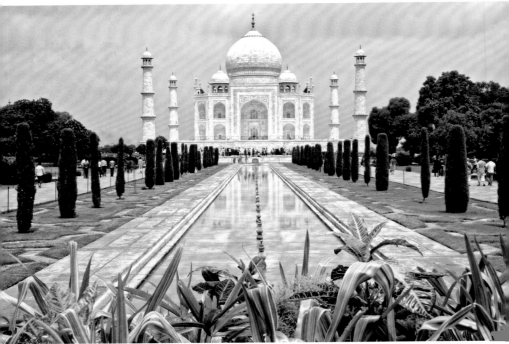

© Martin M303

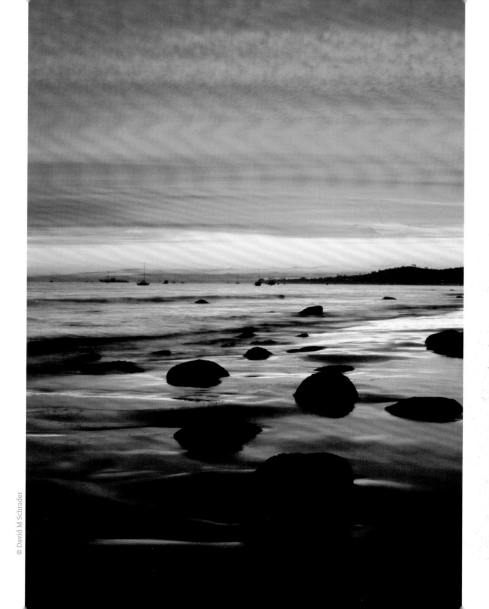

Exposure Modes

All but the simplest digital cameras have enough exposure modes (and specialty exposure modes known as scene modes) to make your eyes spin. But once you have a good understanding of what each of the exposure controls does, it's much easier to sift through the various exposure modes on your camera and choose the one that is best for a particular situation. Each of the primary exposure modes is designed to solve a particular problem and, while you will eventually find yourself relying on just one or two for most of your picture-taking needs, it's a good idea to experiment with each of them early on and get to know their advantages. Here briefly are each of the modes and some of the reasons why you might use them:

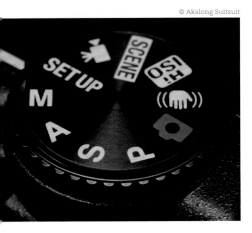

© Akalong Suitsuit

← **Exposure mode dial**
Most digital cameras have a dial like this, though some simpler cameras list modes as menu options. In both cases the icons are typically the same and enable you to quickly match your camera's exposure response to your subject.

AUTOMATIC

Also known as the "green mode" (it's often green on the mode dial) this is the all-encompassing fully auto mode. The camera typically sets the ISO (based on its reading of the ambient lighting) and also sets the shutter speed and aperture. If your camera has built-in flash, it will also typically turn itself on when the camera senses that the lighting level has dropped below what it deems acceptable. The nice part of this mode is that you can concentrate on just the viewfinder and ignore all technical decisions, but the obvious downside is that you've surrendered all creative control. For example, you have no control whatsoever over depth of field or subject motion. Usually white balance is chosen for you, as well. The one override that you may have available to you is exposure compensation.

PROGRAM AUTOMATIC

This mode varies from one camera model to the next, but typically the camera sets both aperture and shutter speed for you. The difference is that you can (often must) set the ISO yourself, so that you are matching the sensor's light-sensitivity to the existing light. The primary advantage in this mode is that, with most cameras, there is a command dial that lets you scroll through the various equivalent aperture and shutter speed combinations. If, for example, the camera sets an exposure of 1/125 second at ƒ/8 and you know that you want more depth of field, you can scroll through the aperture settings to find a smaller aperture. You can also set the white balance manually when using this mode, and make exposure compensation adjustments as you see fit. Another subtle difference is that the flash won't pop up automatically and you will probably have to flip it on manually.

SHUTTER PRIORITY

This is the mode to choose when subject motion is your primary concern, because here you select the shutter speed and the camera chooses the correct corresponding aperture setting. This is the mode favored by sports and action photographers. If the action is fast and needs to be frozen, a fast shutter speed is set; if the intent is to blur the subject as it is moving, longer shutter speeds can be explored until the optimum amount of blur is reached. One caution here is that as you select the shutter speed, you must keep an eye on the shifting depth of field. If, for example, you select a very fast shutter speed of 1/2000 of a second, the camera will likely be forced to select a very wide aperture setting, and this means almost no depth of field. Conversely, if you select a very slow shutter speed—to blur the gate of a racehorse or the flow of a mountain stream, for instance—the camera will select a relatively small aperture which will potentially create a situation where too much of the scene is brought into focus. Check sharpness with your depth-of-field preview button regularly.

APERTURE PRIORITY

Often your primary concern is depth of field. In those situations the Aperture Priority mode is ideal because it lets you select the aperture while the camera selects the appropriate shutter speed.

If you want to restrict depth of field in a head-and-shoulders portrait, you can select a very wide aperture and the camera will match it with the right shutter speed for a good exposure. Or, if you are shooting a landscape and want to have sharpness from near to far, then select a small aperture and, again, the camera will choose the right shutter speed. If subject motion is an issue, you must keep track of the shutter speed that the camera is selecting. You may have to raise the ISO if the camera is setting too slow a shutter speed and your subject is creating more blur or motion that you desire. Also, keeping the camera on a tripod when using small apertures will negate any chances of camera shake during long exposures.

MANUAL MODE

The Manual exposure mode provides the most control, but the least assistance from the camera. In this exposure mode you are responsible for setting both the aperture and the shutter speed. To use this mode you can use the camera's light meter (or a handheld meter) as a guide, but you are completely free to accept or ignore its recommendations as you see fit. The Manual mode is very useful when you are fairly certain that the camera's meter is going to be misled by a complex or contrasty subject and you want to use your experience to override its settings. In photographing a scene that exceeds the sensor's known dynamic range (typically around 10 stops for a mid-range camera), for example, the meter

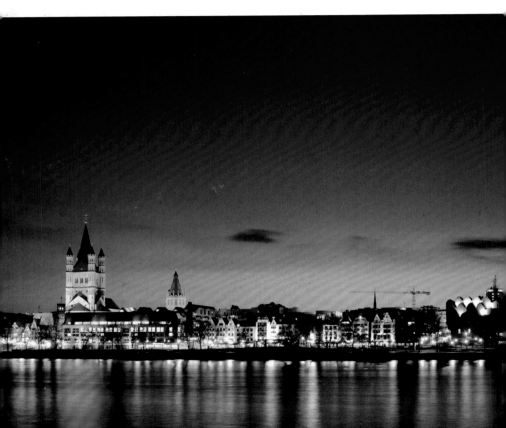

will provide an "average" reading of the scene. But in this case you may have to make a decision to abandon some shadow information to preserve highlights. Also, in all cases when you're using a handheld meter you will have to use the Manual mode because otherwise the meter will ignore your settings and set exposure based on its own readings. There are also many extreme exposure situations—extremely long exposures to capture star trails, for example—when the only way to set such exposure times is to use Manual mode.

↓ **All modes lead to Rome**
Or, in this case, all modes may lead to a great night shot of the Rhine near Cologne, Germany. Any of the main exposure modes could capture this shot, but manual allows the greatest control.

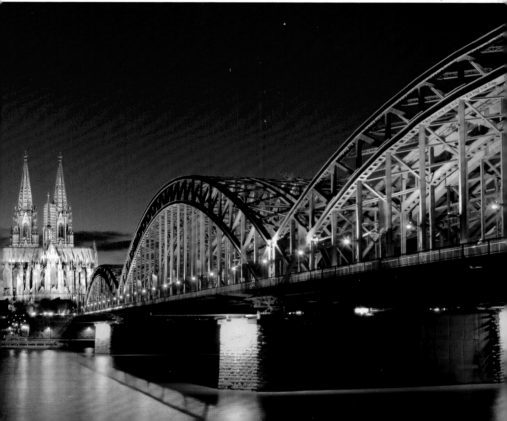

Histograms & Meters

To get the best results from your camera's light meter it's important to understand exactly how it performs it's primary chore—and that you understand both its strengths and its shortcomings. Knowing how your meter measures light and what its limitations are will help you to manipulate and interpret its results. Knowing, for instance, that your camera's imaging sensor has a vastly more limited dynamic range (range of contrast) than your eyes and brain is supremely important in interpreting the information provided by your meter.

READING THE HISTOGRAM

Perhaps the most valuable tool available to you as a digital photographer is the luminance histogram. This chart horizontally maps the tonal values of a scene from pure black at the far left to pure white at the far right—on a scale of 0 to 255. The vertical axis shows the number of pixels in each particular tone. Your camera sensor is limited in its ability to capture only a certain range of tonal values. These limits can be very bright (mostly highlights) or very dark (mostly shadows), but what they can't be is very far apart.

If your camera has Live View, you can observe the histogram as it calculates the exposure of your scene in real-time. If your camera doesn't, you can activate the histogram as you review a shot in playback. You can then see if your tonal values are optimally distributed, adjust your exposure, and reshoot as necessary.

So what is the optimal histogram? The most important goal is to prevent your histogram from bunching up too much at the far ends, which indicates that detail is being lost in pure white or pure black. Ideally, your histogram should start at the bottom left corner, rise into a

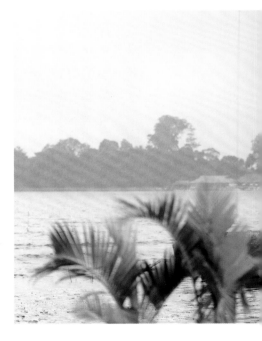

mountain, peaking in the middle of the chart (the mid-tones), and taper off back down to the bottom right corner.

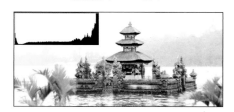

↓→ Finding the middle ground

The top image is overexposed, with hardly any detail in the sky and background. This is visible in the large number of pixels bunched up against the far-right side of the histogram. Likewise, the middle image is underexposed, with most of its pixels slammed up against the far left. The bottom image is properly exposed—in the sense that all of the pixels taper off before overexposing the highlights, and the few pixels cut off in the blacks are not too much of a worry. The majority of the data is safely captured between the extremes of the chart.

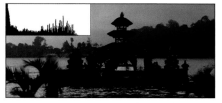

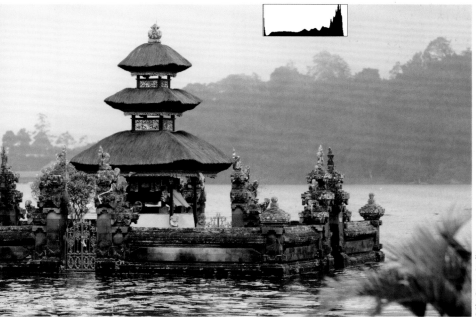

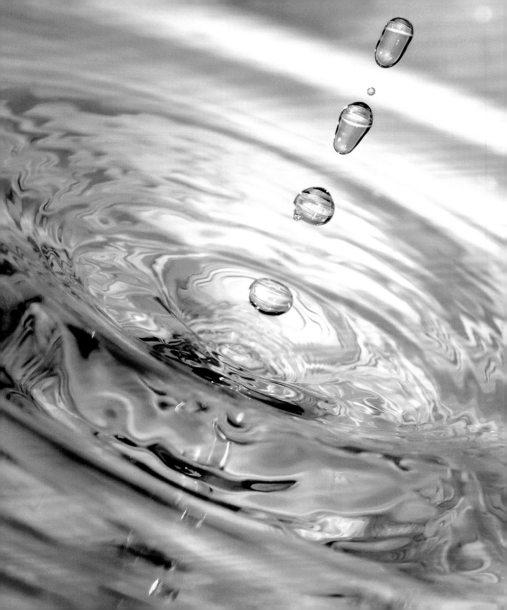

Of course, not all scenes will give you the opportunity to create an optimal histogram, regardless of how delicately you expose the shot—but the histogram will still be an essential tool in helping you combat such high-dynamic-range, high-contrast conditions. The important thing is to understand how your histogram works, and how it reflects the way your camera sensor measures light, and captures and records that light as image data.

TTL METERS

All in-camera light meters fall into one broad common category: TTL-type meters. Standing for Through-The-Lens, TTL metering means that the light is being measured (by a separate metering sensor) after it has passed through the lens and typically is measured at (or close to) the imaging sensor. This system creates an extraordinarily accurate means of light measurement because the light is being measured after it has passed through the lens and any lens filters that you might be using.

← **Flash made simple**
The high-speed flash necessary for capturing these water droplets requires delicate calculations—that fortunately occur in an instant thanks to automated TTL metering.

What the meter sees in terms of illumination is exactly what the sensor will be recording.

Conversely, in pre-TTL cameras if you used a lens filter you had to take the amount of light that was absorbed by the filter into consideration when calculating your exposure. This compensation, known as the filter factor has been rendered virtually obsolete by TTL metering. While calculating the filter factor wasn't difficult, measuring the light after it passes through a lens filter is very much more accurate.

Also, since the light is being measured internally, the meter does not have to make adjustments for other types of lens accessories like close-up extension tubes or telephoto extenders. Even the light from your electronic flash is measured—and the flash output controlled—after the light has bounced off your subject and passed through the lens.

The real beauty of the TTL system, then, is that no matter what lens or filter accessory you employ, the metering sensor doesn't have to compensate (or have to assist it) in any way. For both you and the camera the process becomes one of speed, elegance, and simplicity.

How Light Meters See the World

In preparing to meter any scene, it's important to acknowledge a very significant difference between the way that you see the world and the way that your meter sees it. Until relatively recently, light meters saw the world only in a palette of grays—metering sensors were monochrome, and their goal was to average all the shades of gray they detected, then pick an 18-percent average that would safely (or to the best of its ability) capture both shadows and highlights. (And incidentally, the reason that 18-percent gray is halfway between black and white, rather 50-percent gray, is because the math is based on an algorithmic scale, not a linear one.) The reason that this system works so well is that whatever you aim your meter at, will be recorded as middle gray. If you are careful to meter a subject that happens

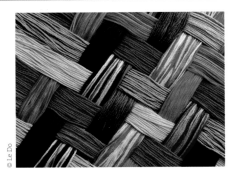

© Le Do

↑ Metering sensors are colorblind
Learning to see each color, and indeed batches of different colors, as shades of gray will help you understand and better use your camera.

to be middle gray then that subject will be exposed perfectly and all of the other tones will naturally fall into their proper place. Those tones that are lighter than middle gray will record lighter and those that are darker will record darker. A perfect system.

↓ Measuring brightness
This diagram shows how brightness measurements relate to f-stops, with middle gray at the center, shading into light and dark indicated by + or - f-stops, respectively.

f-Stops from Average				-3	-2	-1		+1	+2	+3	
Brightness %	0	10	20	30	40	50	60	70	80	90	100
Levels 0–255	0	25	50	75	100	128	150	175	200	225	255

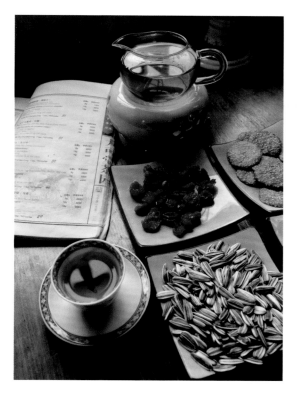

← **A still-life scene**
Daylight coming through a window, falling on a variety of colors each with differently reflective surfaces, with shadows bunched up at the top of the frame. In such a diverse scene, you can either directly tell your camera which tone to treat as middle gray, or have your camera average all those tones together in order to calculate an even exposure for both the shadows and the highlights (as was done for this scene).

Some newer cameras, however, feature RGB metering sensors, meaning they can distinguish between colors. This is useful in a number of ways—for instance, sensors are generally more sensitive to red light, and are therefore prone to underexposing scenes that heavily feature red subjects (including skin tones). Additionally, some metering systems can be set to evaluate the full scene, but be biased toward the area of the scene where the focus was locked, which is usually the main subject of the photo. These can be powerful features in getting successful exposures in complex or changing lighting conditions, but they are also quite complex to set up, and are not necessarily suitable to all shooting conditions. Reading your camera's manual is essential.

In Search of Middle Gray

Finding a reliable middle tone in any scene is simpler than you think. Most outdoor scenes, natural and man-made, contain a number of nearly perfect middle tones for metering, including:

CLEAR BLUE SKY

A dark blue sky on a sunny day makes setting exposure for landscapes easy. Blue skies are particularly useful when the scene contains large areas of light or dark that might fool the meter. Metering the sky is also useful in very contrasty lighting, or when the scene is backlit by strong sunlight. But it needs to be a clear day with a rich, blue sky, clear of haze or cloud cover that could skew your reading.

LIGHT GREEN FOLIAGE

For a scene that has a lot of green grass or light-green foliage, you can set a very accurate exposure by metering those areas, particularly useful for a landscape that contains tones that might fool your meter. For a dark, rocky outcropping with green trees, just meter from the foliage and the rest of the tones will fall into place. If you find your scenes are coming out too light, then use your exposure compensation feature.

GRAY OR RED-BRICK BUILDINGS

Old, unpainted barns are ideal, naturally gray metering targets, as are the boards of an old wooden farm cart or a pile of weathered lumber. An old school house or the side of a red-brick store are also excellent—the key is to make sure they are reflecting the prevailing lighting conditions and not cast in shadow.

→ **Catch the light**
Regardless of which metering target you use to set your exposure, it is always important to make sure the area off of which you are metering is reflecting the prevailing light.

↓ **Abundant green for an easy scene**
One nice thing about photographing nature subjects is that you're often presented with plenty of green reflective surfaces off of which to meter an accurate, reliable middle gray.

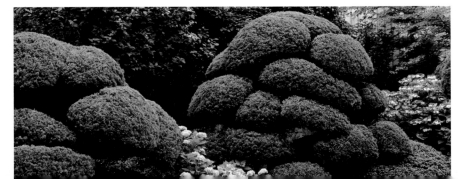

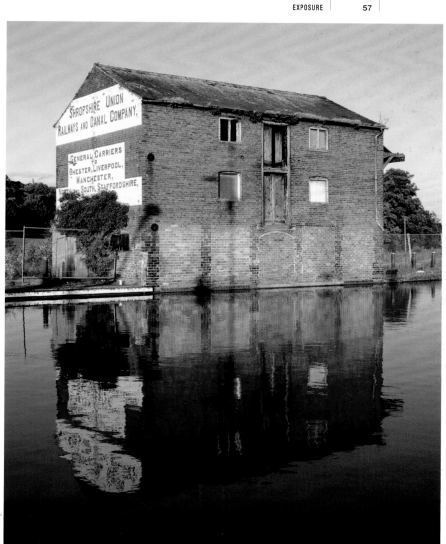

GRAY CARD

One reliable method is to use a mid-toned gray card. These are available from camera retailers and reflect exactly a mid-gray to the camera. The card reflects 18 percent of the light reaching it, and the reason for this number is the non-linear response of the human eye.

LOCK SELECTIVE READINGS

To use any of these naturally occurring middle tones you will have to isolate them from the rest of the scene, either by using a selective-area metering mode, zooming in to fill the frame with just that subject, or simply by moving closer to it. Whenever you meter selectively it's important to lock that reading in before you recompose and shoot the final scene. If you don't, the meter will override you and set the reading it would have chosen. Most cameras allow you to lock a meter reading by keeping the shutter button half-pressed. As long as you keep your finger on the trigger, the meter reading will remain fixed. Because this feature typically also locks focus, it is only useful if the subject you are metering and the one you are shooting are the same distance. If not, you may have to set the exposure directly. Some cameras have a separate exposure-lock feature.

→ **Expose, then compose**
For this scene, the camera was pointed down so the green grass occupied the full frame, then—keeping the shutter release half-way down—the scene was recomposed and shot.

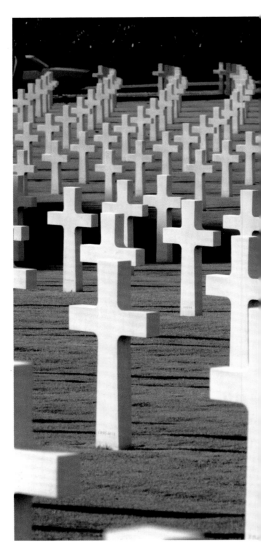

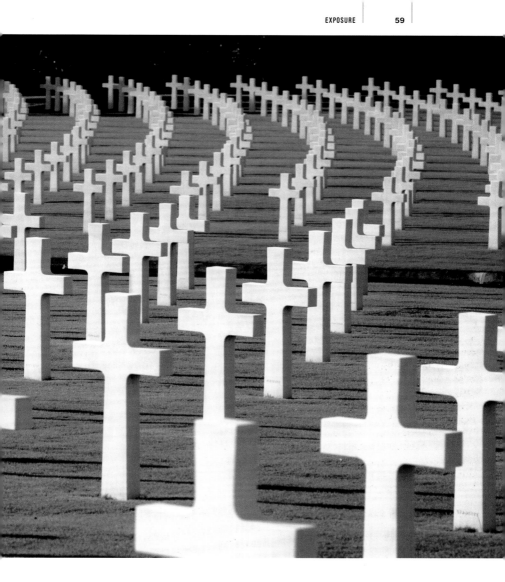

Metering Modes

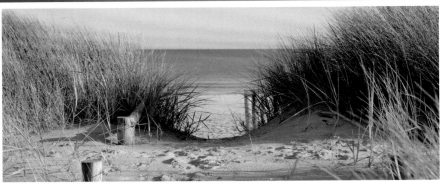

© Joe Gough

All digital cameras contain TTL-type meters that utilize at least one of three different types of metering "modes" to calculate exposure. Compact cameras typically offer only one metering mode, while more advanced cameras may offer all three. The difference in how each mode operates is based largely on how much of the scene the meter is viewing. Switching from one metering mode to another is simple—normally just the press of a button or the turn of a dial. It's worth trying out each mode so that you're comfortable with how to access it and how to use it.

↑ Even exposure
Had only the sand been metered, the camera would likely have underexposed this beach scene. However, including the sky, sea, and particularly the green grass elements helped the onboard computer recognize the scene for what it was and properly expose for it.

MATRIX METERING

Also known as multi-segment or evaluative metering (depending on your camera), in this mode the camera looks at the entire scene and considers the lighting as it reflects from numerous specific areas throughout the frame. This is the default mode used in almost all digital cameras, from basic compact cameras to the most sophisticated DSLR models. It is far and away the most complex and sophisticated form of light metering and is exceedingly accurate in even the most complex situations.

In this mode the meter divides the frame into a set pattern or grid of areas that can range from a very basic half dozen or so segments to more than a thousand on some high-end DSLRs. Once you activate the meter by partially depressing the shutter release, the camera analyzes the amount of light coming from each of those segments and then compares the pattern of illumination to a library of subjects stored in the camera. On some cameras the meter may be comparing the scene to as many as 30,000 exposures that are stored in the camera's memory. In programming the data bank for these meters, the manufacturers include a vast array of both common and complex scene examples—landscapes, portraits, close-ups, etc. Through this comparative analysis of the scene, the camera is able to make a fairly educated guess about exactly what the subject is that you're photographing—and which parts are likely to be most important. If the camera sees a tall, relatively dim vertical area that is surrounded by a bright field of illumination, for example, it may conclude that you're photographing another person standing on a bright sandy beach (or a snowy field). It then calculates an exposure that will moderate the brighter areas while providing adequate exposure for the face. It's amazing technology and works stunningly well (when properly used).

In creating its exposure, the matrix meter will take many related bits of information into account (in addition to brightness levels), including the distance to the subject (based on focusing information from the lens), the direction and intensity of the light, the contrast, RGB values for each segment, and the

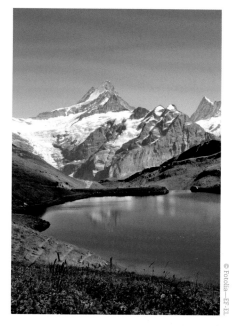

© Fotolia—EF-EL

↑ **Recognize when Matrix is appropriate**
Never forget that your camera is still just a computer. It is up to you to use matrix metering appropriately, and to know which scenes it is best suited for. For instance, this landscape shot, with blue sky, green mid- and foreground elements, and plenty of sunlight is perfectly suited for matrix metering. Ultimately, the key to using matrix metering is to become so familiar with the way it works in your particular camera that you can anticipate the lighting situations where it might have difficulty, or need some compensation input from you.

color of the subject. The camera then goes through a complex series of algorithms to set the exposure—and it does all of this in a fraction of a second.

Selective Metering Modes

CENTER-WEIGHTED METERING

One of the downfalls of matrix metering (which are mild and relatively rare) is that the meter is always considering the entire frame. In most situations this is helpful, but there are times when the most important subject—the one that you want metered accurately—takes up only a small portion of the frame, and this is where center-weighted metering can be very useful.

Though it still considers the illumination information from the entire frame, the center-weighted metering mode biases or "overloads" its readings to a small central portion of the frame. The center-weighted area is indicated by a circle in the viewfinder and typically the meter concentrates 60 to 80 percent of its readings from that area. Center-weighted metering is ideal for situations where a

relatively small, important subject is surrounded by an excessively bright or dark background. If you are taking an informal portrait of a cross-country skier against field of bright white snow, for instance, you can use this mode to meter directly from the skier and thereby reduce the meter's consideration of the surroundings. Similarly, if you are photographing a strongly backlit flower surrounded by bright foliage, you can read directly from the blossom and get a more accurate exposure for the flower.

⬉ Skin versus snow
While it doesn't completely ignore the edges of the frame, center-weighted metering mode recognizes that whatever is in the center (in this case, the portrait subject) is what's important.

↓ Don't worry about the edges
Center-weighted metering mode allowed the edges of the frame to be pushed into the highlights, in order to capture the full tones of the inner folds of these rose petals.

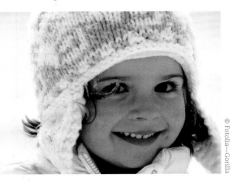
© Fotolia—Gorilla

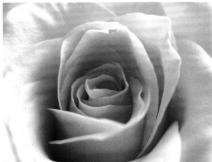
© Sylvia Schreck

SPOT METERING MODE

Spot metering takes the idea of center-weighted metering to the extreme and reads an even smaller area of the frame —usually an area that is between one and five percent of the viewfinder area. On most cameras this area is indicated at the center of the frame, but on some you can change its placement.

One significant difference is that in spot-metering mode the camera is not taking any other portion of the frame into consideration. The meter reads exclusively from the indicated spot area. Spot metering is useful when the subject takes up a very small part of the frame— but when you meter off such a small area, it's important you've chosen the optimal area to read. Remember that the

reading is telling you what settings will reproduce that small area as a mid-tone.

Another benefit of spot metering is that you can compare specific tonalities within a scene. This enables you to measure the true dynamic range of a scene by measuring both its brightest areas and its darkest. You can also use a spot reading to place a very small and specific subject at middle gray.

As with center-weighted metering, it's critical to use your camera's exposure-lock function to hold that reading if you recompose the scene after metering.

↓ Spot-metered silhouettes
Silhouettes are a situation in which you don't want to meter off your subject at all. Here, the colored background was spot-metered, leaving the two figures completely underexposed.

↓ Spotlit subjects
Spot metering is excellent for dramatically capturing a spotlit subject, ensuring only the brightest area is properly exposed and letting the rest of the frame fall off into shadow.

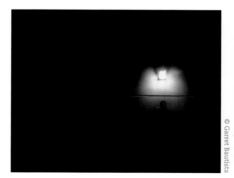

© Garret Bautista

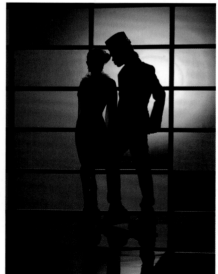

© MikIG

Limit Yourself to Spot Metering

Your camera's spot meter is designed to read a very finite area of the frame—often only a few degrees in angle of view. But isolating those few degrees can be the only way to precisely meter the important areas of a complex scene. By acknowledging that your meter wants to render that area as a neutral gray, you'll know exactly how to set exposure for the most important part of the scene. Whether the surroundings are overly bright, dark or even intensely dappled with both, by metering just the key area you have control over setting the best possible exposure.

↓ **Mont Saint-Michel**
Many monuments and iconic buildings are lit in such a way that spot-metering off their surfaces creates an exposure that accentuates their specific structure while the rest of the frame is left more subdued.

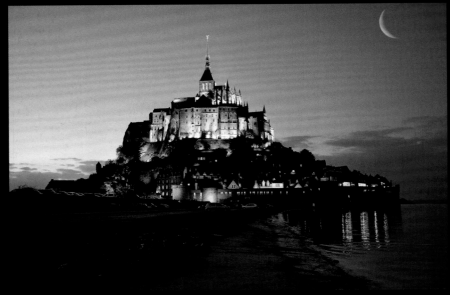

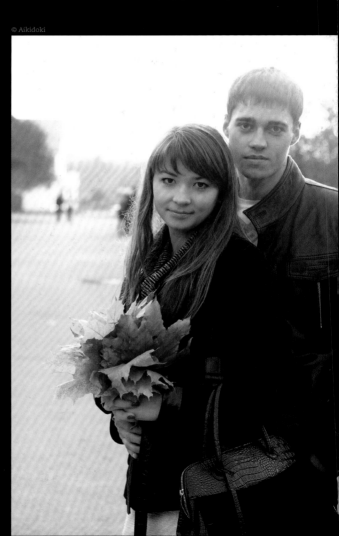

© Aikidoki

→ **Quick fix for a backlight**
The strong backlighting in this portrait shot could easily have resulted in a massive overexposure. But by spot metering off the leaves held in the shadow of the front figure, an accurate metering was easily achieved.

Challenge Checklist

→ In a high-contrast scene, use your spot meter to isolate just the subject that you want to read. You must be careful aiming the lens, since a slight jiggle to the left or right will throw off the accuracy of your reading.

→ Put your camera in Manual mode so that you can recompose the scene after metering your subject. Alternately you can use the exposure-lock feature, but on many cameras the exposure lock and focus lock are combined, so it will depend on how you need to handle both.

→ To read the dynamic range of a scene, take spot readings of the brightest and darkest areas. The difference between those areas in full stops is your dynamic range.

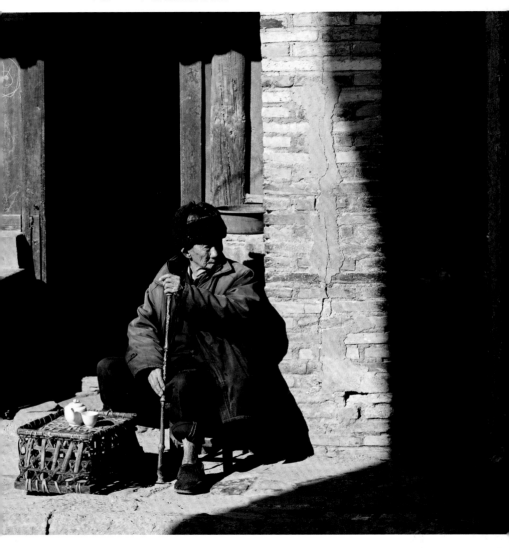

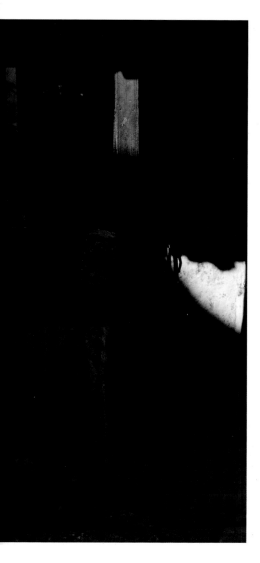

Color Temperature

All light sources produce a unique color of light, and they are rated by their color temperature in degrees Kelvin (a system named after William Thomson, also known as Lord Kelvin [1824–1907]—though it's not likely that anyone will ever ask you). Color temperature numbers increase as the color of light goes from red to blue or from warm to cooler. Sunlight in the middle of the day, for instance, ranges from about 5000–5400K (depending on the latitude and exact hour) and is considerably more blue than tungsten lighting which is at about 3200K. Every light source that emits by burning (such as the sun or a tungsten filament) has a unique color temperature, though in most cases those temperatures vary to some degree—as lamps get older, or as the sun rises and sets, for example.

To the human eye, however, all ambient lighting—natural or artificial—seems acceptably white to us after a relatively short period of exposure to it. Whether

← **Balancing light sources**
As if dealing with the exposure for high-contrast lighting conditions weren't enough, in scenes such as this, where there is an even split between bright daylight and dark shadow, your white balance setting (as explained on the following pages) becomes extremely important. Here, the more significant daylit subject has been given bias, while the shadow area to the right has been forced to take on a slightly blue color cast.

you walk out into the golden light of morning or the bright, much more blue light of noon, all light seems acceptably "white" to your brain. That is because the color receptors in your brain are constantly compensating and correcting for variations in the color temperature of light. And again, this happens so naturally and so quickly that we rarely take notice.

The exact same correction takes place when you walk from natural sunlight into an artificially lit room: the color of artificial incandescent lighting is much warmer in color than most daylight, for example, but once you're immersed in that lighting, you barely notice it's warmth. We've all taken a walk in the blue light of twilight and noticed the reddish warmth of the artificial light spilling out from windows. Yet if you were to walk into any of those rooms, your eyes would immediately make an adjustment and in a matter of seconds you'd be seeing that light as a completely neutral color source. Your brain's ability to create a constant color of lighting helps you to walk through the world with a relatively constant sense of the neutrality of light (as false a reality as that may be).

THE PRACTICAL SCALE
OF COLOR TEMPERATURE

In photography, the important light sources for which color temperature has to be calculated range from domestic tungsten to blue skylight. Precision is difficult, particularly with daylight, because weather and sky conditions vary so much. There are also differences of opinion on what constitutes pure white sunlight.

K	Natural source	Artificial source
10,000	Blue sky	
7500	Shade under blue sky	
7000	Shade under partly cloudy sky	
6500	Daylight, deep shade	
6000	Overcast sky	Electronic flash
5200	Average noon daylight	Flash bulb
5000		
4500	Afternoon sunlight	Fluorescent "daylight"
4000		Fluorescent "warm light"
3500	Early morning/evening sunlight	Photofloods (3400K)
3000	Sunset	Photolamps/studio tungsten (3200K)
2500		Domestic tungsten
1930	Candlelight	

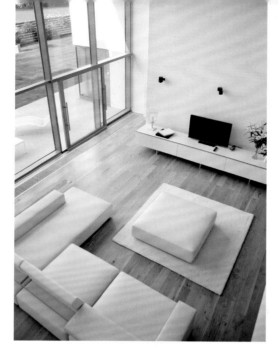

← Bright Whites

In this all-white room, it is exceptionally important to take an accurate reading of the ambient color temperature.

← Temperature vs. Tint

Color temperature reaches from orange/yellow to blue, which you can visualize as the vertical axis shown left. Tint, however, is the second dimension of white balance control, and reaches from green to magenta (see the slider on page 273). The science behind this is complex, but generally speaking, large changes in white balance are made by adjusting the temperature, then small tweaks are made by adjusting the tint—particularly if the image is shot under sodium-vapor light (see page 134).

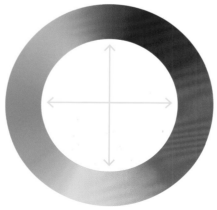

White Balance Control

Digital cameras, on the other hand, have a built-in white-balance control that lets you assign a color temperature so that you can either "correct" the ambient lighting or exaggerate its color. The white balance, in effect, enables you to tell the camera exactly what type of lighting that you are using—daylight, tungsten, fluorescent, etc. Most DSLR cameras even have a further refinement that lets you tweak the color temperature of a given source (setting 3150K instead of 3200K for tungsten, for instance).

The white balance control is a terrific tool when you want to eliminate the color cast of a particular light source. The classic example used to be interior tungsten lighting, which would give a heavy orange color cast if a proper white balance wasn't set. However, CFL (Compact Fluorescent Lamps) and LED (Light-Emitting Diode) lighting is replacing tungsten in many situations, so it's not so clear-cut which white balance should be used even in controlled interior situations.

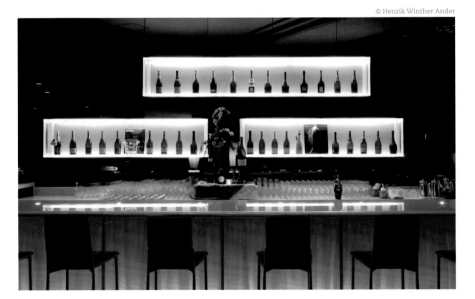

We'll discuss this much further on pages 132–133, but for now it's important to remember that CFL (and all fluorescent lighting) has a broken color spectrum, with spikes that are actually off the color temperature scale, and that therefore sometimes cannot be captured accurately. LED lighting, on the other hand, have adjustable color temperatures, so there is no single White Balance setting that works for all LED lighting conditions.

Fortunately, White Balance is 100% adjustable after the fact, as long as you are shooting in the Raw format. During Raw conversion, you have the ability to choose any color temperature or tint that you want, or to simply click on an area of the image you want to set as your 18% neutral gray. You can even assign separate white balances to different areas of the same image. However, the goal should still be to set an accurate a white balance when capturing the shot.

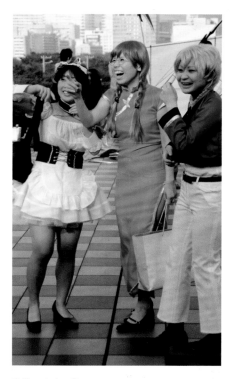

← Neons and fluorescents
Commercial spaces typically use an array of artificial light sources in order to create a dynamic aesthetic. While it may appeal to the naked eye, it can wreak havoc on your digital images. You will often have to experiment with a few different white balance settings, none of which can perfectly match all the different light sources; but perfection isn't always necessary, as the viewer often expects to see artificially vivid colors in such spaces.

↑ Street shooting
Auto white balance can be a huge aid when you are out shooting in rapidly changing, dynamic situations. Between calculating accurate exposures, arranging careful compositions, and looking for decent subjects, you have plenty to worry about besides fixing color casts. Just make sure it's getting it in the ballpark.

**THERE ARE THREE MEANS
OF SETTING WHITE BALANCE:**

(1) Automatic white balance adjusts
the color response of the camera
continuously and automatically. As you
change from one light source to another,
the camera responds instantly. Typically
the auto response will operate in a range
of (roughly) 3500–8000K.

(2) Source-specific white balance presets
let you dictate exactly how you want the
camera to respond by telling it the type
of existing light. These vary from camera
to camera.

(3) Manual or Custom WB mode is the
most precise, because in this mode
you take a test shot and then set that
temperature manually. The specific steps
for creating test settings varies, but the
general idea is constant: first you take
a clean, white surface and photograph it
in the same lighting conditions as your
subject—taking care not to have any
shadows, and making the white target
fill up the frame; then, you instruct your
camera to use that as the custom WB.
For all subsequent shots, the camera
will use precisely the white balance
setting that rendered your target
subject pure white.

→ **Stage lighting**
Elaborate stage lighting setups often require
either a custom white balance to get accurate
whites, or a more lax attitude toward accurate
whites in general, and using the color casts for
creative effect.

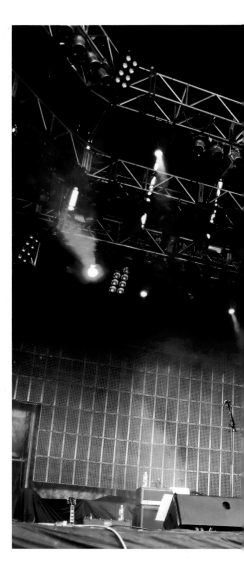

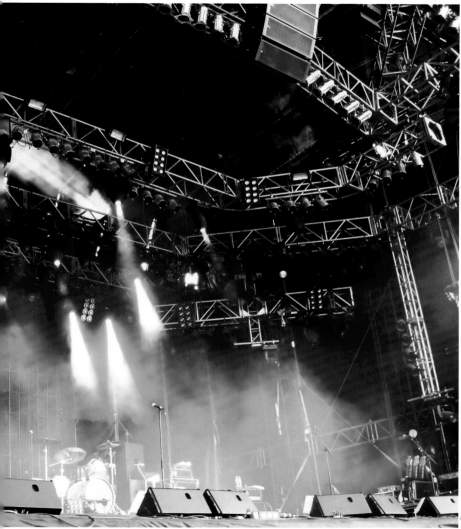

Set a Creative White Balance

Challenge

White balance lets you step into any lighting situation and then balance the sensor's color response to that specific light source. This can be used as a creative weapon to mislead the sensor. You can use the "cloudy day" setting in midday sun to add warmth to a portrait, perhaps. Telling the camera you're shooting in tungsten light when, in fact, you're shooting in sunlight will supply extra blue to the mix. This is one way you might respond to this challenge. Think about the color of the light source and how adding light of a different color (or more of the same) might affect the outcome. What creative visions do you see?

↓ **Don't fight it**
Since sodium vapor is almost impossible to white balance for anyway, indulging in its rich, golden yellow color cast can give roadways and street scenes a supernatural effect.

© Kalabu

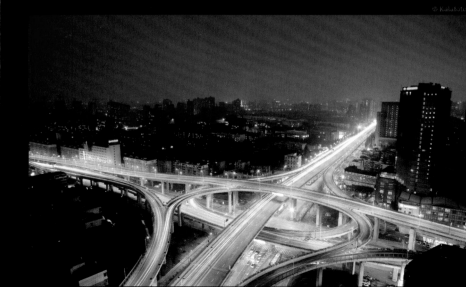

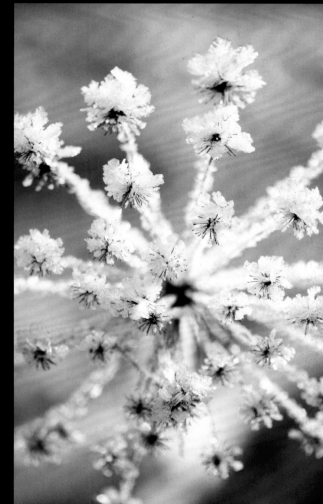
© Kati Molin

→ **Feeling blue**

While white balancing off the snow or ice would have given an accurate coloring, the result wouldn't have had the same chilling effect that this blue color cast gives, which was achieved with a tungsten WB setting.

Challenge Checklist

→ Experiment with white-balance options; shoot in Raw and adjust the white balance during processing.

→ Use reverse psychology when setting a creative white balance: you know that the tungsten setting will add more blue to cool off tungsten lamps, but what if you added more warmth?

→ One of the goals of a correct white-balance setting is to render white subjects as close to a pure neutral tone as possible, but don't be restricted by correctness. If a white church comes out as blue in your twilight effect, so be it.

→ If your camera has the capability, experiment with adjusting the color balance using the color picker found in the white balance menu.

Handling Extreme Contrast

As we discussed, your eyes are able to see and manage a far broader dynamic range than your camera's sensor. Given just a few seconds to adjust, your eyes are able to see and resolve great detail in both the darkest shadows and brightest highlights—a range that approaches the equivalent of nearly 24 stops of light. And because when you view a scene, your eyes are continuously shifting from one portion to another, your brain is able to process that range of contrast almost instantly. Pity your poor sensor, however, limited to a finite range of tonalities—and a range, quite honestly, that's often not adequate to the task at hand.

In fact, with the exception of very low-contrast situations (a foggy or overcast day, for example), many daylight situations in full sun are already pushing the limits of what your camera can handle. And once you get beyond those limits, important decisions have to be made about what is to be preserved and what must be jettisoned beyond the far edges of your histogram. Knowing how to make those sacrifices, what tools are available to deal with extreme circumstances, and which choices work best photographically will help keep you from losing important subject detail for the sake of exposure. Fortunately, there are ways to not only record your subject accurately, but also to take creative advantage of the challenges at hand.

CONTRAST CONTROL:
TOOLS & TECHNIQUES

As you venture into more complex exposure challenges, it's important to know that there are a number of tools and techniques that you can use to help you solve the contrast riddle. Some of these solutions are camera-based (exposure compensation, for instance) while others rely on accessories and light modifiers. Not every tool works in every situation so it pays to experiment and be familiar with each of them.

↓ **Consider what's important**
If the purpose of this had been to represent the textural detail of these dark chairs, it would be a failure. But the purpose was to create a graphic image of strong contrasts, and so the shadows in the seats were allowed to fall into pure black.

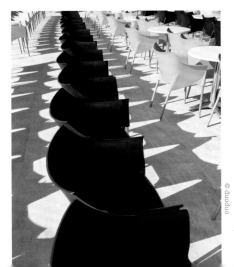

© duoduo

EXPOSURE COMPENSATION

Often the solution to an exposure problem is to add or subtract exposure from the metered exposure setting. The simplest way to do this is by using your camera's exposure compensation feature. This feature lets you add or subtract exposure regardless of what exposure mode you're using or what metering mode is measuring the light. Typically, you can add or subtract exposure by anywhere from three to five stops in one-third stop increments.

Exposure compensation is often used in conjunction with specific types of selective metering such as Center-Weighted or Spot metering (see pages 62–63). By carefully measuring specific areas of a scene and then using exposure compensation to adjust the overall exposure, you can manipulate the tonal values of specific areas within a scene to suit your needs.

Keep in mind, however, that exposure compensation can't magically add or subtract exposure without affecting one of your exposure controls. In Aperture Priority mode, exposure compensation will adjust the shutter speed; and in Shutter Priority mode, it will adjust the aperture. This has two important consequences: one, you need to consider the effect a change in one or the other exposure control will have on your shot, in terms of either depth of field or how motion is captured; and two, there is no

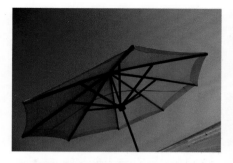

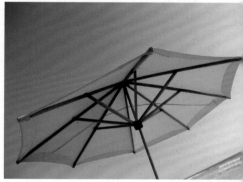

© Tomas Hajek

↑ **A simple fix**
The abundance of direct sunlight made the original photo, on the right, underexposed. A simple exposure compensation of +1.5EV brightened up the umbrella and livened up the shot.

such thing as exposure compensation when you are in Manual exposure mode, as you are controlling every aspect of the exposure. If you want to brighten or darken a scene, you have to do so directly by changing the shutter speed or aperture (or ISO).

Adjust with Exposure Compensation

Exposure compensation shines most when you combine it with your knowledge and experience in setting exposure for difficult but common subjects. For this challenge, you will need to find a subject that would typically fool the meter. If you're photographing snowscape scenes, for example, use the compensation control to see just how much extra exposure is needed to record the snow as a clean white with texture and detail. Getting to know how much compensation is purely a matter of trial and error—so up build your experience.

↓ **Edinburgh Castle**
The camera wanted to expose this shot so the castle was bright and evenly lit, but the original impression was much darker and moodier, which was mimicked by a negative exposure compensation.

© Brian Jackson

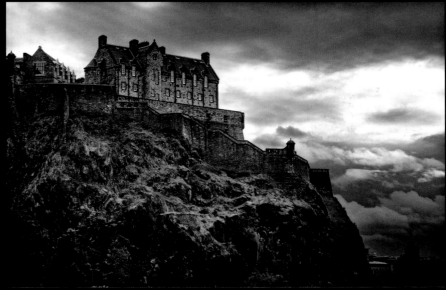

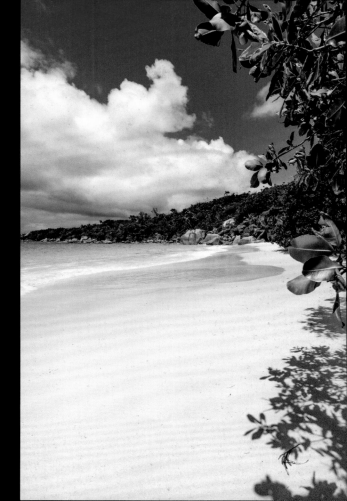

→ Making the whites white
The abundance of light tones in this shot pulled the metering system into underexposing, in an attempt to render the white sands a neutral gray. A stop of positive exposure compensation was all that was required.

Challenge Checklist

→ Your metadata will record how much compensation you used for each shot, so no need to keep notes. But do compare various amounts of compensation to your results and take note of those comparisons.

→ To record dark subjects at their true tonality you must subtract exposure from the metered reading; conversely to bring subjects to their natural light tonality, add exposure. Your meter sees the world as gray, and that is your starting point.

→ Zero out your compensation when you're done, so you don't forget and start your next day's shooting with the compensation set to add or subtract light.

High Dynamic Range Imaging

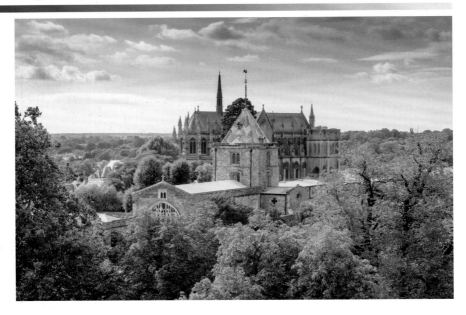

One of the more innovative approaches to solving the extreme contrast riddle has been the ascent of an extremely popular technique called High Dynamic Range Imaging (HDRI). HDRI is simply a process whereby the entire dynamic range, however high, is captured in a sequence of different exposures, and then all of them are combined into a single image file. So far, so good, but this combined image file (saved in a special format such as RGBE or OpenEXR) can still not be viewed on a normal computer or television screen. It needs a second stage of being converted back to a viewable image by a process known as tone mapping, in which you decide where exactly to distribute the full tonal data that you've collected throughout the limited dynamic range capacity of a given viewing platform (i.e., a paper print or a digital display).

The simplest way to capture the requisite exposures is to set your camera to its Autoexposure Bracketing mode, in which the camera will take a series of shots (i.e., a bracket) with only one being

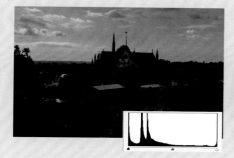

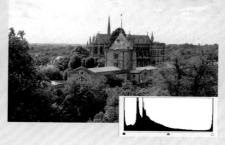

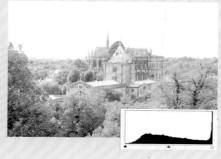

←↑↗↘ **Three-exposure bracket**
This scene is a classic high-dynamic range situation: bright midday sun in the mid- and background, but a shadowy foreground—precisely where the autumn colors were so vibrant. So the best exposure option was to bracket three exposures—one for the highlights, one for the mid-tones, and one for the shadows—which were then combined into a single image in Photoshop.

at the proper exposure (as determined by the metering system), and the others covering some predetermined range of over- and underexposure. You can usually set precisely the range covered by your bracket in your camera. Typically, a three-shot +/-2-stop bracket is sufficient—this means that the first exposure will be properly metered, the second will be overexposed by +2 stops and the third will be underexposed by -2 stops. The effect is that you have now

expanded your dynamic range by six stops: three in the highlights, and three in the shadows. Depending on your camera—and the processing power of your computer—you can shoot extremely wide brackets of, say, a dozen shots covering a vast range of tonal values, but this is almost always going to be overkill. Usually, expanding your camera sensor's native dynamic range a few stops in either direction is sufficient, and the resulting files easier to process.

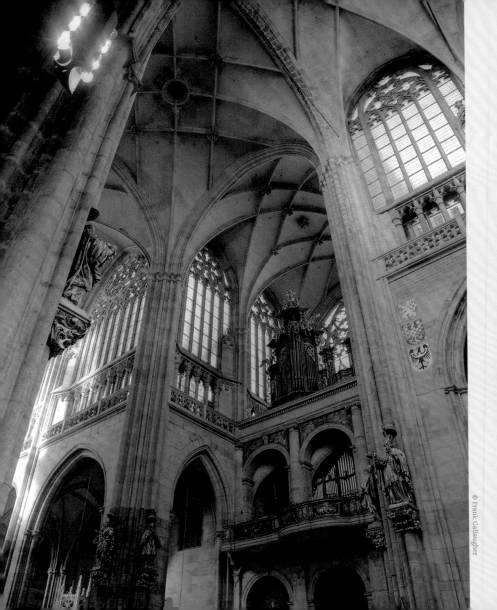

HDR PROCESSING

There is no shortage of processing software options available for combining your bracketed exposures into a single HDR image, from dedicated programs like Photomatix (www.hdrsoft.com) to built-in tools and plugins available in Adobe Photoshop or Lightroom. Regardless of the software used, the basic process is fundamentally a matter of deciding where to put what information from which exposure in the final image. For instance, in Photoshop you are given four options in 8- and 16-bit modes: Local Adaptation, which gives you the most control and allows you to construct a custom tone curve to most accurately spread out your exposure information across various areas of the frame; Equalize Histogram, which globally spreads out all the exposure information gathered across the full frame; Exposure and Gamma, which lets you manually adjust the brightness and contrast; or Highlight Compression, which attempts to restore blow-out highlights of one exposure with detail from another.

← **Improvised ND filter**
Interiors are another classic situation where HDR can be a big help. The light coming through the beautiful windows was far brighter than any of the interior lighting, so in order to capture detail from the ground level all the way up to the roof, three exposures were combined into a 32-bit Tiff, then tone mapped in Adobe Camera Raw.

Another option entirely is to combine your three exposures into a 32-bit Tiff, which you can the tone map in Adobe Camera Raw. This gives you the familiar set of exposure controls (see page 265), but each of those sliders will have a much larger effect than usual, because you are now manipulating considerably more lighting information than what was possible to capture in a single exposure. It's rather like creating an archive of all the lighting information in the original scene.

If you begin to explore HDR imaging in full, you will soon realize that the abundance of information captured across multiple images can be combined in many more ways than one, and that given such a wealth of exposure options, your rendition of your final image quickly becomes a matter of personal, creative interpretation. It becomes very easy to push what was a normal scene far into the bounds of heavily processed, surrealistic artistry. However, it's strongly recommended that you begin by performing the most photorealistic processing that you can. For one, that is much closer to the purpose of this book (i.e., using HDRI as an exposure tool, first and foremost); and second, because it is all too easy to get carried away with surrealistic interpretations, it's best to establish a firm foundation before moving on to higher levels of experimentation.

Combat the Contrast with an HDR Image

Although the sensor in your camera has a finite dynamic range, that just means it can only record a certain tonal range in one frame. That is the secret to this challenge: You will make separate exposures for two or more distinct tonal regions of your scene and then combine them into one HDR image in processing. The final photo will contain a tonal range that greatly exceeds the limitations set by your camera. So seek out extreme contrast—the wider the range, the better. Then tame the contrast by expanding the dynamic range of your images.

↓ **Balancing land and sky**
The severe underexposure required to capture the rich, saturated tones in the sky meant the foreground dock would have to be almost pure black. So a simple HDR combination of one shot exposed for the sky, and one shot exposed for the foreground, meant all the tones could fit into a single, final image. Anti-ghosting tools kept movement in the waves from being distracting.

© Fyle

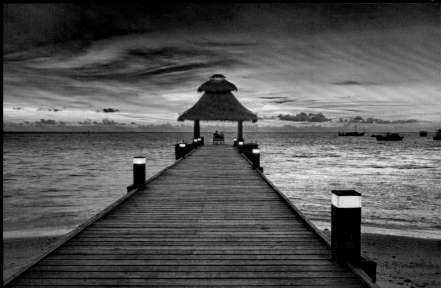

→ **Go for a graphic take**
This shot demonstrates a subtle use of HDR, in which one shot is exposed for the outside and pillars, with a second capturing detail in the graphic pattern along the vaulted roof at the upper-left of the frame.

Challenge Checklist

→ A tripod will help, but auto-alignment features will be a big help; just do your best to remain steady between shots.

→ One fast way to fire off several shots at various exposures is to use your autoexposure bracketing feature. Just be sure that the primary exposure is set correctly for the mid-tones, and then bracket widely enough to capture images of both the shadow and highlight areas.

→ If your camera has a built-in HDR mode, try it. But try to create the multiple exposure manually too, and then compare the results.

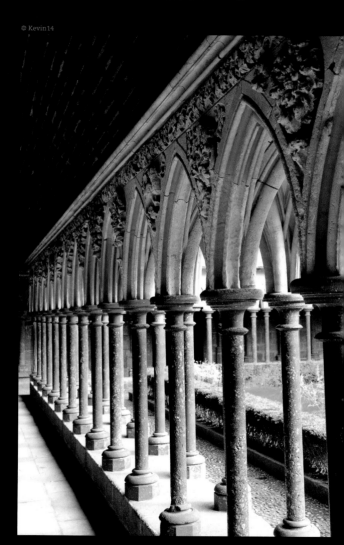
© Kevin14

The Zone System in a Digital World

One of the pioneers of creative exposure was the American landscape master Ansel Adams. In addition to redefining nature photography through his powerful wilderness compositions, Adams, perhaps more than any photographer before him, elevated the principles of exposure to a high skill. It was his articulate writings on the topic of vision, exposure, and their interrelationships that have now given generations of photographers a thorough understanding of the power of exposure.

In 1939–40, Adams and fellow photographer Fred Archer created an exposure method called the Zone System—a system that provided a means by which one could use the tools of exposure to predictably translate their personal vision to the final print. As Adams explains, however, it wasn't so much an invention as a "codification of the principles of sensitometry." Adams also coined the term "visualization" (often misquoted as "pre-visualization")

to describe this process of translating one's vision to the final print. Finally, Adams used the Zone system in conjunction with under- and overprocessing, which with film and when combined with the appropriate amount of over- and underexposure, respectively, altered the contrast of the negative. The digital equivalent is much simpler—i.e., at its most basic, moving the Contrast slider.

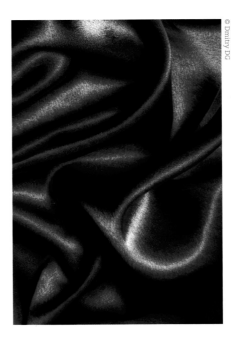

© Dmitry DG

→ → → Zones III, V, and VII
Digital photography saves you a lot of time concerning yourself with all 10 distinct tonal regions and their associated definitions. In fact, once you understand the principles of the zone system, you can concentrate mostly on just these three zones. They are, as illustrated here from left to right: Textured Shadow (Zone III), Mid-tone (Zone V, the pivotal value), and Textured Brights (Zone VII).

Though originally developed for use as an aid in exposing and printing black-and-white negative films, the core aspects can be adapted very well to digital photography. And though many books have been written on the Zone System and some have made it appear hopelessly complex, it isn't.

In fact, understanding and applying the basic premise can make getting a good exposure—even with your digital camera—a very simple process. Moreover, it creates a reliable and fast method for placing tones exactly where you want them in your photos.

The fundamental concept of the Zone System is that the world around us could be divided into 10 distinct tonal values (though there are a few variations of the system that use either 9 or 11 values). The values range from zone "0" which is pure black with no detail to zone "IX" which is pure white with no texture at all. The middle tone in this system is Zone V and it represents a midway point that is exactly halfway between pure black and pure white. As we discussed briefly earlier, this middle zone is what photographers refer to as "middle gray."

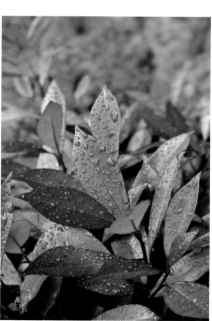
© Florelena

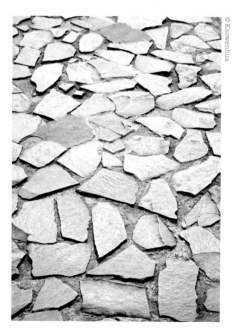
© Kaowenhua

Here is the interesting aspect of the 10 distinct tonal representations on the Zone System scale: each zone in the scale represents a tone that is either half as bright or half as dark as the one adjacent to it (depending on which direction you're moving).

As you should remember from our discussion of basic exposure controls, each time that you move from one exposure stop to the next, you either halve or double the amount of light getting to your sensor. And as you have probably guessed (and correctly so), each time that you change exposure by one stop (again, either aperture or shutter speed) you shift every value on the Zone System scale to the next value. In other words, every zone on the scale is exactly one stop away from the one next to it. By shifting exposure, you can shift exactly where specific tones land in that 10-stop tonal range.

If, for example, you meter a subject of a particular value (say a red apple), you are placing it on Zone V. But if you open the lens by one stop (or slow the shutter by one stop) the apple would be placed one tonal step lighter. Instead of being placed on Zone V, it will now be shifted to Zone VI. The reverse is also true: close the lens by one stop (or make the shutter speed one stop faster) and the apple is now placed on Zone IV—exactly one stop darker. You can see the power this gives you over the tonal placement of any subject—and it is an exacting science.

The beauty of this system is that you know that whatever you meter is going to land on Zone V. To make it darker, all you have to do is underexpose from that meter reading. To make it lighter, increase exposure. It doesn't matter

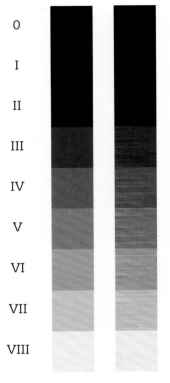

0

I

II

III

IV

V

VI

VII

VIII

IX

whether you adjust shutter speed or aperture, but for each stop that you alter the exposure, you shift every tone either up or down the tonal scale. Your creative decision is on the initial placement of your mid-tone; then all the other tones fall into their respective zones. That's the Zone System workflow: place, then fall. Combine judicious mid-tone placement with a full understanding of where the rest of the tones will fall as a result, and you'll master the Zone System in no time.

THE ZONES

An alternative version of the Zone System has 11 zones instead of the 10 shown here, and yet another has 9. Note that we show two versions of the scale here, one of solid tones, the other with an added texture. One school of thought holds that textured zones are closer to the reality of a scene, and so are easier to judge.

ZONE 0 Solid, maximum black. 0,0,0 in RGB. No detail. In digital photography, the black point goes here.

ZONE I Almost black, as in deep shadows. No discernible texture. In digital photography, almost solid black.

ZONE II First hint of texture in a shadow. Mysterious, only just visible. In digital photography, the point at which detail begins to be distinguished from noise.

ZONE III Textured shadow. A key zone in many scenes and images. Texture and detail are clearly seen, such as the folds and weave of a dark fabric.

ZONE IV Typical shadow value, as in dark foliage, buildings, landscapes.

ZONE V Mid-tone. The pivotal value. Average, mid-gray, an 18% gray card. Dark skin, light foliage.

ZONE VI Average Caucasian skin, concrete in overcast light, shadows on snow in sunlit scenes.

ZONE VII Textured brights. Pale skin, light-toned and brightly lit concrete. Yellows, pinks, and other obviously light colors. In digital photography, the point at which detail can just be seen in highlights.

ZONE VIII The last hint of texture, bright white. In digital photography, the brightest acceptable highlight.

ZONE IX Solid white, 255, 255, 255 in RGB. Acceptable for specular highlights only. In digital photography, the white point goes here.

Low-Key Images

In most situations, the choices that you make in either accepting or altering the exposure settings your meter indicates are decisions made to place the tonalities of specific subjects where most viewers would feel that they normally belong. You're simply tweaking the exposure to correct for "Zone V" metering—adding exposure to keep white subjects white, for instance, or reducing exposure to keep dark subjects dark. But there are times when diverging from a middle-of-the-road exposure creates some very dramatic images. Typically, such extreme variations are made to enhance a specific type of subject or to exaggerate an emotional climate. Of course, if you get too extreme in your variations people will view your exposures as mistakes rather than creative choices, but it's only by experimenting that you can find the parameters of your own creativity.

Any time a photograph is dominated by darker tones and has a limited number of light or middle-toned areas, it's referred to as a low-key image. Low-key images can (and usually do) have highlights and, in fact, often need the contrast of limited brighter tones to better exhibit the richness of the darker regions. The overall tonal range, however, tends to be quite dark and subdued—a portrait set against a dark shadow background or a still life made up of deep, rich colors.

Low-key photos tend to elicit a brooding or melancholy emotional response because of their inherent darkness, and are often seen as mysterious or intriguing. Our eyes are tend to linger longer on dark-toned images because our brains are searching for clues about the missing brighter areas.

→ St. John's Chapel, Tower of London
Here, the deep shadows on this chapel are allowed to contrast with the flaring sunlight through the window, in order to reproduce the actual sensation of this medieval architecture.

↓ Playing off the shadows
In this shot, there is a faint trace of highlights along the model's upper arm and cheekbone. The colors fall in the mid-tones or darker, and as they contrast against the pure black background and shadows they appear richer and bolder without actually undergoing any saturation boost.

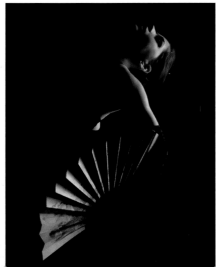

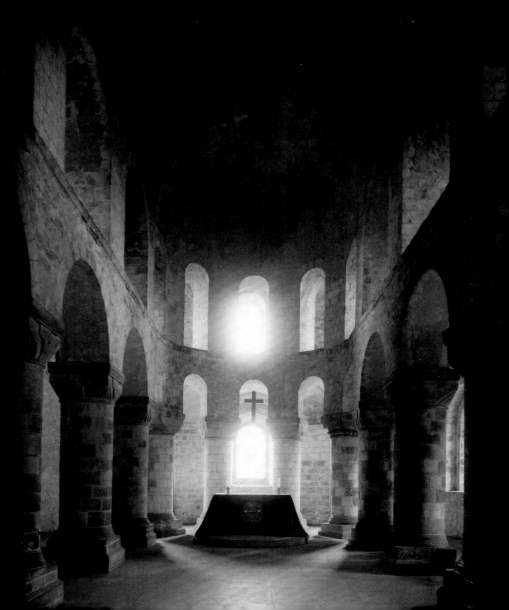

EXTREME UNDEREXPOSURE

Imagine that you're photographing an approaching thunderstorm. Recording the tones as they appear may be enough to show that what you're photographing is a storm-laden sky. You can, however, greatly exaggerate that mood and intensify the drama of the moment if you intentionally underexpose the scene by two or three stops. By doing so, you will significantly reduce the scene to one of gray, almost black skies, and large areas of deep shadow. The entire image—including all but the brightest highlights—will shift into a palette of deep grays.

The trick to recording very low-key scenes, however, is to not go so dark that you can't resolve a certain amount of minimal shadow detail during processing. If details in storms clouds are lost, it's probably of no concern, but if foreground details are reduced to pure black then you've lost all sense of texture and detail, and your image will lack a sense of place and context.

Such deep underexposure can also be used to subdue more colorful subjects, as well, in order to draw out the richness of the colors and use darkened shadows to enhance surface textures. For a street produce market, for instance, a "normal" exposure will record a colorful and cheerful scene. But by reducing the exposure several stops, shadows begin to dominate, people fall into dark shapes

and the colored produce seem to be oddly abstract shapes. By making an extreme shift in exposure you've altered the mood—which is entirely your creative right as a photographer.

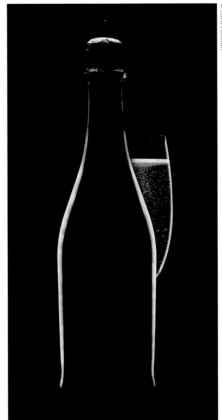

© Luca Fabbian

↙ Engaging product shots
Though it might seem counterintuitive
to hide the main subject in a product shot,
it is an effective technique for pulling in
the viewer's attention—one well-used by
art directors.

↓ Storms above the Isle of Skye
There isn't a single highlight in this stormscape,
though the clouds, waterfall, and midground
elements appear brighter by comparison.
Limiting the palette to the left side of the
histogram, elicits tension from the view.

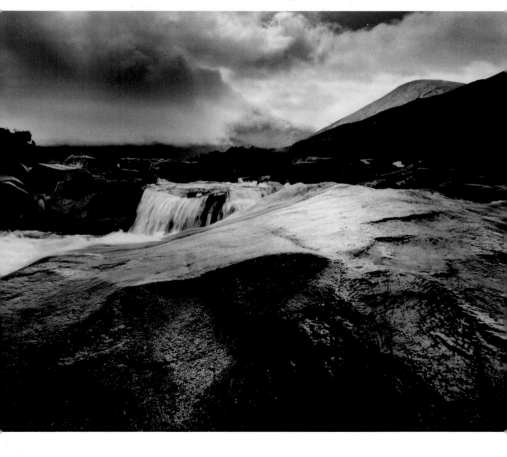

Shoot the Shadows with a Low-Key Shot

Challenge

Dark and dreary, dank and gloomy, that's one way to think of a low-key shot. But low-key scenes can also have a dramatic regal flair—a palette and lighting style through which Rembrandt brought illumination to his vision. In completing this challenge you will no doubt discover that even the darker side of the tonal scale has its emotional light. You have to see strength and emotion in places that are not screaming for your attention. But once you learn to design from the mid-tones down and embrace the shadow world, you'll find much visual magic hidden in those secret lairs.

↓ **Contrast is key**
It's ironic how often a low-key shot is composed around a light source, but a shadow isn't a shadow without a contrasting area of light.

© Andreiuc88

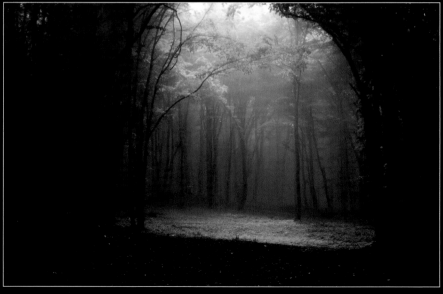

→ Leave it a mystery

A couple more stops of exposure and it would have been possible to see into the archways and windows, but leaving them pure black has a more engaging and mysterious effect.

Challenge Checklist

→ Low-key images are not without highlights. Often a sliver of highlight draws greater attention to the dark balance of such scenes. Indeed, even a white rose can be photographed using a low-key recipe by grossly underexposing it's natural brightness.

→ If you're shooting a portrait indoors, use a sheet of black seamless paper as your background. Dress your subject in deep tones and you'll further enhance the low-key effect.

→ Underexposing landscapes on an already gloomy weather day is a great way to exaggerate the mood of such scenes. A quick shortcut: take a reading from a mid-tone and then use two or more stops of negative compensation.

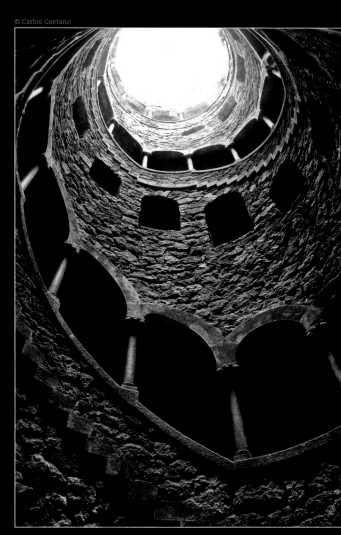
© Carlos Caetano

High-Key Images

A high-key image is one where the overwhelming balance of tones range between lighter mid-tones and the very whitest highlights. In exposing for high-key scenes, it's fine to let some of the brightest images wash-out completely, as this tends to enhance the airy and romantic look of the pictures. Again, it's not a fault to have a certain number of mid-tone or darker areas, but high-key images do work better when their contrast is moderate and dark tones are kept to a minimum. High-key images definitely tend to have a cheerful, upbeat quality to them. The technique is particularly well suited to portraits, both formal and informal, because it gives them a gentle, dream-like quality.

⬉ High-key high fashion
There are two immediate side effects to this portrait's use of high-key lighting: the skin is so blown out that it needs no retouching in order to appear smooth; and the reds of the lips and fingernails are accented and emboldened.

↓ Cheery interiors
When photographing interior spaces—particularly domestic ones—it is often desirable to represent them positively, with a feeling of cleanness and comfort. Letting an abundance of light spill through the rooms achieves this.

© Valua Vitaly

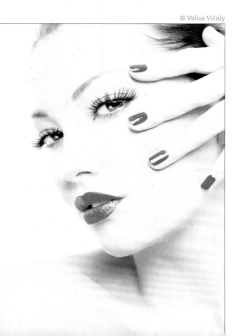

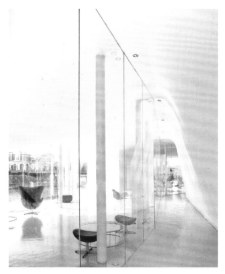

EXTREME OVEREXPOSURE
& HIGH-KEY IMAGING

It's typically harder to find subjects that work well with overexposure because usually it means sacrificing a high percentage of highlights and lighter tones. Therefore, the idea works best with subjects that are atmospherically or emotionally matched to the technique— yellow and white flowers swaying in a summer breeze, for example, or girls in white dresses dancing in a meadow. In these situations, mood trumps highlight detail and if you capture the right moment, then the airiness of the scenes can have a powerful emotional impact.

Again, by allowing lighter areas to blow out, you are inviting critiques from people who will see the images as simple mistakes. But if you were to scan the calendar and greeting card racks you would see that this is actually a very popular technique in establishing a bright, cheerful, and upbeat mood. Art directors often see this as a welcome technique for creating a clean, positive representation of a given subject.

One interesting byproduct of extra exposure is that colors tend to shift toward a more pastel range that further increases the welcoming mood. While this is a delicate craft, as almost all hues weaken with increasing brightness, the eye will pay correspondingly more attention to subtle nuances of tone and contrast—and these subtleties are very

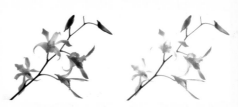

↑ **Not quite clipped**
Illuminated by a studio flash aimed directly toward the camera from behind a sheet of Plexiglas, these orchids are bright, but not blown out (or "clipped"), and you can clearly follow the distinct lines around the edges of each petal, tracing the overall shape of the flowers.

↗ **Definitely clipped**
Here, the exposure was increased by just one stop, but the difference is dramatic. The petals appear translucent, with a shift toward brighter pastels. Indeed, this high-key shot sacrifices shape in order to stress color and light.

much where high-key photography thrives. The more that you increase exposure, however, remember that you are also tossing aside things like surface and edge detail as well as texture in the lighter regions. And you are shifting what would normally be the darker areas into a range of middle tones or even above-middle tones. Accordingly, the high-key technique is not appropriate for accurate representations of subjects with significant detail in shadow areas. Also, if your subjects are backlit, you will begin to lose shape as the edges are eroded by backlighting. If you push this effect far enough, you can obliterate large mounts of edge detail, and have your subject appear to be floating in mid-air, bursting forth out of the clouds.

Hug the Highlights with a High-Key Shot

Challenge

With their cheerful tones and luminescent glow, it's no wonder that high-key images are the staple of the greeting card industry. That is the charm of photos that are created from a wash of bright tonalities—a sense of joyful abandon and an aura of purity. One of the keys to mastering this challenge will be your ability to see or create compositions that are dominated almost entirely by tones that are lighter than middle gray. And one way of exaggerating their glow is to abandon detail in some of the brightest ranges—intentionally abandoning detail and texture in favor of establishing an upbeat and innocent mood.

⇩ **Show off the subject**
The challenge of adequately lighting a close-up shot is often remedied by simply going overboard and bathing the subject in a soft, enveloping light for a high-key interpretation.

© Azteca

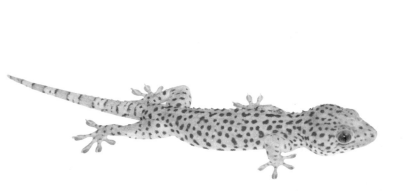

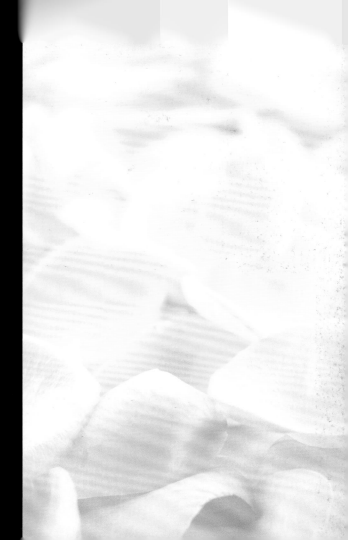

...soft contours
...gh-key interpretations
...ite the viewer to
...preciate what little
...tured detail remains,
...d so a subtly over-
...posed approach can
...en be more effective
...an a proper exposure.

Challenge
Checklist

...f you're thinking of
...etting up a high-key still
...ife, picture yourself in a
...market picking props.
...What would you choose?
...ggs? Gardenias? White
...pottery?

...Don't panic when the
...highlights begin to run
...off the right edge of your
...histogram with high-key
...images—remember that
...you're allowing some
...detail to escape in favor
...of setting a mood.

...Shooting a portrait? Use
...a white bed sheet as your
...backdrop and second one
...as a wrap for your model.
...ust be sure to use plus
...compensation from
...whatever you meter to
...push the tonal range up
...several zones.

CHAPTER 2 | Light & Lighting

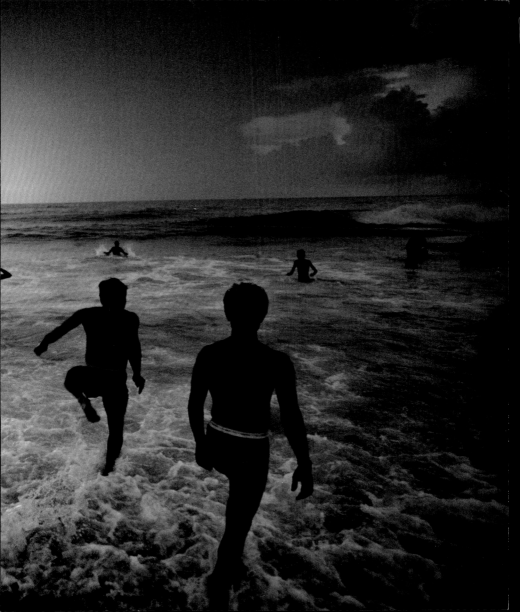

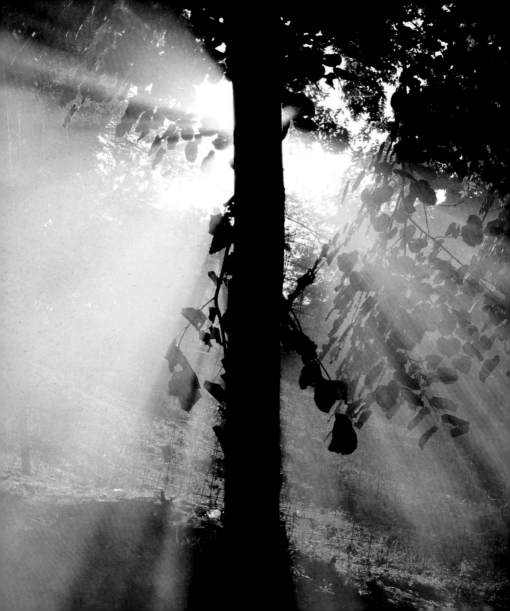

Introduction: Light & Lighting

It's easy to underestimate the significance of light, as it's basically ubiquitous in our waking lives. If we aren't outside during the day being guided by the sun, we're constantly battling back the darkness with our own artificial lights. Even scenarios we consider quite dark will almost always have some source of light in them, like a path through the woods at night being ever so faintly illuminated by the moon. As such, most people take light for granted. Either it's there or not; the lamp is either on or off. And if it's there, it's either bright or dim, simple as that.

Photographers, of course, know there's quite a lot more going on, and that's what makes light and lighting such a fundamental element of photography. Light is like our own photographic language, and becoming fluent in it is an essential step in building photographic skill. Photographers sometimes speak of their ability to "see" or "read" light. On the surface, this is a rather obvious statement; of course you can see light, everyone does. But what they are referring to is their ability to observe the fine and subtle qualities of light, then capture them and make them work creatively in an image. Photographers notice the color of different light sources, the density and length of shadows, the angles of light and corresponding times of day—the list goes on and on.

In most situations, there is usually some degree of control over the light. But even in photojournalistic or naturalistic situations where there's either no time or desire to influence the light directly, you still have decisions to make as to how your camera responds to and records that light. How dense do you want your shadows? Do you need to preserve detail in the highlights? Should you color balance for the warm tungsten lights or the daylight coming through the window? Gradually, as you become fluent in the language of light, these questions will be less like obstacles, and more like creative tools you can use to achieve your particular vision.

Light is the single element that will always make a difference in a shot. A scene may be boring or commonplace in one kind of light, but change the angle or intensity, and suddenly it's something more. Sometimes the light is so striking that it becomes the subject of the photograph itself. It's impossible to isolate precisely what kind of light is flattering or aesthetically pleasing and why (though there are general trends to look out for, such as the golden light at the beginning and end of the day); such universalities are hard to come by in art. But you will learn to recognize the exceptional qualities of light when you see them, and to make the most of those situations as you encounter them.

Bit-Depth & Tonality

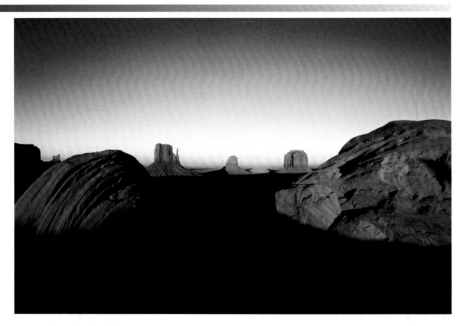

In digital imaging, each and every tone and color value is assigned a definite, discrete numerical value (as opposed to film, which exists in an analogue continuum). The basic unit for computing is called a "bit," short for "binary digit." These bits are either on or off, ones or zeroes, black or white—there is no in-between (hence the "binary" terminology). So a single bit could indicate that a pixel is either pure black or pure white, but that doesn't leave any room for the infinite gradations of gray

↑ **Lots of skyline**
The gradual lightening of the blue sky as it moves from the top of the frame toward the horizon is a large part of what makes this image work. Had the image not been saved with sufficient bit-depth, that delicate gradient could easily have appeared as a series of stripes across the sky, with obvious jumps across tonal values.

in between these two extremes. To fill in the gaps, we can put a string of bits together and combine them to give us a greater number of intermediate values. If we put 8 bits together, that gives us 256 (2^8) discrete values in which we can store information. When applied to digital images, that range of values is called the "bit-depth" of the image.

Recall from the discussion of dynamic range on pages 80–83 that in the creation of an image file, the imaging sensor assigns a numerical value to each pixel, usually in a range from 0–255. Now you can see where that number comes from: The image file (in this case) is constructed using 8 bits. Now that may not seem like a lot; certainly we can perceive more than just 256 colors and shades in an image. Each pixel is interpolated out of the data from three different photodiodes, one per primary color. So in fact, a color channel contains 256 x 256 x 256 different levels of information, resulting in 16.7 million possible colors, far more than we are able to perceive with the human eye.

While 16.7 million colors may seem more than adequate for all our image needs, that is not always the case. Take, for instance, a wide-angled shot that contains a vast expanse of blue sky and a horizon line with some darker landscape at the bottom of the frame. As the sky approaches the horizon, its blue tones gradually get darker. The difference between the light and dark areas of the sky may not be very great, but it is stretched out across the majority of the frame. So rather than using

16.7 million discrete levels to illustrate this gradient, the image may use only a few dozen. The resulting image will probably exhibit a phenomenon called banding: obvious and perceptible jumps between tonal values across a large area of the frame. Even if it is not terribly obvious at first, any significant adjustments in post-production would exaggerate these abrupt jumps between tonal values, and the results would be distracting and unrealistic.

INCREASING BIT-DEPTH

We can mitigate this banding effect by working in a greater bit-depth. The 8-bit format we've been discussing so far is just the base level for building digital image files—used by JPEGs, in-camera histograms, and most LCD displays. If you shoot in the Raw format, today's imaging sensors are capable of saving images in 12- or 14-bit formats. This gives you 65,536 discrete values per channel, or 281 trillion colors to work with—quite enough to protect even the most subtle of gradients from exhibiting banding.

Of course, Raw files must be processed before they can be displayed, and if you plan on manipulating them further in image-processing software, you should make sure that you continue to work in a

large enough bit-depth. In Photoshop, go to Image > Mode and make sure that either 16- or 32-bits/channel is selected. However, keep in mind that most displays and printers will still only use 8-bits per channel, so you will need to save the file back down before displaying or printing the image—but don't worry, you are still making use of the greater original bit-depth and range of tonality; you are just doing a better job of distributing that tonality across the areas of the frame that need it most.

It's worth noting that there is a clear distinction between dynamic range and bit-depth: While we can increase the number of discrete values into which a given range is divided, we are not actually expanding that range. Which is to say, working in greater bit-depths does not increase the dynamic range of the sensor—black is still black and white is still white. Rather, greater bit-depths simply give us more room to exhibit the differences between those extremes.

→ **Plenty of space**
Not every scene requires a full 281 trillion colors in order to capture an accurate representation —and sometimes, if you are going for a high-contrast look, you'll be throwing out a lot of those in-between values anyway. The key is to recognize which scenes exhibit a large gradient that requires greater bit-depths and shoot accordingly. Of course, shooting in Raw is generally a good idea regardless, as you will always have the option to make use of the greater range of tonality if it's needed.

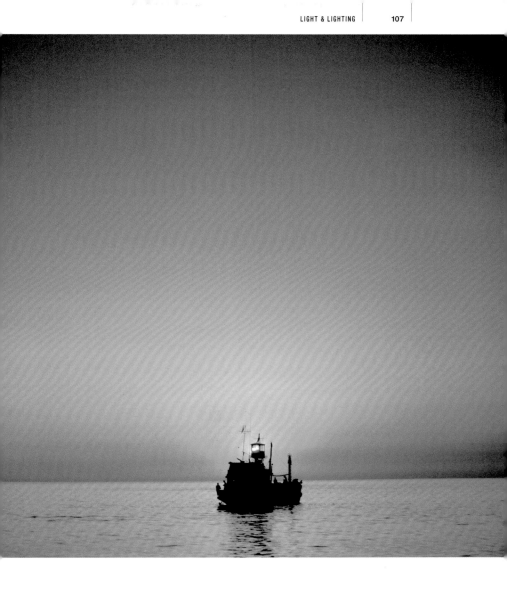

The Sun Throughout the Day

The time of the day will be the most important factor contributing to the role of sunlight in your photography. Sunlight shines at a very low angle early and late in the day, gradually rising to a harsh, high-angled light around noon (depending on Daylight Saving Time).

DAWN AND DUSK

If you've ever raced against time to a scenic vista in order to view a sunset, you know how quickly light can change as the sun approaches the horizon. The movement of the sun, while barely perceptible across the vast expanse of a full sky, seems expedited at the beginning and end of the day. In reality, the sun moves at a constant speed, of course; it is merely the stationary reference point of the horizon line that lets us perceive its motion. But the quality of its light does indeed change rapidly, affected by the extreme angle at which it is shining on a scene. These changes can be unpredictable and dramatic, and you must work quickly to observe their effects and make use of them.

The sun appears red at the beginning and end of the day because its light is passing through more atmosphere, which scatters the blue and violet wavelengths. Additionally, any clouds present along the horizon have a farther distance to travel before they get out of the way, so there is a greater likelihood that red sunlight will be diffused through radiant, fiery cloudscapes.

MIDDAY SUN

At noon, the sun reaches its zenith and is at its brightest intensity. It is also at its most perpendicular angle to the earth, and so the shadows it casts are particularly harsh, creating high-contrast exposure situations. Delicate metering is essential in order to capture the full dynamic range of such scenes. In landscapes, various filters can help capture the high-intensity blue of the

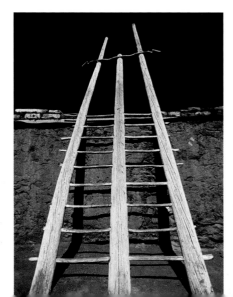

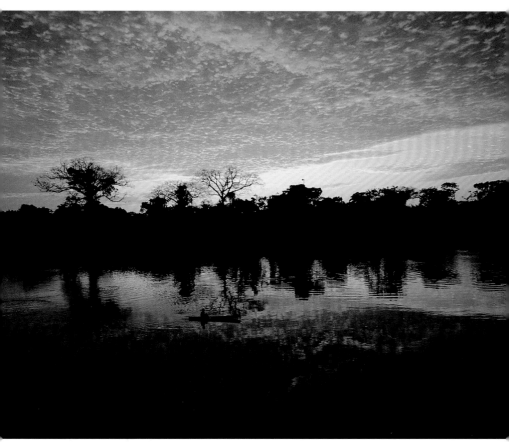

← Strong contrasts
Black-and-white photography invites the use of strong contrast, and harsh shadows can be a compelling element of the composition, even if detail is lost in them.

↑ Sunrise and sunset silhouettes
Sunsets are a traditional favorite time for photography, but as a subject in itself, a sunset alone can be rather commonplace. Using the brilliant lighting conditions of dusk as a backdrop for another subject, however, allows you to flex your creative muscle. Here, the brilliant skyline is reflected in the Amazon river, casting the lone boat and tree line in a moody silhouette.

sky while still preserving the mid-toned greens of rolling hills and shadows cast by trees or buildings. Portraits can be particularly challenging, as the direction of this sunlight casts unflattering shadows down on a subject's face. These shadows can be filled in by flash or reflectors, or mitigated by diffusers.

On the other hand, if you embrace the contrast, midday sun can create punchy, dynamic images. Black-and-white photography is particularly suited to such conditions, as shadows and highlights are often expected to lack detail and be rendered pure black or white, respectively. But embracing high contrast usually means accepting dense, featureless shadows.

THE SPACE BETWEEN

Recognizing the particular challenges presented by the extremes of light throughout the day, it follows that the light in between these times, especially early morning and late afternoon, is often easier to photograph. Not too high and not too low, this sunlight is perceived by the human eye to be both attractive (good for a variety of subjects) and neutral white (making white balance adjustment a simple matter).

→ **Early morning and late afternoon**
When the sun is lower early in the morning and late in the afternoon, the light is not so bright as to overwhelm the delicate yellows and greens in the trees, nor so angular as to make the shadows a major part of the composition.

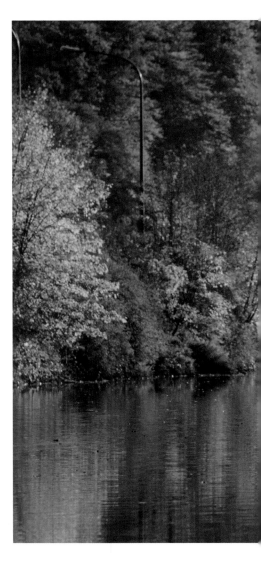

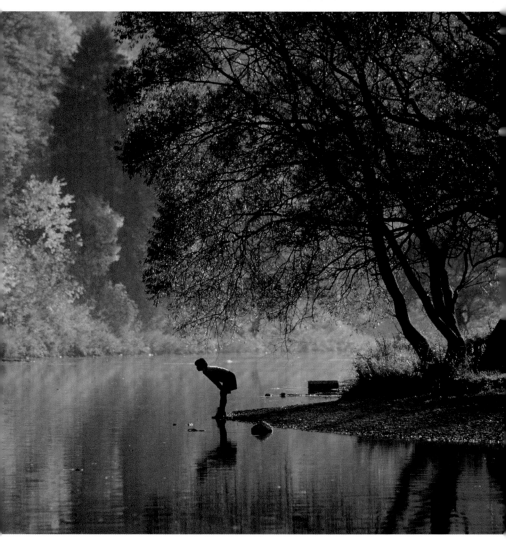

Dealing with Strong Sunlight

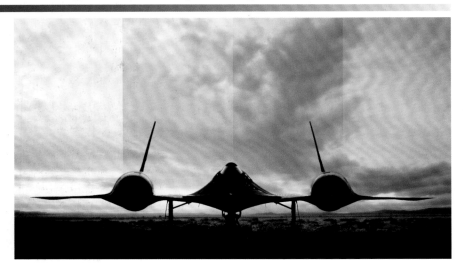

↑ Filter effects
Grad filters help balance bright skies against shadowed foregrounds, and can also be used to add a color cast. This composite image shows the effects of various grad filters, from left to right: no filter, neutral density, blue, and yellow. Much more cloud detail is captured with filters.

It is all well and good to speak of the patience required for photographing a scene in ideal sunlight, but as a photographer, you are not completely at the mercy of nature. On the contrary, you possess a variety of tools and techniques to manipulate the light given to you so that it is optimal for any given subject.

GRADUATED FILTERS

In many landscape shots, the top of the frame is dominated by an extremely bright skyline, much brighter than the mid-tones and shadows occupying the bottom half of the frame. To squeeze all this dynamic range onto your camera's sensor, you can use a graduated (grad) filter to block some of the brightest light at the top, while allowing progressively more light to pass through as it moves down the frame. The most common is a neutral density filter, which blocks a certain amount of light without adding any color cast. You can slide these filters

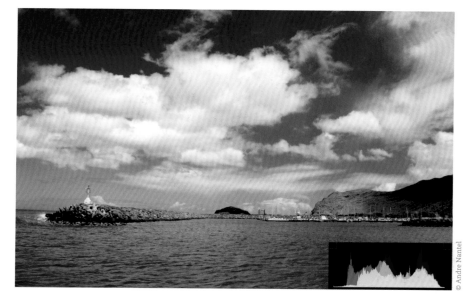

© Andre Nantel

↑ **Saturated skies**
A polarizing filter makes the clouds pop against a vivid blue sky, and keeps bright sunlight from reflecting off the water. The wide-angle lens means the intensity of the polarizing effect varies, with the blue sky getting progressively more saturated toward the upper-left corner.

up and down the end of your lens, in order to line up the gradation level with the horizon of your scene. The effect can be seen in the histogram: as the filter slides down over the lens, the right side of the histogram will gradually approach the right edge. The goal is to get the highlights as close to this right-side edge as possible without clipping them off.

POLARIZERS

Another method of blocking some of the light in a scene in order to prevent overexposure is the use of a circular polarizing filter. These filters will darken skies and make clouds pop, and are most effective at right angles to the sun. By rotating the filter on the end of your lens, you can adjust the effect of the polarizer to suit your particular exposure situation. Be sure to pay attention to the other effects the filter has on your scene, as polarizers also reduce reflections from glass and water, and cut through atmospheric haze.

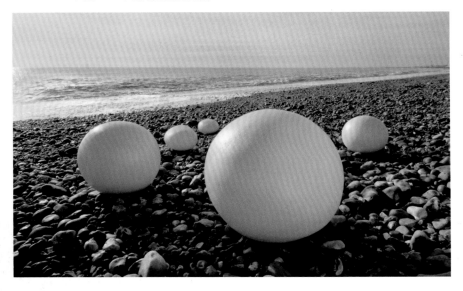

FILLING IN SHADOWS

Whereas neutral density and polarizing filters mitigate high-contrast lighting conditions by decreasing the intensity of the highlights, another option is to increase the intensity of the shadows and bring them closer to the highlights. This is called "filling in" the shadows, and can be accomplished in several ways. First, you can fire a flash and directly add light to the scene. This use of fill flash is effective, as the color temperature of flash is close enough to daylight that the two can usually be mixed without looking unnatural. But it takes a delicate touch to balance the amount of flash with the ambient light.

REFLECTORS

At its simplest, a reflector is any surface that can bounce daylight onto a subject. You can direct where the reflected light falls by adjusting the angle of the reflector. White reflectors bounce the most light and are therefore the most common, though golden and silver reflectors can also be used if you want to add a particular color to your subject. By allowing you to directly observe their effects in real time before the shot is taken, reflectors can be much easier to use than fill flash. Lightweight and cheap, most reflectors also collapse for easy storage, making them an essential piece of equipment.

← **Rounding out the light**
The light shining on this beach scene was strongly directional, so a collapsible silver-fabric reflector was used from off-camera right to fill in the shadows on the backs of these painted stone objects (by artist Yukako Shibata).

↓ **Natural diffusers**
This portrait uses the natural diffusion of light through a bamboo forest to soften the shadows cast on the subject's face. The single streak of direct sunlight also adds dimensionality and ambience—but needs to be delicately color corrected in relation to the rest of the face, lest the subject appear too blue (from the color temperature of the shade).

DIFFUSERS

A diffuser is anything that scatters light from a given source such that it falls more evenly across a subject. In outdoor portraiture, for instance, positioning a large, semi-transparent panel in between the sun and your subject will distribute the sun's light evenly across their face, lifting shadows and toning down highlights.

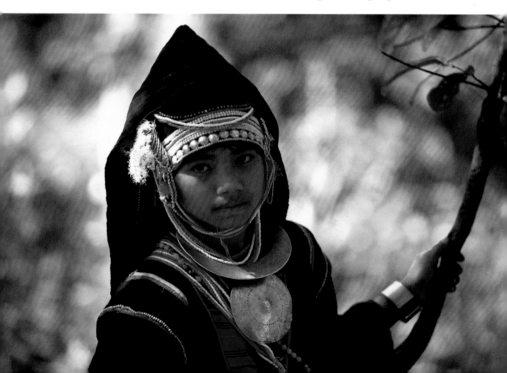

Shooting Into the Sun

Technically, everything about pointing your camera at the sun for a shot is wrong: Images strongly tend toward overexposure, color detail is easily lost, and textures are rendered flat. But creative manipulation of these conditions can deliver atmospheric and successful images. If the sun is visible in the frame, the extremely high dynamic range will mean you have to make a judgement call as to exposure—either your subject will be illuminated and your skies will be blown out to pure white, or your skies will be properly exposed around a shadowed, silhouetted foreground. Matrix metering may assume an overexposure and overcompensate by making the whole image too dark. Spot metering lets you indicate which area of the frame will be properly exposed. In any case, delicate use of the histogram is essential to achieving the look you want.

If you frame the shot so the sun is masked by an element in the scene, that element (which will appear as a silhouette) will be framed in a light radiating out from its edges. This edge or "rim" lighting accentuates the shape of that element and lends a strong graphic emphasis to the image.

Shooting into the sun is technically known as backlighting, although unlike in a studio, the height of the backlight is chosen for you by the position of the sun. For this reason, many outdoor backlit shots are taken at dawn or dusk when the sun is at its lowest. At other times of day the photographer can lie on the ground and shoot at an upward angle in order to backlight a subject.

↙ Facing dusk
Allowing these subjects to be cast as under-exposed silhouettes greatly enhances the mood of this image, and means the distant sky can fit into the exposure and contribute to the atmosphere.

↓ Runway at dawn
Peeking through a gap in this airplane fin, the sun is given a definite shape that would otherwise be lost in overexposure. The under-exposed, angular shape in the foreground becomes a strong graphic element, keeping the scene from being just another sunset photo.

© Frank Gallaugher

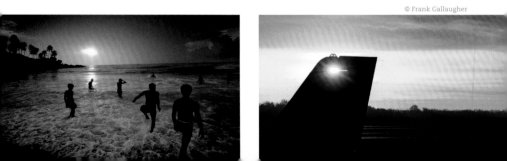

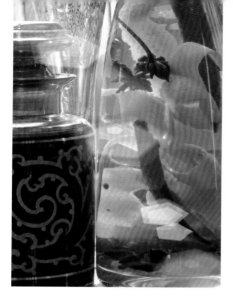

FLARE

Any time you shoot into the sun, you are inviting excess light to be reflected off the interior surfaces of your lens, creating streaks and artifacts known as flare. The wider the aperture, the more prone to flare the resulting image. You can use a lens hood to shade the edges and keep light from striking the front at too extreme an angle. The hood itself is often lined with nonreflective material. However, no lens hood is perfect, and even the best ones have little effect when the sun is directly in frame. Post-production will give you the opportunity to manually remove small amounts of flare, depending on how prevalent it is in the final image.

← **Pentagonal flare**
This still-life makes use of strong backlit colors, and the line of flare artifacts (pentagonal from the aperture shape inside the lens) add to the graphics and colors, particularly because they occupy a central diagonal.

CREATIVE USE OF FLARE

Technically, flare is an error. But judicious and intentional use of flare can deliver some very pleasing effects. Flare can add a cinematic quality to a shot. The difficulty is that it is impossible to judge how images will turn out until they have been taken, and often the frame will be so bright it can be difficult to compose the shot. A useful technique is to shield a portion of the lens with your hand, adjust your composition and focus to your liking, then take your hand away before firing the shutter.

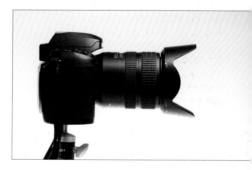

↑ **Proper Equipment**
In addition to improving image quality and preventing unwanted flare, lens hoods can also protect the front lens element from bumps and scrapes.

Face the Sun Head-On

Challenge

For this challenge you'll be shooting directly into the sun, but carefully setting up the shot to prevent total overexposure. The easiest way to achieve this is to block the sun by placing some element in between it and your camera. The object will be rendered as a silhouette, but the rest of the scene will still hold detail. The metering mode will depend on your scene, but you will need to keep a close eye on your histogram and be ready to override any autoexposure readings. Positioning is also key. Scouting ahead will help; you won't have much time to set up your shot before the sun moves.

↓ **Flare for effect**
Polygon stripes are hard to avoid if you shoot straight into a bright sun, but they can be made to work. Remember that they spread out from the light source in a line, so positioning the sun here in the top corner made them run diagonally. We're all so used to seeing flare that it's no longer a mistake, but something to help the mood—flare is often added artificially for just that reason.

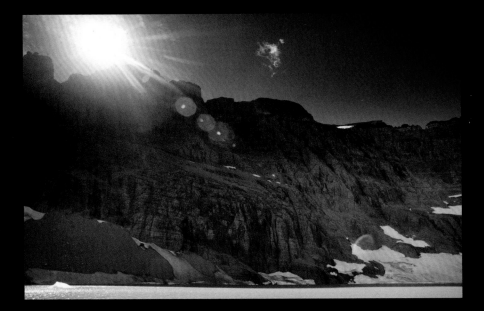

→ Radiant mist

Note that while they appear similar, these radiant beams of light are not flare artifacts, but rather ambient fog that is catching part of the light as the sun beams through it. By hiding the sun's actual disc behind the tree trunk, more of the tonal range of the beams has been captured, and there is less highlight clipping.

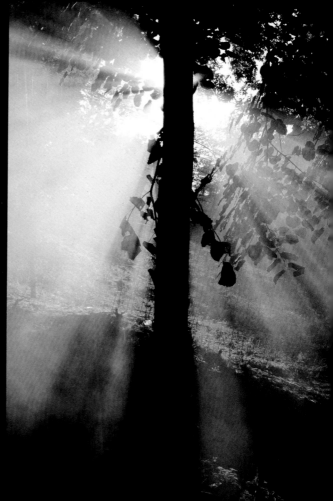

© Darko Novakovic

Challenge Checklist

→ If you have one, mount a lens hood to limit flare and help you see the frame as you are composing.

→ If you are completely unable to avoid flare in your shot, don't fight it—embrace the flare as a compositional element in itself and work with it, without allowing it to completely obscure other important elements.

→ Check your histogram after each shot and make sure your shadows and highlights aren't getting unintentionally clipped.

Golden Light

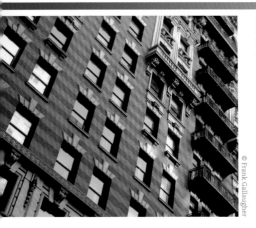

← **Urban reflections**
Frontal golden light brings out rich, saturated colors, and the windows of this New York high-rise reflect the shimmering blue of a clear sky above.

The brief period of time when the sun is just above the horizon but still below about 20 degrees offers a distinctly warm, golden color of light—typically between 3500K and 4500K (see pages 66–68). The richness and saturation of the resulting colors, combined with long shadows cast by such a low-angled sun, create a signature look that is much beloved by photographers. Indeed, golden light is so popular that it risks becoming a cliché; and if your intention is to deliver images that are unique, it may not be your first choice. But it is nevertheless an essential part of your photographic repertoire, and a safe bet for getting a memorable image. Because we see the world this way for only a brief period of time each day, golden light imparts a sense of ephemerality to a scene. Accordingly, you must work quickly to make the most of this light, which usually lasts for only an hour at the beginning and end of the day. Scouting locations and planning your composition ahead ensures you can concentrate on tackling exposure.

THE THREE-ANGLE CHOICE

In addition to its flattering tonality, golden light is loved by photographers for the variety of angles it offers for any given subject. While the low angle of the sun stays constant, you can control how that light strikes your subject by moving the camera. Shooting into the sun creates a backlit scenario, with opportunities for silhouettes or edge-lit portraits. In backlit shots, shadows dominate the frame, such that very few directly illuminated areas are available to give the image any local contrast, resulting in the loss of fine detail.

If you shoot away from the sun, you have full frontal light that brilliantly reflects the natural colors of your subject, giving it an intense, grandiose appearance. Shadows get tricky with this angle, however, as your own shadow is now

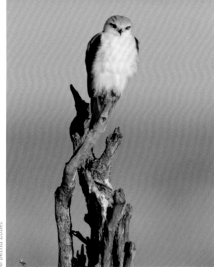

© Bernd Zoller

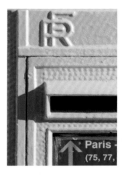

← Parisian post
Close-up shots with strong side lighting make the surface texture obvious and tangible, and shadows running horizontally across the frame lend a graphic quality.

← Suitably majestic
With no strong shadows cast by this kite to anchor it to an environment, this shot feels like it is hovering in space—particularly suitable for its avian subject.

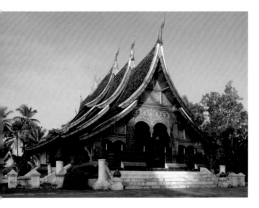

↑ Laotian temple
Golden light communicates a sense of majesty, and is well suited to many architectural subjects. In this shot, the light serves its purpose without having to cover the entire building; the shadows speak to the surrounding environment and prevent the photograph from becoming a cliché.

falling in toward the scene. This may not be an issue with a telephoto shot, but with a wide-angle lens, you may need to either compose the scene so your shadow is out of frame, or blend your shadow into shade cast by some other element—a tall tree or building, perhaps. Additionally, if your subject is framed such that you cannot see its shadows at all, the frontal light can make your image appear flat, as it doesn't offer the viewer any reference for the subject's depth.

In the interim 180 degrees between backlighting and frontal light, you have a plethora of side lighting options. This angle of light exaggerates depth and is defined by the long, horizontal shadows crossing the frame. The resulting high levels of contrast create ideal conditions for revealing fine texture in surfaces.

Clouds & Light

Almost everything we've discussed so far about the role of daylight in photography has ignored a major factor: clouds. On a perfectly clear day without a cloud in sight, you can use the previously described rules and patterns to predict exactly where and when a certain kind of light will shine with reasonable accuracy. Clouds, however, are giant floating variables that literally change with the wind and will consistently keep you on your toes.

Sometimes a blessing, sometimes a curse, clouds interact with light in several key ways. Overcast days with uniform cloud cover are commonly (and unfairly) perceived as dreary and bland.

Some of this is simply human perception, which associates bright white light with natural beauty. Beyond that, without any point-source light in the sky, there is nothing to cast distinct shadows, and scenes can appear flat with little detail. However, by spreading and softening the sunlight, the clouds are acting as an immense diffuser in the sky. The resulting soft light means you can take a portrait almost anywhere without worrying about unflattering shadows or high-contrast exposure problems. Indeed, it means you have a lot less to worry about in general, as the entire landscape is evenly lit with a consistent light that won't be dramatically changing from hour to hour. And while colors won't pop with the same intensity that they do under direct sunlight, the soft light does make it much easier for your sensor to capture subtle and nuanced color variations in your subject.

CLOUDS AS REFLECTORS

At certain angles, tall cumuliform (compact and dense) clouds that extend vertically upward in the sky can even act as light sources themselves, reflecting the light of the sun onto a scene below. Huge banks of such clouds can fill in

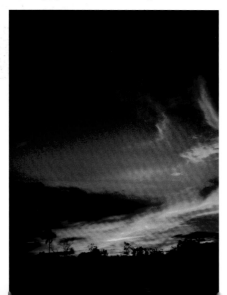

← **Saturated skies**
The vivid colors of a sunset are best captured by a bit of intentional underexposure, which will in turn render objects on the earth as silhouettes.

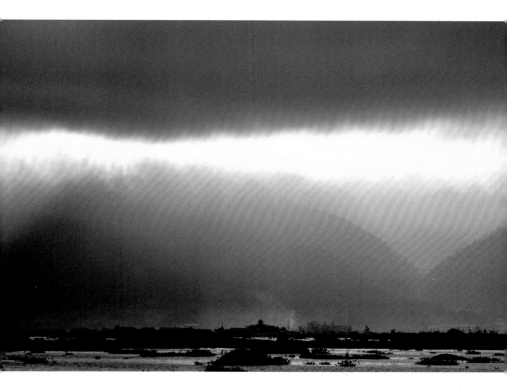

shadows and help even out the exposure—particularly if the sun is shining upon them from the opposite side of the sky, as in mid-morning or mid-afternoon (earlier or later and the sun is already too low in intensity to have much effect). Even if the light is not strong enough to completely fill in shadows, it can still lower the color temperature of the shade and bring it closer to the temperature of the

↑ **Looming clouds**
Besides casting everything below in a diffuse light, heavy clouds like this can also become a major part of the composition itself.

surrounding daylight, making these shadows appear less blue. Broken clouds are often unpredictable in the way they scatter light, and this can make them more exciting and also more complex to photograph. This complexity is enhanced in situations when different

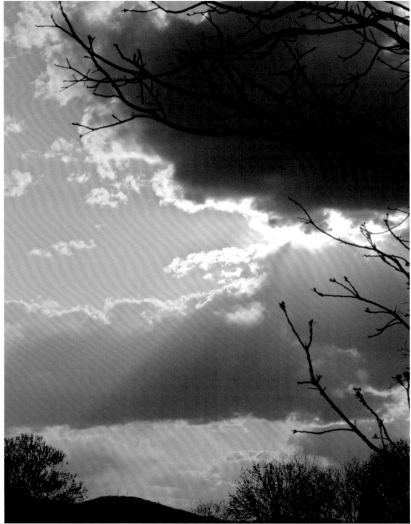

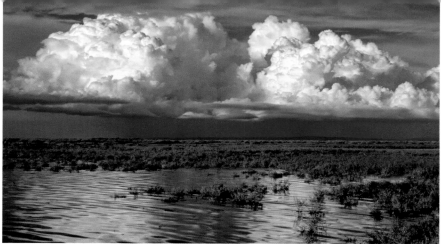

layers of broken cloud hang at varying depths throughout the sky. A scene with distant mountains, for example, could have a bank of heavy cloud hanging in the distance, but scattered lighter clouds in the foreground.

BROKEN CLOUD COVER

In between a perfectly clear day and a heavily overcast one, there are days of mixed daylight, in which a bright blue sky is interspersed with clouds of varying shapes and sizes. Compact and dense clouds (called cumuliform) can dramatically alter a scene for

← Breaking through
Clouds can create truly spectacular lighting effects depending on their interaction with the sun. Here, strong edge lighting gives these clouds a radiant outline; and they in turn transform the sunlight into radiating beams of light, which would otherwise be invisible against a clear sky.

↑ Cumuliform composition
These tall cumuliform clouds reflected enough sunlight to evenly illuminate the marshes below, and are also reflected themselves in the water, where they emphasize the textural qualities of the ripples along the surface.

brief periods of time as they pass in front of the sun. In an open scene, the blue sky reflection (10,000K) is usually overwhelmed by the intensity of the sun (5200K); but by blocking and lowering the intensity of the direct sunlight, a cumuliform cloud will momentarily equalize the color temperature to around 6000K, delivering a brilliantly lit foreground that keeps the deep tonality of a blue sky overhead. Of course, these dense clouds also cast quite distinct shadows of their own, particularly if they are low in the sky, which can create high-contrast exposure situations if those shadows are kept in frame.

Weather Extremes

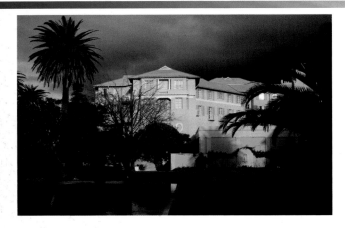

← **Ominous contrast**
A momentary break in cloud cover fully illuminated this old Cape Town hotel, contrasting strongly with the heavy, morose storm clouds above. A few seconds earlier or later and the whole scene would have simply looked dull and dreary, with no point of comparison to illustrate the power and magnitude of the weather conditions.

Extreme weather can be hard on your camera but simply because it's extreme and less usual, can offer good opportunities for strong imagery. Simply take the necessary precautions against water, sand, condensation, or whatever else, and look for one-of-a-kind images.

STORMS

The default lighting condition of rain or thunderstorms is basically the same as that of an overcast day, only darker. Even though the clouds themselves may look vast and intimidating, they require a contrasting light source to illustrate their contours and bring the scene to life. This happens during momentary breaks in the cloud cover, when the sun cuts through as a strong, directional spotlight that illuminates a single subject amidst a sea of darkness. You must act quickly to seize such opportunities, as the natural windy conditions of the storms mean they will be short-lived.

Approaching storm clouds on the horizon can make for a dramatic landscape, with massive, multilayered cloud formations looming over and contrasting with an otherwise tranquil scene in the foreground. A successfully captured bolt of lightning is also a dynamic element to add to a scene, but unless you get lucky, you will need a long shutter speed to negate the uncertainty of when it strikes. Fortunately, the dark conditions of heavy cloud cover make such long exposure times feasible—provided you use a steady tripod.

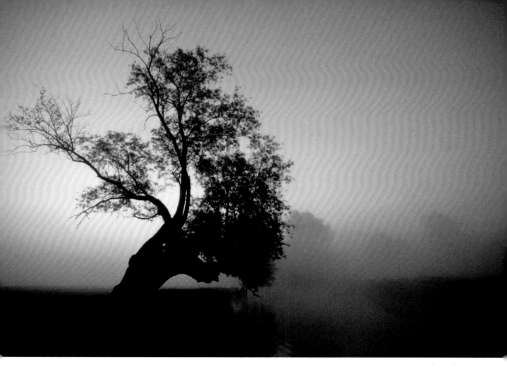

MIST AND FOG

Thick mist or fog swathes a scene in vapor particles that scatter the light and act like a ground-level diffuser cloud. Like most weather extremes, these conditions are usually fleeting—particularly the mist formed overnight by still air cooling over wet ground, which quickly evaporates in the morning sun. Fortunately, you needn't worry too much about exposure, as these scenes are typically low in contrast and easily captured by the sensor. You even have

↑ Ethereal early mornings
Early morning fog, just barely illuminated by the rising sun, creates dreamy, otherworldly environments. To get subjects in sharp focus, you must be physically close to them—shooting across a distance with a telephoto lens introduces too much atmospheric haze for crisp results.

some wiggle room—exposing for the whites of the fog will make it glow and appear luminescent, while less exposure will deliver gloomy, eerie results. Shooting through mist introduces depth, with objects gradually appearing paler and less detailed the farther away they are.

SNOWFALL

The pristine conditions of a fresh coat of snow make for idyllic imagery, and present a unique lighting condition in which every available surface acts as a reflector. The abundance of white befuddles the camera's metering system, which will interpret the snow to be neutral gray and render the scene accordingly. To prevent this dull underexposure, add one or two f-stops of exposure compensation while keeping an eye on your histogram, until the scene appears correctly on the LCD. On the other hand, you should have little to no problem with unflattering shadows cast on your portrait subjects, and can photograph freely even in direct, midday sunlight.

COLD BATTERIES

Extreme weather conditions can take their toll on your equipment, and cold temperatures in particular will sap battery strength quickly. Keep a spare battery warm inside your jacket and periodically switch it out with the one in use to extend the life of both batteries.

→ **Nowhere to hide**
With properly calibrated white balance, a snow-covered scene serves as an ideal backdrop for showing off vivid colors and textures, such as this European red fox's fur coat. The fox is also evenly lit on all sides by the reflected daylight.

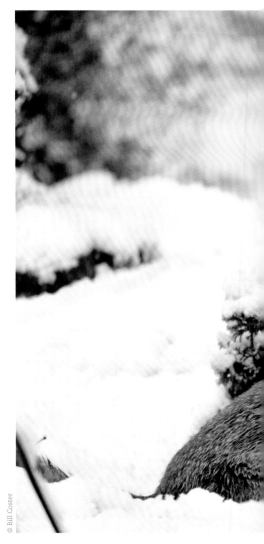

© Bill Coster

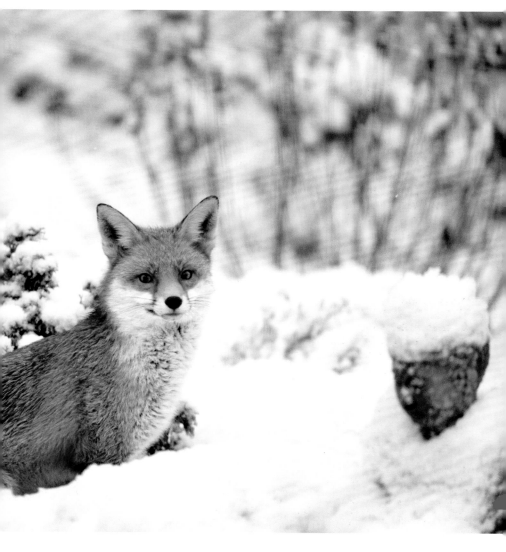

Incandescent Light

Anything that emits light as a result of being heated is said to be incandescent. Fire is the most obvious example of this type of light, and the warm glow of a flame is its signature color. Today, the most common light source used in interior spaces is still traditional incandescent light, but candles and gas lamps have been replaced by tungsten bulbs. These are the classic light bulbs containing a tungsten filament encased in a sealed glass bulb, which is heated by an electric current that warms the wire to a bright glow. The resulting orange/yellow color is (counter-intuitively) relatively cold and falls at the bottom end of the color temperature spectrum.

This method of generating light is exceedingly inefficient, however, as a great deal of energy is wasted in the production of heat rather than light. As a result, numerous sources of incandescent light are required in order to fully illuminate a space, which means a greater likelihood that those light sources will appear within the frame of any given interior shot. The resulting high dynamic range means you will have to approach your exposure with a discriminating eye—either leaving the area nearby the light sources overexposed, or filling in the shadows by adding your own light to the scene.

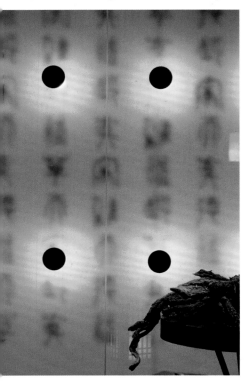

← **Incandescent decorations**
This decorative screen in a restaurant was diffusing the light from several tungsten lamps on the other side. Another color would have been far less interesting, but the same warmth that made the restaurant feel comfortable and inviting makes this image evocative and exotic.

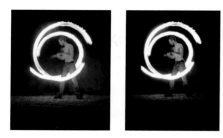

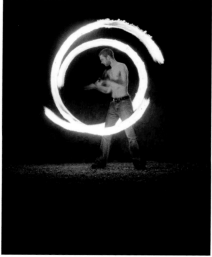

↑ ↗ → Three takes on color correction
The flames twirled about by this fire dancer cast a quintessentially incandescent light. The picture above left shows how strong the resulting color cast can be if not corrected. Auto white balance, shown in the middle, gets the white balance almost perfect, but the result lacks ambience and feels (ironically) artificial. The custom white balance set for the image shown right strikes a decent balance, and appears very much how the scene felt at the time.

© Frank Gallaugher

INCANDESCENT COLOR CORRECTION

As with any artificially lit scene, it is imperative to keep a close eye on your white balance settings to avoid unwanted color casts. Your digital camera's incandescent/tungsten WB preset is usually around 3200K, but this is calibrated for studio lamps. Domestic light bulbs have no such standard color temperature—a 40-watt tungsten bulb is cooler than a 100-watt one, and candlelight glows at an even lower temperature than either. To completely eliminate the orange-yellow color cast,

you will need to manually dial in a lower white balance setting, or set a custom white balance.

However, you may find such precise adjustments unnecessary and even undesirable, as a perfectly balanced incandescent scene can often appear sterile and artificial. Our eyes are long accustomed to incandescent light, and associate its orange color cast with warmth, familiarity, and comfort. It can lend a sense of intimacy to a group shot, and make an interior feel inviting. A delicate touch is still essential.

Fluorescent Light

Fluorescent light is far more efficient than tungsten bulbs, using less energy to create brighter light. Due to their efficiency, fluorescent lights are popular in industrial and commercial spaces, and are making their way into energy-conscious homes as well. This is good for the environment, but rather unfortunate for photographers, as fluorescent light is considered unflattering. Besides the fact we've come to associate it with sterile, commercial spaces, it is also completely unnatural—in fact, it had to be shoe-horned into the color temperature spectrum between early morning/evening and afternoon sunlight. In reality fluorescent light is not continuous the way incandescent or sunlight is. Rather, it is comprised of distinct spikes in the blue and green channels, with gaps in the reds. Your mind does a good job of filling in these gaps such that it is perceived as normal, but imaging sensors have a harder time of it. That said, fluorescent bulbs have come a long way. Special care has been taken to make their phosphors emit a hotter light that more closely approximates natural white daylight, and their power-up mechanism is smoother, preventing the headache-inducing flicker so loathed in traditional fluorescents. These compact fluorescent lights (CFLs) are so-called because their tube is wrapped up in a spiral or loop, making them much smaller and able to fit in traditional tungsten lamps.

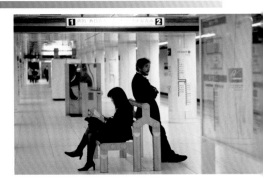

↑ **Tokyo underground**
Public spaces are often lit with fluorescent lamps. In such locales, getting the white balance absolutely perfect isn't always necessary, as long as the color cast isn't overly distracting.

↓ **Tungsten vs Fluorescent**
The graph below illustrates the continuous spectrum of tungsten light, and the fact that it is comprised of all the different colors of light means it can accurately illuminate each of those colors in an image. Fluorescent light's spectrum, on the other hand, is broken and discontinuous, with sharp spikes in cool colors and much lower in the warmer ones. Among other things, this is why fluorescent lights are so unflattering for showing off skin tones (which are themselves mostly comprised of reds and yellows).

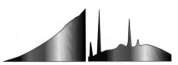

Tungsten light   **Flourescent light**

FLUORESCENT COLOR CORRECTION

As usual, your first tool in compensating for the green hues of regular fluorescent lights is your camera's corresponding WB preset (usually around 4000K). But even if you set a custom white balance specifically for a given fluorescent lighting condition, the gaps in that light may nevertheless result in a scene with slight deficiencies in color accuracy that remain perceptible to the viewer. Fortunately, the spaces in which you typically encounter such light are often expected to be rendered with those characteristic green hues—the viewing public has simply grown accustomed to perceiving light in these spaces this way.

Domestic residences in which you typically find daylight-balanced CFLs, on the other hand, need special care to avoid casting an otherwise inviting home in a lifeless, impersonal light. Newer cameras often have a separate WB preset specifically for these lamps called Fluorescent H, which is slightly warmer at around 4500K. But given the unpredictable and inconsistent quality of these lights (the color of which can even change based on the currency of the mains outlet into which it is plugged), your safest bet will be to set a custom white balance with a gray card and shoot Raw, enabling the most leeway for fine-tuning adjustments in post-production.

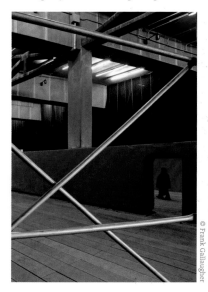

↓ ↘ → A happy medium
The camera initially rendered this warehouse interior with an unappealing green color cast due to the fluorescent lights above. Auto white balance, applied in post-production, went too far in the other direction, with too much magenta. In the end, a custom white balance set for a cool blue cast was preferable, as it speaks to the industrial feel of the scene.

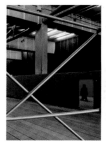 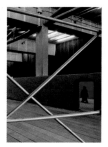

Vapor Discharge Light

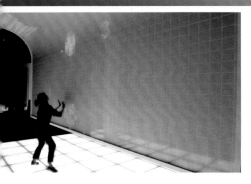

↑ **Color science fiction**
This technological display was illuminated by mercury vapor lamps, and the uncorrected blue color cast suits the subject well, communicating a futuristic and alien atmosphere.

Illuminating large, outdoor spaces like city streets, parking lots, and football fields requires a high-intensity light source beyond the capabilities of tungsten or fluorescent lamps. Vapor discharge lamps meet this challenge by creating a powerful arc of electricity between two electrodes housed inside a sealed tube. Once the arc is formed, it evaporates metal salts that are contained in the tube, creating a luminescent plasma. The color of the resulting light is dependent on the metal salts used. Because it takes time for the metal to evaporate, these lights initially cast one color when they are first turned on, gradually shifting to another as more metal is evaporated.

MERCURY VAPOR LAMPS

The most common vapor discharge lamps, their glowing mercury emits a broken spectrum of light much like fluorescents. Though perceived as a cool white by the eye, their color starts off as a strong green before shifting to a bluer hue. The intensity of these blue-green spikes is greater than that of fluorescents, and more difficult to correct.

SODIUM VAPOR LAMPS

The light emitted by plasma-state sodium starts as a strong orange before shifting to yellow, with severe deficiencies in all other color channels. As a result, they cannot be color-corrected to perfectly balanced white, because there is no other color to recover. These are the most common light sources in urban areas like city streets—their cumulative effect is what makes cities shine yellow at night when seen in an airplane.

MULTI-VAPOR LAMPS

By combining different metals, these lamps emit a cold white light that can appear quite natural—even to a sensor. For this reason, these lamps are used as studio lights when high-intensity light is needed. They are also used in sports stadia, where photographers need them to capture accurate white balances.

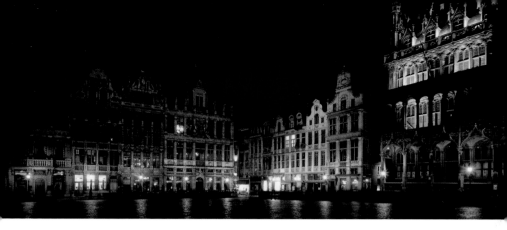

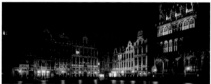

←↑ La Grande-Place

The intricate architecture of Brussels' Grand Place deserved better treatment than the limited spectrum of yellow sodium vapor lamps could afford (left). Of course, nothing could be done about it at the time this was shot, but in post-production, the yellows were isolated and shifted to a warmer, more grandiose hue (above).

VAPOR DISCHARGE COLOR CORRECTION

With the exception of multi-vapor lamps, getting accurate color from vapor discharge light is usually a nightmare. Your camera probably lacks a WB preset for these, so setting a custom WB and shooting Raw is your best bet for color correction. However, in the conditions in which you typically encounter vapor discharge light, perfect rendition of color isn't always necessary. We're used to viewing street subjects in the yellow hues of sodium vapor; and industrial settings often benefit from the greens and blues of plasma-state mercury, so consider your given subject.

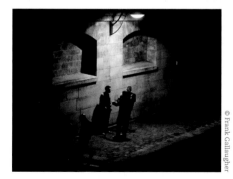

↑ A scene on the Seine

In the streets where sodium vapor lamps are most common, the light is often localized, with discrete patches of illumination that can serve as excellent compositional elements.

Mixed Light

The real world is rarely lit by a single, uniform light source (day-lit landscapes notwithstanding). Rather, many spaces reflect light from multiple different sources, each with its own color temperature and characteristics. Generally, there are three approaches to dealing with mixed lighting, the easiest being to simply set your camera to Auto White Balance and let it determine an average color temperature for the scene. Depending on how diverse the various light sources are, this can work quite well—grays and whites may be skewed a bit, but no single color will be completely off-target. Or you can go the opposite route and set your white balance for only one particular light source, leaving all other colors to shift accordingly. This can be a good approach if one light source

is dominant, and the inaccurate colors aren't too distracting. The final and best option for color correcting mixed lighting involves adjusting each light source separately, and can be done only in post-production. There are a few different approaches here, but the most effective is to use the Replace Color tool (see page 300). This allows you to isolate one particular color and shift its hue, saturation, and lightness independent of all other colors, bringing it into harmony with the rest of the scene.

↖↓ Balancing window light

This interior needed to feel warm and inviting, so the original white balance was set for tungsten, disregarding the daylight from the windows. However, the resulting blue color cast on the right side of the frame was too distracting; so in post-production, that particular blue light was isolated and then desaturated to a neutral white.

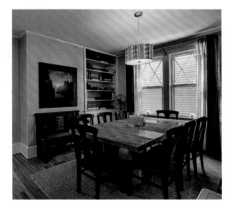
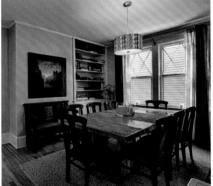

→ **Diverse cityscapes**
Fluorescent in the office windows, tungsten and vapor discharge at street level, all interspersed with radiant neon signs—the bombardment of light within a city is all part of the appeal. This diversity is what makes them so photogenic, and the innumerable color casts are testament to the excitement and randomness that characterize a metropolis.

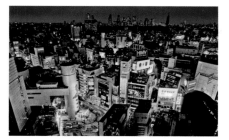

CITY LIGHTS

City lights can be considered the ultimate style of mixed lighting. Vapor lamps are common in municipal areas, and require a deft diagnosis of which variety is being used. In combination with this, a shop-lined street will often feature a row of tungsten-lit frontages, while neon is used overwhelmingly in certain other districts.

COMMERCIAL SPACES

The light within shops, malls, and other commercial buildings is designed to encourage consumers to linger, persuade them to move on more quickly, or plot a particular course. For this reason, the trend is to use a mixture of incandescent, vapor discharge, and fluorescent lighting to achieve the desired effects, and this must be accounted for. Fortunately, the effort put into the lighting design pays off with a well composed and delicately balanced scene, which is often simple to photograph. Indeed, high-end shops and galleries go to great lengths to ensure their ambience is worthy of their expensive goods and services, offering up lush photographic subjects.

↓ **Arcade interiors**
The Galeries Royales Saint-Hubert in Brussels is illuminated by daylight through its gigantic glass roof. The mix of warm sunlight from above and artificial lights in the shop windows makes for a dynamic and grandiose subject.

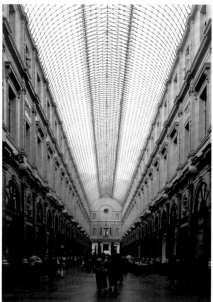

© Frank Gallaugher

Camera-Mounted Flash

This type of flash can refer to two things: either the built-in flash that is a part of your camera, or an external flash unit mounted in the camera's hot shoe. Built-in flashes are by their nature extremely limited, and are designed almost exclusively for portability and convenience. They can illuminate only a relatively short distance in front of the camera, and their close proximity to the lens axis means a strong, frontal light that is unflattering for many subjects—particularly portraits.

External flash units, on the other hand, overcome many of these limitations and add a number of features as well—though these depend on the particular model used. Professional external flash units are considerably more powerful, and so are able to illuminate wider angles and reach farther distances. They are also positioned much higher above the lens axis, and can be rotated up or down and side to side in order to facilitate bounce flash.

HOW FLASH WORKS

Flash units consist of a power source (batteries, usually), a capacitor, and a gas-filled tube. When the flash is activated, the capacitor builds up a rapid charge from the battery; and when the flash is fired, the charge is released into the tube, where it creates a brief arc of electricity that emits a "flash" of light. The duration of the flash is extremely short, which becomes a problem when using fast shutter speeds with a camera that has a focal plane shutter, like a DSLR. Such shutters are composed of two curtains that travel across the sensor in sequence—the first curtain exposes the sensor, and the second (or "rear") curtain covers it back up. The time it takes for the curtains to cross the sensor falls well below the full range of shutter speeds necessary for most images; so for faster speeds, the rear curtain will start covering up the sensor before the first curtain has finished its crossing. This means that only a sliver of the sensor is exposed at a time. If a flash were to fire at such high shutter speeds, only that sliver between the two curtains would capture its light. For that reason, the fastest shutter speed at which the sensor can be fully exposed is called the camera's Flash Sync Speed, and is the upper limit at which you can fire a flash at full power (often between 1/180 and 1/300 second).

To get around this limitation, external flash units often have a feature called High Speed Sync, which fires several bursts of flash during the course of an exposure—the idea being that the sensor can be fully illuminated by the flash in increments, with one flash per sliver of exposed sensor area. This works well,

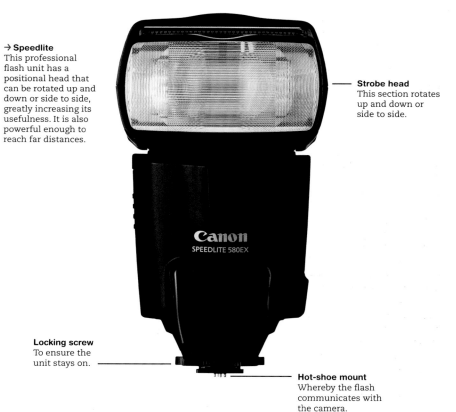

→ Speedlite
This professional flash unit has a positional head that can be rotated up and down or side to side, greatly increasing its usefulness. It is also powerful enough to reach far distances.

Strobe head
This section rotates up and down or side to side.

Locking screw
To ensure the unit stays on.

Hot-shoe mount
Whereby the flash communicates with the camera.

and allows the use of high shutter speeds with flash; but there's a trade-off: in order to fire such a rapid succession of flash bursts, the intensity of each burst is decreased, so the overall power of the flash is diminished. Fortunately, this is usually an acceptable compromise, as the use of fast shutter speeds typically indicates an abundance of light anyway.

INVERSE SQUARE LAW

It is common sense that light gradually decreases in intensity (or "falls off") as it travels greater distances. If you're going to be adding your own light to a scene, it is essential that you be able to precisely predict that degree of fall-off to make sure your subjects are adequately lit. Toward that end, flash photographers work according to the inverse square law, which states that the intensity of light falling on a subject is inversely proportional to the square of the distance from that source. While that may sound like a mouthful, in reality it's quite straightforward.

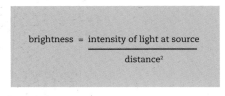

$$brightness = \frac{\text{intensity of light at source}}{\text{distance}^2}$$

For example, if you have two subjects of equal size, one of which is twice as far from a light source as the other, the more distant subject will receive only 1/4 as much light as the closer subject. In lighting terms: doubling the distance cuts the light down by two f-stops.

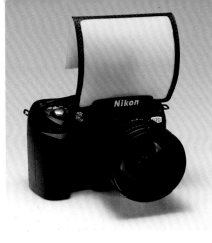

© LumiQuest

↑ **Mini-diffuser**
Built-in flashes are undeniably handy, and can be made even more useful with simple accessories like this miniature diffusion screen. This will prevent both the red-eye effect, and soften the light output, avoiding the deer-in-headlights look so characteristic of these flashes.

RED EYE

This well-known effect occurs when the flash bounces off the retina of a human subject, and increases in likelihood as the angle of flash approaches the axis of the lens. An automated solution is to fire a series pre-flashes in advance of the main flash in order to make the subject's pupils contract. This Red-Eye Reduction feature is generally both annoying and disruptive, causing your subject to squint and announcing to everyone nearby that you are taking a picture. It is further negated by the ease with which red eye can be fixed in post.

↓ **Background blackout**

While the inverse square law may seem mathematically complex, its principle is quite familiar. And it can be used to great effect—for instance here, where the flash was just strong enough to light up the dog's face, but weak enough to fall off very shortly thereafter, rendering the background pure black.

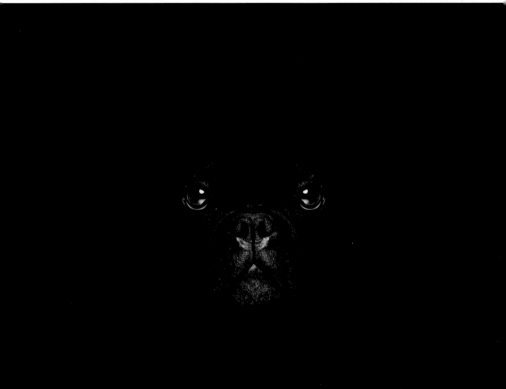

Balancing Flash to Ambient Light

Camera-mounted flash is best used as a supplement to ambient light, rather than the primary light source. Backlit subjects, for example, can have the strong shadows cast toward the camera brightened up. This is called fill flash, because you are "filling in" the shadows by introducing another light source. You will need to use Forced Flash or Manual mode in such conditions, as auto modes will read an abundance of light and disregard flash as a necessity. You want to delicately balance your flash to the existing light conditions without overpowering them. An appropriate ratio of flash to daylight, for instance, is around 1:3 or 1:4.

BOUNCE LIGHT

In dim interiors, your flash is a handy way to augment the ambient light; and by their nature, interiors give you an abundance of reflective surfaces with which to work. By angling your flash up toward the ceiling or to the side at a wall, you can bounce your flash off those surfaces and back toward your subject. The results are far more flattering than frontal light, both because of their angle and the fact that they are diffused into softer light. As the light now has to travel a farther distance to your subject, high-powered, professional flashes are typically used at full output. Another issue is that the angle of the light may now cast shadows on your subject, and

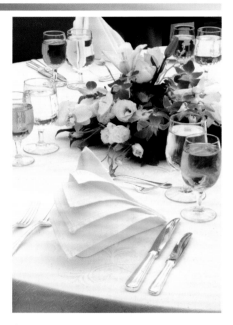

↑ **Interior festivities**
Indoor event spaces are frequently quite dim. Fortunately, they do offer a giant reflector card in the form of a ceiling, off which you can bounce your flash to cast a diffuse, flattering light.

you can't fill them in with your flash because it's already being used for bounce. A quick fix is a bounce card—a reflective surface that need be no bigger than a playing card. This attaches to the back of the flash and reflects some of the light forward, while still allowing most of the output to radiate up for bounce.

REAR-CURTAIN SYNC

The two-stage nature of focal plane shutters affects the role of flash at high shutter speeds. You can "sync" the flash to either the first or second curtain, so that the flash fires at either the very beginning or very end of the exposure. First- or front-curtain sync is fine for stationary subjects, but if there is any movement in the frame, it means a sharp subject, captured crisply at the start of the exposure, will be obscured by motion blur that overlaps the initial capture. The solution is to sync the flash to the rear curtain (rear- or second-curtain sync)—the very end of the exposure. With motion subjects this is ideal, as the flash will capture a sharp moment that overlaps any blur. The resulting trails of motion blur are quite dramatic and effective. Rear-curtain sync isn't only about communicating motion though; it is also a method of including distant backgrounds in a dark scene with a nearby main subject. Capturing a sense of place and environment is often essential, and helps avoid the isolating, black backgrounds so typical in poor flash shots. It takes some practice to perfect this rear-sync technique, but the results are often stunning.

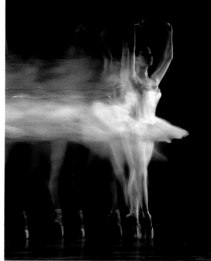

© Adastra

↑ **Motion trails**
The blur of motion on the left of this photo was captured without flash. When it fired at the end of the exposure, the ballerina was momentarily fully illuminated, and the resulting sharp image was the last bit of light captured by the sensor.

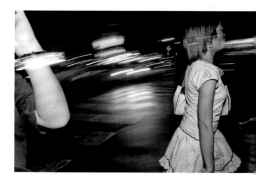

→ **Street sync**
There's a lot of both camera movement (from left to right) and subject movement (in the street background) in this shot, but the woman crossing the frame stands out sharp amid it all—the trademark look of rear-curtain sync.

Studio Flash

Whereas on-camera flash is used to make the most out of a difficult lighting situation, studio flash gives you total control over how your subject is illuminated. The trade-offs are obvious: You will need space to set up your flash equipment, and time to test and balance its effect. But for optimal lighting, there is no substitute.

Studio flash can begin by taking your camera-mountable flash unit, attaching it to a tripod or some other light stand, and controlling it from the camera. High-end digital cameras can, in fact, control several external units at a distance, letting you adjust the intensity of each from the camera's LCD screen.

But that is, of course, just the beginning. Dedicated studio flash equipment comes in every shape and size, and gives you the ability to choose exactly the right kind of lighting appropriate for the shot.

↓ **Tools of the trade**
Professional studio lighting is versatile, powerful, and reliable. It is also invariably expensive.

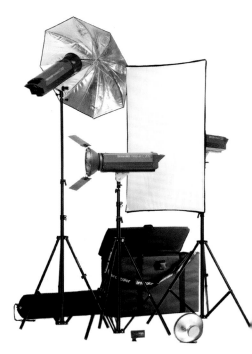

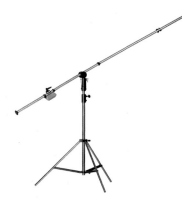

↑ **Extra reach**
Superbooms like these can extend high above a subject, facilitating top lighting without the need for climbing up a ladder.

↓ **Support mechanisms**
Elaborate setups can be built
by assembling these arms,
brackets, and bars into whatever
configuration is required. Lights
can then be clamped on wherever
they are needed.

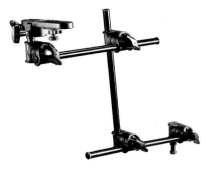

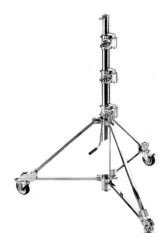

↑ **Winch mechanism**
The wheels on the bottom
of this stand make large
adjustments in position
easy—they can be clamped
down once placed to prevent
them from drifting around.

TRY BEFORE YOU BUY

While the cost of professional studio
equipment may seem prohibitive, there
are alternatives for photographers on a
budget. Some studios will rent lighting
setups by the day (or even hour) so you
can try out equipment for a fraction of
the purchase price. If you're just starting
out, this lets you get a feel for which
equipment you'd find most useful,
without committing to buy.

LIGHTING SUPPORTS

As with all photographic lighting, studio
flash units must be precisely positioned
according to the needs of each shot.
Beyond that, because there is a definite
trial-and-error component to working
with flash, the units need to be easily
adjustable as well. Toward that end,
proper and sturdy supports are just as
important as any other piece of studio
equipment.

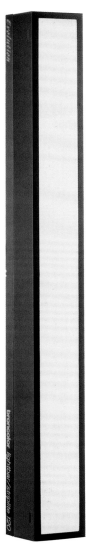

MODELING LIGHT

Calculating and visualizing the effects of studio flash can be difficult, particularly as you add multiple units, because their light can't be seen until the shot itself is taken. Obviously, the instant review option of digital cameras mitigates this hassle to some degree, but professional studio flashes also include a feature to help you see their effects in advance. A small continuous light, called a modeling lamp, is often imbedded in the unit, right next to the flash tube, and it can shine continuously while you set up your shot. They don't always shine at the exact intensity of the flash itself, but they are a huge help in deciding the angle and distance each flash unit should be from the subject.

← **Striplights**
Ideal for illuminating large backdrops, striplights produce a very even light along their entire length—usually around 3 feet (1 m).

TYPICAL STUDIO FLASH EQUIPMENT

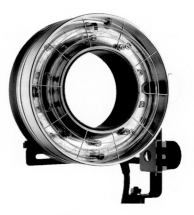

↓ High-power heads
So powerful that they often have their own cooling fans built in, high-power flash heads can shine across great distances, or diffuse across a wide open space. They can even compete against sunlight in outdoor setups, and are purpose-built for large shots. In smaller setups like macro, they are usually overkill.

↑ Ringlights
Though technically still on-camera flash, the light from a ringlight is completely shadowless, as it is evenly emitted from all angles around the lens. These are excellent for macro photography, and also portraiture.

→ Small heads
These discreet flash units can be hidden behind objects within the frame, allowing you to shine light in places where a larger piece of equipment would intrude into the shot.

Continuous Light

These light sources work according to the WYSIWYG principle (that is, What You See Is What You Get). You can observe their effects in real time as you move and adjust them into a proper configuration. This eliminates the guesswork and inverse square law calculations that are necessary in flash photography, and can allow for much more precise and nuanced setups. A lot of this technology was developed in Hollywood, for the obvious reason that a continuous, multiple-frames-per-second movie can't be lit using flash.

Working with continuous lights can be a much more satisfying experience than flash. Because it is a constant presence in the studio, the light tends to take on a tangible quality. It starts feeling like a set piece. Additionally, you can walk throughout your setup and observe its effects from all angles, rather than only through the captured image on an LCD screen as with flash.

Any discussion of continuous studio lighting will overlap with much of what was discussed in the pages on artificial light, as these lights are incandescent (page 130), fluorescent (page 132), or vapor discharge (page 134). The difference, of course, is that they are purpose-built for photography, and their color temperatures are calibrated to emit a specific, predictable kind of light.

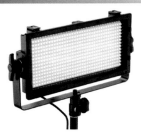

↑ **LED Panels**
Whereas other light sources require accessory gels to modify the light and match it to the ambient color temperature, LED units can simply be adjusted to match without any modification needed.

LED (LIGHT EMITTING DIODES)

Despite LEDs being relatively new, they are well on their way to dominating the artificial photographic lighting industry. This is mostly due to their versatility: they range from high powered studio units to portable ones that fit in a camera's hotshoe. They are energy efficient, and compatible with existing accessories. Most importantly, however, their color temperature can be adjusted for technical accuracy or creative effect.

INCANDESCENT

Simple, rugged, and foolproof, incandescent studio lights are easy to work with. Their continuous spectrum means they can be balanced to other light sources with the use of filters, and

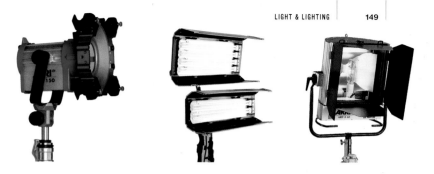

are easily shaped by accessories to offer either soft, diffuse light or a tight, focused beam. However, they do have a significant and even dangerous drawback: heat. On the surface, this can simply be an inconvenience. Portrait subjects can start sweating, makeup can melt, and a long day's work in the studio can get quite uncomfortable. Beyond that, their heat can gradually yellow and char an otherwise white surface like a wall; and if extreme caution isn't taken, they can even set fire to any accessories attached to them. Toward this end, if you plan on working with extensive incandescent setups, safety is essential.

HMI

Vapor discharge lamps designed for photography use Hydrargyrum Medium-arc Iodide (HMI) as the metal salt, and the resulting light is a clean, pure white. This is ideal for balancing with ambient daylight—such that these lights are commonly referred to as Daylight lamps. They can be powerful enough to use outdoors in direct sunlight, and you needn't worry about heat dissipation. The nature of their technology, however, requires that they are bulky and cumbersome—not to mention expensive.

FLUORESCENT

If designed with photography in mind, fluorescent lamps will include coatings matched to the spectral sensitivities of imaging sensors that cast precise, easily captured color temperatures. Their long tubes are also ideal for light banks that evenly illuminate a large area—often used for still life and product photography. To augment this tendency toward diffusion, concave reflectors can be placed behind a row of lamps to further the spread of light. The other side of the coin is that fluorescents are not easily shaped into focused, directional light. And while they are more energy-efficient than incandescents, they tend to cost more up front—particularly in replacements. They do not emit a great deal of heat, and so worries of dissipation and fire need not be a major concern.

Lighting Accessories

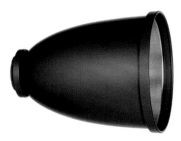 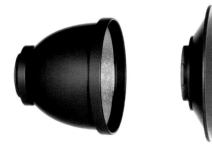

↑ **Reflector shapes**
Each reflector, mounted to the front of a light source, determines a distinct angle at which that light will shine on the subject.

A studio light source, be it flash or continuous, is just the beginning of light in a studio scene. Between the source and the subject, that light can be manipulated in any number of ways. On page 114, we discussed using reflectors to bounce natural light and fill in shadows. In the studio, large, flat reflectors can be used similarly—in fact, the typical studio is painted pure white, allowing the wall, floor, or ceiling to be used as a reflector. When it comes to studio lighting accessories, however, reflectors take on a different role and allow you to work with a great degree of precision.

UMBRELLAS

Commonly seen in portrait studios, umbrellas use the same principle as bounce light discussed on page 142. The light source is pointed away from the subject itself and into the parabola of the umbrella interior, which reflects that light back toward the subject across a wider area. The result is a softer light, flattering for portraits. The light also takes on the qualities of the material used in the umbrella interior—silver for the strongest light, golden for warmth, or white for the softest effect. And just like a rain umbrella, these accessories collapse for easy storage.

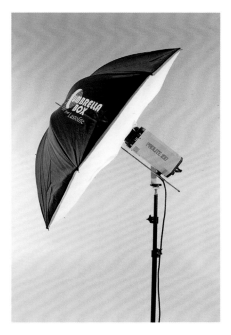

← Not meant for rainy weather
Extremely effective at creating soft, flattering light, umbrellas are easy to work with, as their light is diffuse enough that precise positioning isn't as necessary as it is with other point-source lighting equipment. They do require a tripod on which to be mounted.

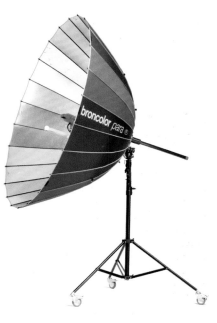

REFLECTOR DISHES

Attached directly to continuous light sources, a reflector dish molds the light at its source, preventing it from spilling over at the edges and focusing its output at a definitive angle (commonly called "spill kill"). The reflective inner surface augments the strength of that light, depending on its color—shiny silver produces a strong, hard light; matte white weakens the light, making it softer.

↑ Parabolic reflectors
The parabolic dish works a bit differently from other reflectors, allowing the light source itself to be moved closer to or farther from the center of the shape. The quality of the light changes according to its position.

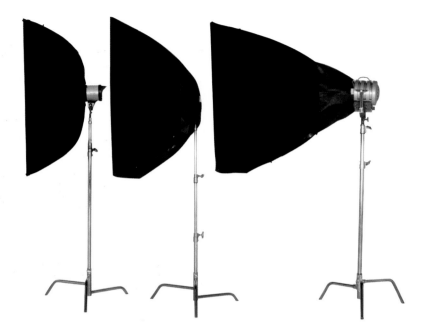

SOFTBOXES

These accessories catch the light from a single-point source within a confined, reflective space, and then transmit it out across a defined surface. They can be quite small, appearing rather like a household shelf lamp, or extremely large, becoming the primary light source and mimicking the powerful but soft, diffuse light of a sunlit window.

↑ **Softbox sizes**
The depth of the softbox affects the angle of light emitted, with deeper boxes casting a narrower, more focused light. Though these pieces of equipment look almost comically bulky, they are in fact extremely lightweight and collapsible.

They can also have any number of materials attached to their front, which will impart certain characteristics or textures to the light as it shines on a subject.

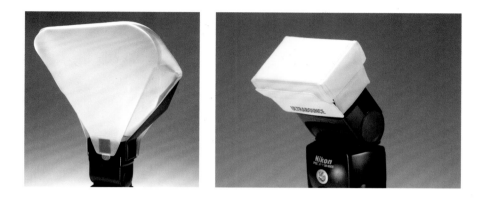

EXTERNAL FLASH UNIT DIFFUSERS

A trademark of the paparazzi, these portable accessories attach to an external flash unit to soften the harsh, directional light characteristic of this light source. They still allow the flash to be rotated, and can thereby be used in conjunction with bounce light. While available in a variety of shapes and sizes, the most effective ones are quite bulky, and can be cumbersome to work with in tight spaces as a result.

SNOOTS

A funny name for a funny-looking piece of gear, the snoot turns your light source into a spotlight, funnelling its light into a narrow beam.

↑ **Bigger is better**
As you might expect, the bigger the diffuser, the more effective it is at spreading out a nice, even light.

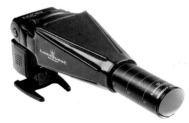

© LumiQuest

↑ **Narrow your flash beam**
The snoot pictured here is mounted to a flash unit, but they are also available for continuous light sources of all shapes and sizes. This particular model has an extendable arm, allowing you to control the focus of the beam without having to reposition the flash itself.

Home Studio

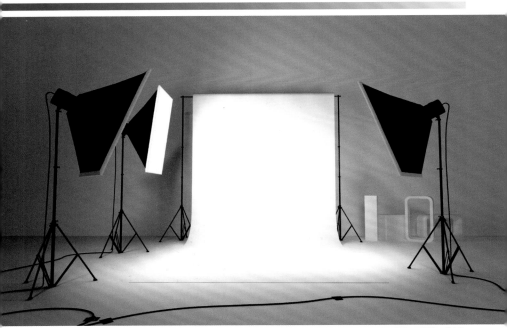

© Secret Side – Fotolia

↑ A Typical Studio
It may surprise you how easily you can mimic the results of a giant studio with tens of thousands of dollars worth of high-end equipment. This studio, for instance, is really quite simple: nothing but white, nonreflective surfaces and a few softboxes. Replace the whitewash paint with some bedsheets, set it up next to a northern window (which has the most even light throughout the day), and you're most of the way there.

A professional studio can easily cost a small fortune to set up, but they are designed to accommodate any possible assignment and spare no expense in the process. Setting up a small studio in your home need not be such a colossal task, nor is it prohibitively expensive. It is entirely possible to build a highly functional studio on a budget, which will provide you with a great base from which to experiment.

KEEP IT SIMPLE

It's easy to get lost in the many options for equipment and setup, but when designing your own home studio never lose sight of the most important issue: control of the light. Studios are all about total creative control, and managing the variables that affect the light is key. Windows are great for natural sunlight, but they should have black curtains to limit their effect. Any colored surface will contribute a color cast as light reflects off it; but if you're not feeling up to a big paint job, white bedsheets can go a long way—just be sure they are stretched tight enough to prevent any textural shadows. Overhead lighting can be useful for setting up a shot, but be sure that when it is turned off you still have enough light. Finally, keep a keen eye out for any other variables that may exist— for instance, even the breeze from a ceiling fan, while irrelevant to the light, can disturb a delicate still life and introduce motion blur.

IMPROVISE

Before you run out and spend your paycheck on high-end gear, it can be a valuable experience to assemble a photo studio with items on hand. Household tungsten lamps can be fitted with quality bulbs of varying intensities to become continuous incandescent light sources—

though if you are using multiple lamps, be sure the bulbs are of the same make and model. Bedsheets can be backdrops, and posterboard can be used for reflectors—particularly if you wrap one side with aluminum foil. Experiment with what you have available, and see what you can achieve—but of course, safety always comes first. Don't get anything too close to your lamps, and if anything starts feeling too warm, cut the power and let everything cool off.

EQUIPMENT

When you have experimented enough with improvised setups and are ready to commit to buying your own equipment, start small and make sure you make the most of each piece of gear. If you feel comfortable with the nuances and calculations involved in flash photography, external flash units are a good place to start. For one, they are useful out of the studio as well, as they can be mounted to the camera and taken on the road with ease. Also, many DSLRs act as a fully functional control panel, allowing control of multiple flashes by infrared or radio waves. You will still need to acquire quality tripods with flash mounts, of course, as well as some diffuser accessories.

If you plan on making your home studio a dedicated photographic space, however, it pays to take the dive and start purchasing professional continuous lights. As with most things, you get what you pay for in the world of photographic lighting, so the particular type of lamps can correspond to your budget. Two lamps is a good place to start, as together they offer you an enormous range of possible lighting setups. You will also want a way to diffuse them, so at least one softbox or umbrella will let you achieve any soft light required by your subjects.

A roll of black cinefoil is also an inexpensive and extremely versatile tool that will let you mold the light exactly the way you want it. Cinefoil is made of completely nonreflective material, and feels rather like aluminum foil, meaning it can be bent and formed into any shape you require. Roll it into a simple tube, attach it to the end of your flash, and you've got a snoot. Mount four separate sheets on the sides of your continuous lamp, and you've got barndoors. It can also serve as an ideal backdrop, as you needn't worry about any distracting reflections.

↙↓ Still-life setup
Still lifes are an excellent subject to shoot when you're first starting your studio, as inanimate objects are considerably more patient than models in costume and makeup. This simple setup uses a large softbox positioned above and to the left of the figurine, which is then balanced by placing a small reflecting card very close on the right.

→ Finished miniature
After some light post-production work, the finished shot is worthy of inclusion in any fine-art catalog.

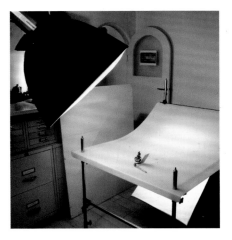

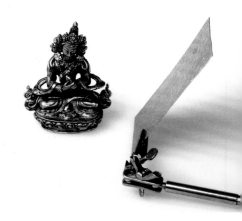

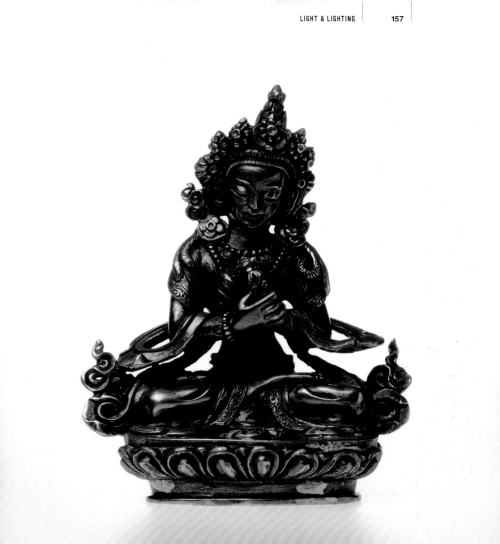

Positioning the Light

With a thorough understanding of all the different sources of photographic light, you can now consider their use in composing a shot. No longer limited to a single light source (be it a built-in flash or the sun in the sky), you must think in a three-dimensional, comprehensive manner, and choose both the angle and intensity of the light as it falls on every side of your subject.

Using the diagram on the opposite page, you can imagine an infinite variety of lighting setups. The key is to decide which is best for the scene you want to create. Do you want to accentuate texture and add drama with a strong side light? Or do you want to completely eliminate shadows by combining diffuse frontal light and backlight, making your subject appear free floating and weightless? While experimentation is essential, and can indeed be a lot of fun, you will save yourself hours of work if you decide in advance what you want to achieve, and then calculate an appropriate approach to that end result.

FRONTAL LIGHT

We know from our discussion of built-in flash that this is the least flattering angle of light, chiefly because the resulting lack of shadows means our eyes have no reference for depth, and the subject appears flat and dull. However, frontal

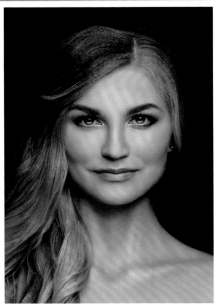

© Salim October

↑ **Classic portrait**
The three-quarter setup described opposite was used for this portrait subject: Source light above and slightly to the right of the camera (which you can see reflected in the eyes), balanced by a light on the opposite side of the model, and with a reflector underneath the camera filling in the area under the model's chin.

light is invaluable in combination with secondary or tertiary light sources, when its obvious directionality makes it easy to adjust in order to balance the other lights.

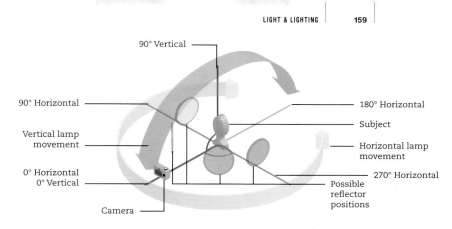

90° Vertical

90° Horizontal

180° Horizontal

Subject

Vertical lamp movement

0° Horizontal
0° Vertical

Horizontal lamp movement

270° Horizontal

Possible reflector positions

Camera

↑ **Lighting in the round**
This diagram can help you imagine the various approaches available as you decide how to light a subject (here, a person's head and shoulders). Keep in mind that as you move around the vertical and horizontal arcs, in reality your lamps can be placed closer to or farther from the subject, affecting their output in accordance with the inverse square law (see page 140). You may even keep this diagram in mind as you photograph outdoors, imagining the blue vertical arc as the sun's path across the sky, and your camera position relative to the subject falling somewhere along the yellow horizontal arc. Of course, in the studio, the blue arc continues underneath the subject as well.

THREE-QUARTER LIGHT

The most common lighting position of all, three-quarter light has the source slightly above and to the side of the camera. From this angle, light can lend a sense of depth without casting obvious shadows. Building on this fundamental setup, you could add a second light at a three-quarter angle on the opposite side of the camera, and then adjust the intensity of each to achieve a precise balance. Then you could add a reflector underneath the front of the subject to bounce up the light from the two sources, filling in any unwanted shadows.

RIGHT-ANGLED LIGHT

Light shining directly on the side of your subject will cast shadows across the frame, unless it is balanced by a stronger frontal light—excellent for revealing textures, but distracting in most portraits.

BACKLIGHT

Alone, backlight gives you silhouettes and edge lighting. But balanced with a frontal light, backlighting can give your subject a well-rounded appearance, excellent for emphasizing contours.

Light a Portrait

Challenge

You may have taken a portrait or two for some of the previous challenges. This challenge, however, is all about specifically setting up and controlling the light for a portrait. This may not necessarily mean you need to build a studio and coordinate multiple light sources—you may want to use the soft light of a window to naturally light your subject. The point is to think about light in terms of portraiture, and to position your subject in that light so that they are captured flatteringly.

↓ **An engaged subject**
Without flash, this shot would have been heavily backlit and the subject would have remained in shadow. But off-camera flash set to rear-curtain sync allowed for a slightly longer shutter speed (to capture the sunset) while still capturing the model sharp at the last moment of the exposure.

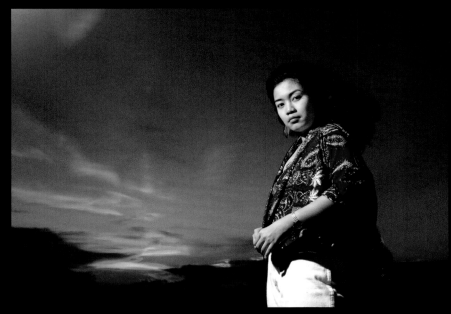

© Kariinpard

→ **Staring off to the side**
Portraiture is just as much about positioning your model as it is about positioning your lights—indeed, what was a side light becomes a frontal or three-quarter light as soon as your model turns their head.

Challenge Checklist

→ First off, you'll need a portrait model. With any luck they'll be patient while you experiment with different angles and adjust your lights.

→ Keep your model comfortable and at ease while you are working. Conversation goes a long way toward making them relax, and a relaxed model will always photograph better than a nervous one.

→ While diffuse light is usually the name of the game, if you feel the urge to try out some more dramatic lighting—such as a strong side light for a dramatic shadow—indulge that creative instinct.

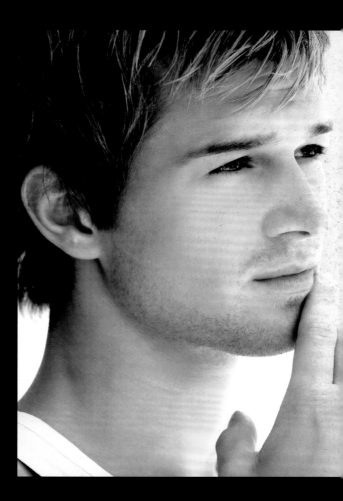

Soft Light

Be it from sunlight diffusing through clouds, flash bouncing off an umbrella, or multiple incandescent lamps evenly illuminating an interior space, soft light is characterized by its lack of obvious directionality and the evenness with which it illuminates a subject. Indeed, soft light is most effective when it is hardly noticeable at all—which is to say, when the light itself is not an essential compositional element of the photo. Light almost always originates from a point-source, meaning there is a single point from which the light radiates outward. Because light travels in a straight line, the direction from which the light is shining becomes obvious as it falls onto a subject; the shadows will all orient at the same angle, and the viewer is able to reconstruct where the light originated. Decreasing this obviousness so the light seems to come from all around is the essence of soft light.

Introducing a translucent material (a diffuser) between the light source and the subject will scatter the vectors of light so they are no longer all radiating out from a central point. What was a series of straight lines becomes a jumble of different angles of light, some of which can illuminate one side of the subject, while others from a different angle can light the other side. The light can now turn those corners and fill in every shadow, resulting in an evenly lit

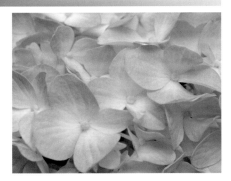

↑ **Diffuse close-up**
With no harsh shadows to give obvious directionality to the light source, this bundle of flowers seems to float effortlessly, and at this close distance one can imagine that they go on endlessly outside of the frame.

subject. Reflectors, working from the other side of the subject, achieve the same thing—reflecting the light so it can shine into spaces that would otherwise fall into shadow.

It is also worth noting that, in terms of exposure, soft light is much easier to work with—provided it is properly set up for the scene. By its nature, this lighting style is low in contrast, meaning you have quite a bit of room to maneuver between the highlights and the shadows. It is still important to make sure that your mid-tones fall at the center of your histogram, but you needn't worry too much about the dynamic range exceeding the capabilities of your sensor.

SOFT LIGHT FOR PORTRAITS

When you remember a human face, you are recalling its shape, the position of its features, its complexion, and so on. The image in your mind does not include deep shadows under the eyes, or a single bright beam of light across a forehead, because such elements are not an inherent part of the face itself. Generally speaking, most portraiture seeks an idealized representation of the subject, in which the person's face is allowed to speak for itself. You would no more let a distracting shadow obscure half of their face than you would let them wear a ski mask for the shoot. It's all about showing them in the best possible light, which for portraiture, is soft light.

Because it can shine around corners and doesn't accentuate hard edges, soft light hides wrinkles and helps your subject appear if not younger, then at least less weathered and aged. Likewise, you must position and diffuse your lights such that their eye sockets are just as illuminated as the rest of their face, and their chin isn't casting shadows down along their neck and chest.

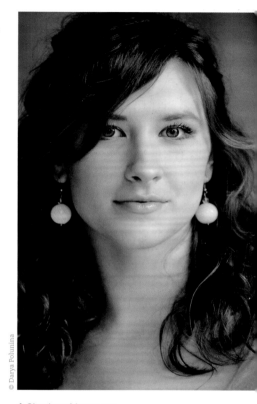

© Darya Polunina

↑ Simple softbox setup
This classic head-and-shoulders portrait, softly lit from the right by a softbox, just barely indicates the direction of the light with subtle shadowing on the left side of the face—just enough to add depth to the image without obscuring the face or becoming distracting.

Enveloping Light

Taken to the extreme, soft light can be set up to completely surround a subject, bathing it in total diffuse light that fills in every nook and cranny, eliminates every shadow, and makes the subject appear lightweight and buoyant. This enveloping light is a particular style, and not necessarily suitable for all subjects. For instance, you may think that if soft light is ideal for portraits, then completely suffusing your subject in an abundance of soft light is all the better; but that can too easily result in overly surreal and unrealistic portraits. Keep in mind that enveloping light is rarely found in nature, and your eye will recognize it as exceptional.

That said, there are many cases when enveloping light benefits a subject, and it is a useful tool when dealing with particular lighting problems. For instance, if you are photographing a highly reflective object, it may be impossible to set up the shot without having studio equipment appearing in the frame, reflected off the object's surface. For this reason, enveloping light is often used for still lifes and close-ups.

The easiest way to cover a subject from all angles with soft, diffuse light is to use a light tent. These lighting accessories are a simple affair, and involve surrounding the subject with a diffusing material of some sort—white fabric is

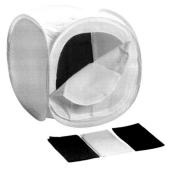

© Creative Light

↑ **Home- vs ready-made**
The definition of a light tent is not strict; any structure will do so long as it results in a complete diffusion of light from all angles in its interior. The portable light tent above, designed by Creative Light, collapses down for easy transport into the field, and comes with a selection of translucent backdrops that can attach to the interior with Velcro.

the most common, but any translucent material will do. Arranged correctly, the light tent will diffuse any light coming from outside the frame, meaning you can use point-source lights and move them freely around the set until the desired effect is achieved. The lights must be positioned far enough away that they do not create perceptible hot spots on the tent's surfaces, but still close enough to give sufficient illumination for an adequate exposure. This is particularly important with macro and close-up photography, which often use small apertures for an abundance of depth of field, at the expense of available light. Once the light is diffused inside the tent, it continues to reflect across all the interior surfaces, further evening the spread of light on the enclosed subject.

Light tents can be set up outdoors, where they can diffuse otherwise harsh sunlight. This is particularly suitable for capturing small insects or flower specimens. By surrounding them in artificial material, they will lose their sense of environment; but the effect can also evoke the classic look of natural history illustration, with its clean, idyllic portrayal cast against pure white. Light tents in the field may also simply be a necessity for capturing subjects that you could not otherwise move into the studio—for instance, many gardens don't look kindly on you plucking out their prized orchids or stealing their wildlife.

Improvised light tents are simple enough, you need only a clean white sheet and a stand from which to hang it. Circle the sheet around the subject, and poke your camera through the slit where the two ends meet. However, for best results that avoid any textured surfaces, a dedicated light tent is the way to go. These come in a variety of sizes, and are collapsible.

↓ **Precious stones**
These gems, shot from directly above and scattered across a white velvet background, still indicate a slight directionality of the diffused light coming from the upper left, but only just enough to give them a sense of place and show off their polished surfaces with a slight glare. The velvet itself was dense enough to soften and absorb most of the shadows.

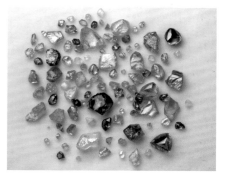

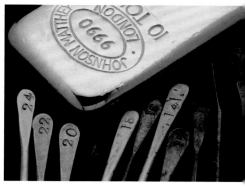

→ **No reflections**
Anything less than completely encircling this gold bar with diffuse light would have resulted in clearly visible reflections of the surrounding studio equipment in its shiny, polished surface. For contrast, a black backdrop was used at the base of the light tent.

Hard Light

If soft light is the absence of obvious lighting effects, it follows that hard light establishes in a photograph a prominent and palpable presence of light in the scene. This is when light takes on a material quality, either in its strong reaction to a subject or as a compositional element in itself.

Hard light generally indicates a lack of obstruction between the light source and the subject—no clouds, no diffusion screens, and no reflective surfaces bouncing the light around. Light strikes the subject at a definite angle, indicated by shadows falling in a common direction. Thus, it becomes clear that hard light is just as dependent on the subject as it is on the source itself, for if the subject offers no edges or contours to cast shadows, there is no way for a photograph to indicate the directionality of the light.

By definition, hard light is going to increase the contrast of a photograph. Some areas of the frame will be brightly lit, with others falling into dark shadows.

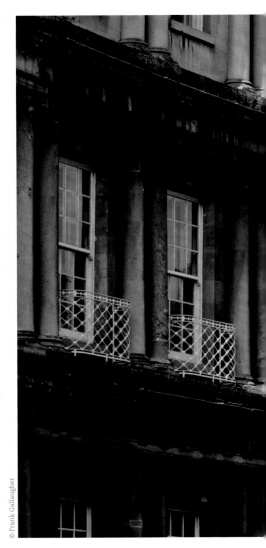

→ **Georgian lighting**
Architecture often benefits from a hard light, where it throws structural elements into harsh relief and accents the design of the building. For instance, the circular orientation of the Circus in Bath, England is accentuated here, where hard, angled light progressively falls into shadow as the building curves around up and to the left.

© Frank Gallaugher

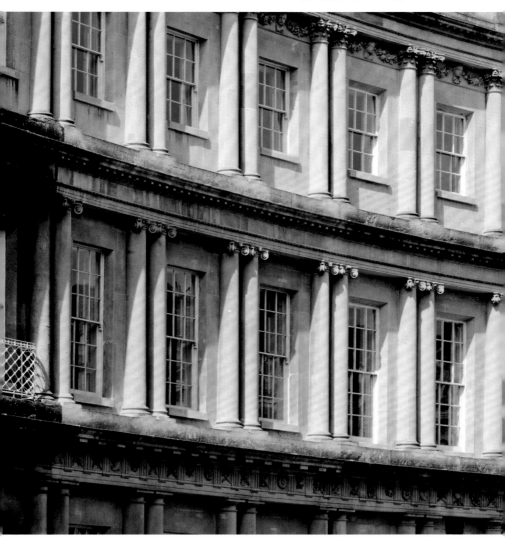

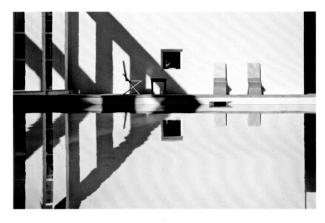

← **Shapes, lines, and shadows**
In viewing this image, your eyes register the design elements first: obvious diagonals, permeated and reinforced by verticals, all reflected symmetrically across a horizontal axis. These elements were emphasized in post-production by increasing contrast and clarity. Only secondarily does the reality of the subject itself come into play.

Careful calculation of proper exposure is therefore all the more important, as the higher dynamic range means you must keep a close eye on the histogram to ensure that your sensor captures detail throughout the full range of light intensities. On the other hand, you can make a creative decision to accentuate this contrast by completely losing detail in the shadows or highlights (or both). We discuss this chiaroscuro approach in the following pages.

Finally, because hard light gives the eye more clues as to the direction of the light source, it also gives a photograph a corresponding sense of time and place. We discussed the flattering aspects of golden light on pages 120–121. Whether you realize it or not, you recognize long shadows as occurring early or late in the day.

GRAPHIC DESIGN

By emphasizing hard edges and bringing shapes into stark relief, hard light gives you the tools to emphasize form and design over content—meaning they are less about an accurate rendition of the subject itself, and more about lines, shapes, colors, and contrast. Letting the geometry of the composition take precedence over its underlying subject can give a surprising, exciting, and energetic feel to your photography.

This style requires you to deconstruct a scene, as it were, into its constituent parts. Where a casual observer may simply see the side of a skyscraper, the graphic stylist sees a line of repeating squares, angled at a diagonal from the low perspective, with beams of light cutting through a neighboring structure and punctuating the building's surface with negative space. Telephoto lenses often help with these kinds of photos, as they can isolate particular elements out of their natural surroundings, which can assist in discarding the material subject's preeminence. Seeing the world this way can become quite addictive, and while it is hardly appropriate for every subject, it gives you the chance to infuse even the commonplace with a dynamic and robust style.

GOBOS FOR PATTERNS

You can add a graphic or textural quality to the light yourself by using a type of stencil called a gobo, which stands for GOes Before Optics (they are alternately called cookies or flags). These patterned screens throw a certain shadow onto your subject, depending on their design.

They occur naturally as well—you can consider the repeating pattern of lines cast by blinds on a window to be a gobo effect. Gobos can be used for obvious graphic design elements, where the shape taken on by the light becomes an object in itself; or they can impart a less obvious texture to the light, which will spread out across the subject, taking on its curves and rounding off its edges.

↙ **Texture designs**
A small sample of different gobo designs. These can be small enough to fit on the end of a flash unit, or large enough to cover a window.

↘ **Molten light**
There are two gobos at work here: the window frame is casting the strong, crisscrossed lines diagonally across the frame; and the imperfections in the glass are changing the quality of the light itself into a wavy, fluid pattern.

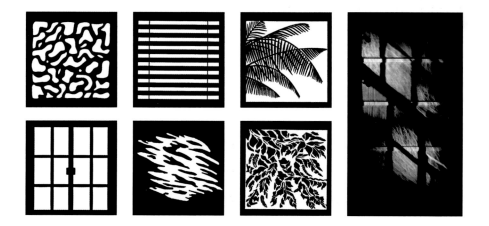

Chiaroscuro

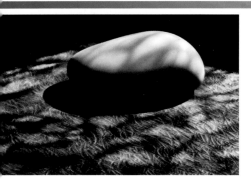

← **Shadow play**
Black-and-white photography lends itself well to the chiaroscuro lighting style, as your eye concentrates only on the subtleties of gradation from light to dark without getting distracted by color.

A beautiful Italian word for a beautiful lighting style, chiaroscuro literally means light-dark. It is a Renaissance art term, pioneered by the painter Caravaggio, in which shapes are created not by outlining their edges, but by using subtle gradations of light and shade to create rounded, three-dimensional forms. By nature of its high contrast, it is a type of hard light, but a very delicately implemented one. A single, point-source hard light will fall off too sharply at the edges of a shape, and the definitive lines it casts are not the defining characteristic of this lighting style.

Rather, chiaroscuro is something of a balance between hard and soft light. It must be hard enough to cast deep shadows, in which you may choose to completely lose all detail and create large blocks of black, out of which the subject rises. And it must be just soft enough that the edges and contours of the subject are apparent, with the light gradually falling from the highlights off into the shadows.

Mood and drama are inseparable from chiaroscuro lighting. An otherwise mundane still life of a bowl of fruit on a table will, when set against a pure-black backdrop with obvious side lighting, take on a timeless and painterly quality. It can also contribute a sense of dread and foreboding, as the mind is forced to speculate as to what may lurk in the deep shadows that constitute a large part of the composition. Consider the lighting style typical of film noir, for instance, where the cynical and deviant themes of crime drama were illustrated by consistent chiaroscuro lighting, making a half-lit character appear shifty and untrustworthy, and the shadows cast across a room insinuate foul play and hidden agendas.

CHIAROSCURO LIGHTING SETUPS

In the studio, chiaroscuro lighting is relatively simple to achieve, as it embraces the contrast and deep shadows that other lighting styles seek to eliminate by employing copious diffusers, reflectors, and multiple light sources.

For the simplest setup, place your subject against a black backdrop, and light it from a three-quarter angle with a strong point-source lamp with a diffuser attached. The light will reach the backdrop at different distances, creating a gradation from light to dark against which your subject can stand out.

Depending on the effect you want to achieve, you may rotate the backdrop so it isn't perpendicular to the camera, which will create a gradient along the length of the background itself.

Metering a chiaroscuro setup can be tricky, given the abundance of contrast. Spot metering off the highlights is the simplest approach, provided you want to lose detail in the shadows. That said, it is often a safer bet to capture as much detail as possible throughout the dynamic range of the scene, as shadows and highlights can always be pushed down or blown out in post-production. Try spot metering first off a shadow, then off a highlight area, and use your camera's exposure readout to find a happy medium between those two extremes.

↓ **Dark profile**
The setup for this shot couldn't be simpler: A single light source shining from upper left, and a black background. The textured face and beard suit the lighting style, giving lots of detail in which to see the progressive darkening of tones.

↓ **Emerging from the dark**
To capture chiaroscuro lighting outside of the studio, keep an eye out for single light sources in otherwise dark environments. This artist was working by a small spotlight during an intimate music concert, and by spot metering off the canvas, the surrounding falls off sharply into shadow.

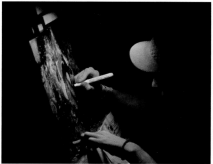

© Frank Gallaugher

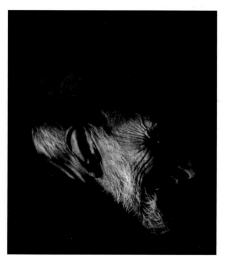

Kick It Up a Notch with Hard Light

Challenge

For this challenge, you should embrace a strong, directional light source and feature its effects at the forefront of your photo. As you've seen on the previous pages, there are a few different approaches to making the light a preeminent element of the image—you can zoom in on particular detail and compose the shot so that it has an obvious graphic quality, or you can spotlight a subject and experiment with the delicate craft of chiaroscuro lighting. If you have the time and control, you can try cutting out your own gobos and capturing their effects as their shadows fall on a particular subject.

↓ **Dune shadows**
The dynamic range between the sun-facing right side of the dunes and the shadows on the left required a careful exposure, with one eye firmly on the histogram.

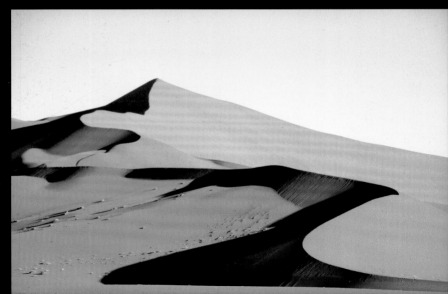

On angular subjects like buildings you'll easily see the contrast created by hard light, which illuminates one side while the other falls into shadow. This was upped in post-production as it adds to the grandiosity of this subject.

Challenge Checklist

→ You'll need to start, obviously, with a hard light source. If you're setting up the shot, this can be a straightforward lamp of any variety. Otherwise, mid-morning and late afternoon will give you plenty of long, dramatic shadows to play around with.

→ Watch your exposure, as always, but don't be afraid to let some of your shadows block up into pure black if that's what you envision.

→ This might be an excellent time to try your hand at black-and-white photography, as it speaks completely through light alone and doesn't let your viewers (or you) get distracted by irrelevant color information.

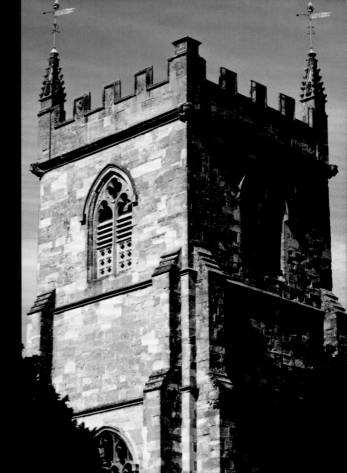

Side & Edge Lighting

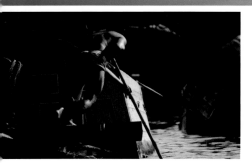

↑ **Leaning into the light**
The distant setting sun serves as a strong edge light cast against the side of this boat, and molds around the contours of the sailor's taut muscles to communicate his physical exertion.

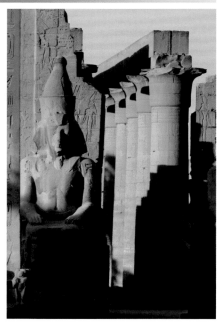

↑ **Side-lit Luxor**
The monumental form of the columns and statues is best brought out by the strong side lighting of the rising sun. A careful exposure was required to keep detail in the shadows.

The long shadows typical of strong side lighting are evocative, dramatic, and highly effective at showing off fully rounded shapes. This lighting style is most apparent when the light source is shining at an exact right angle to the camera axis; but you can experiment with slight variations on that angle to see how the light interacts with your subject. It may be necessary at times to fill in strong shadows, which is often an easy task and requires only a reflector on the opposite side of the light.

As a point-source side light moves farther away from the subject, it gradually dims such that only the very edges are illuminated in a sort of outline. This is when side light becomes edge lighting, and is most effective with dark backgrounds that won't compete with the thin slivers of illumination. Likewise, it is best if the edge light doesn't have to compete with any other ambient light sources. Generally speaking, the simpler the shape and contour of the subject,

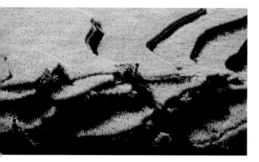

↑ **Texture from afar**
As distance between the subject and camera is increased, the intensity of the side light must also be increased if there is to be any discernible texture in the image. A diffuse light would have lost all the sharp detail in the blades of grass in these rice terraces.

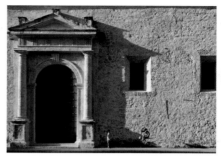

↑ **Grandiose doorway**
There are two types of shadows here: the larger, graphic one cast by the enormous doorway; and the infinite tiny shadows falling in all the indentations in the surface of the wall. A frontal light would be unable to illustrate those fine textural details, and the wall to the right would become an uninteresting component of the composition. As it is, however, you feel quite as if you could run your finger across the page and feel each groove and bump.

the cleaner and clearer its outline will be when edge-lit. Too many elements at varying distances to the camera will each pick up their own edge light and obscure a clear, underlying shape.

TEXTURE

Being a two-dimensional representation, a photograph must use a number of tricks to communicate depth. Chiaroscuro lighting does this with fine gradations of light to dark, which is excellent at communicating full shapes and figures; but textures are a much finer and smaller affair, and require strong side light at a very shallow angle to the

subject's surface in order to cast myriad tiny shadows on a micro scale. Toward that end, getting closer to the subject, either physically with a macro lens, or by zooming in with a long telephoto, makes it easier to discern the fine textural details brought out by a strong side light. Emphasizing texture also helps render a common subject in a more interesting way—what may look like just another concrete wall can, in the right light, reveal intricate patterns of crumbling masonry, chipped paint, weathered surfaces and so on.

Bring Out the Texture

Challenge

Most subjects can be said to have some degree of texture, but it's not always easy to capture it in every lighting condition. Strong side lighting will be the most apt lighting style for this challenge, which you can create in the studio or out in the field—either from artificial lamplight or from a low-angled sun. But unlike your challenge to capture golden light, the lighting itself is not the most important element of this challenge; rather, it's all about finding the right subject that will show off its three-dimensional qualities and come alive under the right conditions.

↓ **Color close-up**
Contrasting colors can impart a textural quality to a photograph all their own, and often the side lighting does not need to be terribly strong in order for them to take on an effective, three-dimensional appearance.

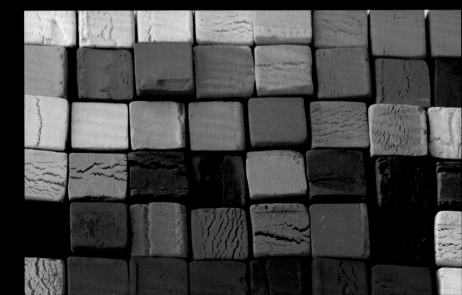

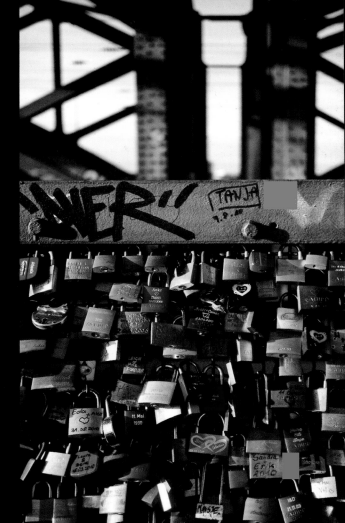

→ Love locks on a bridge

Bringing out the texture
often means taking
something that might
otherwise be busy or overly
complicated and making it
the center of attention. This
would have been a terrible
portrait backdrop, for
instance, but as a subject in
itself, this wall of padlocks
gives the eye multiple
nooks and crannies to
investigate.

Challenge
Checklist

→ Macro and close-up shots
   lend themselves well
   to textural studies, and
   you can add a side light
   by either positioning a
   lamp in the right place,
   or by using an external
   flash unit attached by an
   accessory cord, which
   you can hold with one
   hand off to the side.

→ Longer, telephoto focal
   lengths are the natural
   inclination for textural
   shots, but keep in mind
   that most wide-angle
   lenses let you focus quite
   closely as well, and you
   may be able to get an
   interesting composition
   that pits large
   foreground elements
   against an expansive
   background.

CHAPTER 3 | Composition

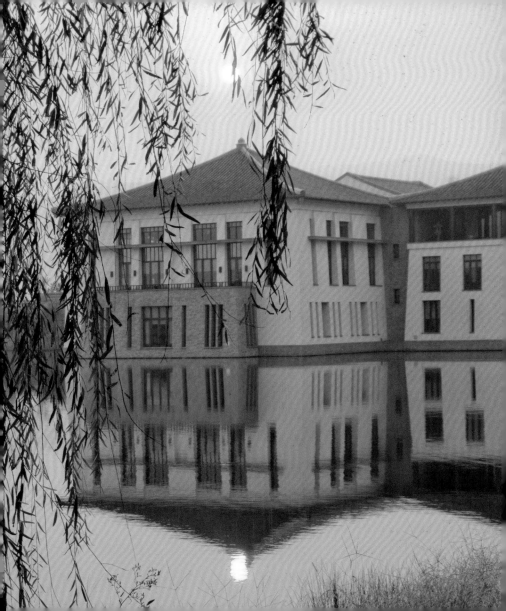

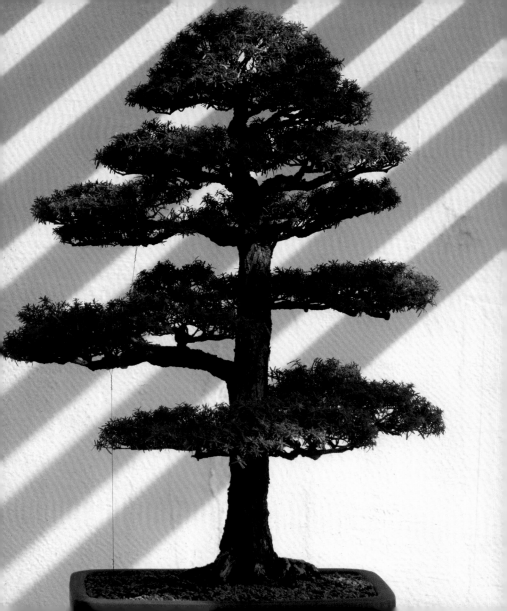

Introduction: Composition

Composition pertains to every photographer using any type of camera. This chapter will apply to you and your photography regardless of the camera in your hands. It won't matter if you're snapping something with the camera in your mobile phone because that's what you have to hand, or if you've progressed to the dizzying heights of a medium-format camera: The principles behind composition remain the same, and they are the foundation of taking stunning and meaningful photographs.

A photograph is your interpretation of an event or scene; it's your expression of a story. Consequently, the basis of a good photograph is its composition, or how you—the photographer—bring together everything that you are trying to say and relate it effectively as a whole. If a photograph is a narrative, then it relies on a strong composition to be conveyed.

Just like photography itself, composition is the synthesis of the technical and the creative. It's where geometry and artistry collide head on and in the resulting explosion they make something gorgeous. If you haven't studied math since high school and the idea of geometry strikes fear to your core, don't worry. When you look at it in the context of taking a photograph and can see how it helps to elevate your images from something ordinary to something special, it's not nearly that daunting.

This chapter builds on the skills and techniques that you learned in previous sections, and gives you the opportunity to put them into practice, too. Of course, if you just wanted to check on a principle or read up on a specific technique, there's nothing to stop you from doing that. All the same, the idea is to have you taking better-composed, beautiful photographs by the end of it.

Pick Your Subject

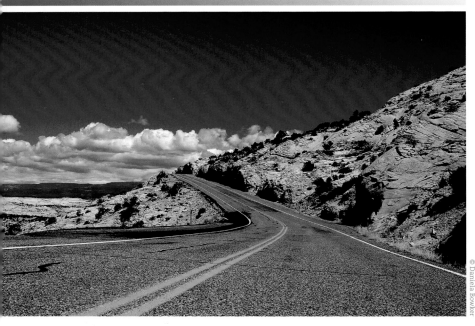

© Daniela Bowker

Choosing what to photograph is the first step; this is where your intent begins, and it influences everything in the shooting and processing that follows. Your subject can be a single object, a group, a large scene, a moment of action, an abstract pattern, almost anything. What will elevate your photography, however, is making your subject part of something else—a project, a theme, a broader aim of some sort.

↖ **Open road, open interpretation**
Here, the subject is clearly a road, but there are also themes of openness, possibility, but also of emptiness and being lost. It conveys a sense of isolation or even loneliness. Anyone looking at the image can get a feeling of being the only person in the world, and that the road heads onward, unending and deserted.

ENHANCING THE SUBJECT

When you've established your subject, you can then determine what is essential to your image, what is the background, and what is superfluous. By working out these key elements and how they interact—for example, how the background accentuates the subject—you will ensure that your photograph is saying just what you want it to say and everything will harmonize toward that end. You will be on your way to composing better images before you've even released the shutter.

If the photograph of the lonely road opposite had a train of cars heading along it they would detract from the feeling of emptiness and change the overall narrative. You might even find that the cars then become the subject, rather than the road. But an isolated building or a solitary car might contribute to the sense of desolation. Whatever you place in an image should be contributing something and complementing the subject, not diminishing it. Sometimes it might mean hanging around for a bit to get the perfect shot, or changing where you stand; but it will be worth it.

Making something the subject of a photo isn't just about placing it in the center of the frame and clicking your shutter. There is an entire gamut of techniques and tricks to draw the eye to the subject of an image, techniques that we'll

explore throughout the course of this chapter; but the starting point is where to place your subject in the frame. While it might seem to make sense to place the subject of your photo slap-bang in the middle, this doesn't necessarily make for the best photo. First of all—and very bluntly—this sort of composition is boring if you use it repeatedly.

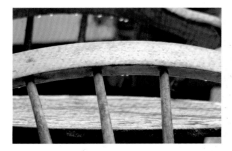

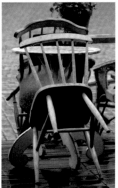

←↑ **Two takes**
What's the subject here? The individual drops of water, clinging to an arch that forms a graphic image? Or a more literal presentation of forlorn furniture left out in the rain?

© Daniela Bowker

Filling the Frame

For the moment, let's disregard a vast number of other possible types of images and concentrate only on one: a single, obvious, self-apparent subject positioned directly in front of the camera. How to frame it? There is a scale of choice: from getting in tight so the photograph is dominated entirely by the subject, to the wider view that incorporates the surroundings. The first option gives you the opportunity to capture much more detail in the subject, and is easier to compose if the subject is large enough to fill up the frame. It is also better suited to subjects that are self-evidently interesting or unusual—such as a rare bird or an exquisite work of art. The second, wide-view option, on the other hand, invites a study of the relationship between the subject and its context, and so the surrounding environment must be relevant somehow.

Perhaps the subject needs some other point of comparison so the viewer can judge its relative size, or maybe there is other action occurring that contextualizes the subject's movement or expression. Neither of these approaches is superior to the other; it's about what you prefer aesthetically, what you want to communicate, and what best suits the circumstances. Don't be afraid to experiment and shift your precise focus, but do know exactly what it is that you want the picture to communicate.

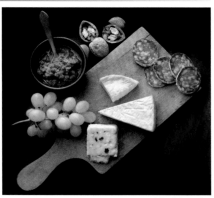

© Daniela Bowker

↑ **Edge to edge**
A simple still life, photographed top-down, where the framing is dictated entirely by the subject: fill the frame from edge to edge, rather than concentrating on any one element.

Keeping in mind the questions of how much of the frame to fill and with what is what differentiates the thoughtful photographer from the casual shooter. You should continually ask yourself these questions, and they will eventually become second nature as you learn to consider both your subject and its environment simultaneously, and decide how much of each to fit into frame. In any case, the bottom line is to maximize the amount of meaningful information in the shot—there shouldn't be anything extraneous in the scene. Whatever you see in a picture should be accentuating the subject, not detracting from it.

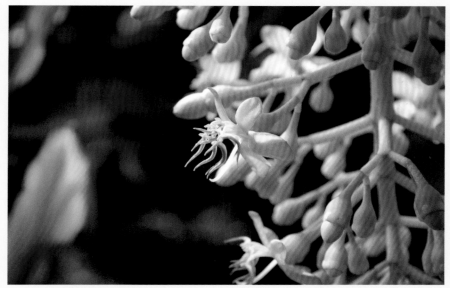

© Daniela Bowker

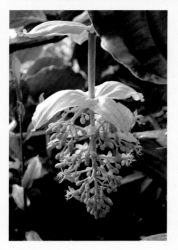

←↑ **Get closer**
What's the subject? The flowers,
of course. While the image on the left
shows the overall shape of the plant
and includes a bit of its surroundings,
the one above isolates the fine
detail within the buds and flowers.
One isn't better than the other, they're
equal alternatives to a common subject.

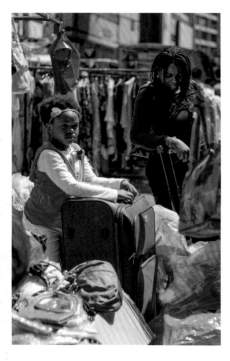

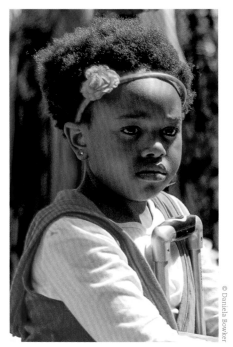

© Daniela Bowker

ORGANIZING THE FRAME

By introducing some tension into your image not only do you make it more aesthetically interesting, but you also create a relationship between your subject and background. Tension is something that will continue to come up throughout this book, but in this particular case, tension is what we mean by capturing the interaction between subject and background, which then introduces some direction or movement into your composition. This will draw your eye into the image so that it doesn't feel static.

Diagonals and strong divides that run through your photographs, together with your subjects' eye-lines, can all contribute to tension. If you're aiming for an environmental photograph, the relationship between subject and background is all-important. The background provides context for the subject and they need to work together in order to tell the story of the image.

If you've never tried off-center focusing with your camera, it isn't nearly as scary as it sounds. If you're using manual focus, focus first on the subject of your image and then recompose the frame to set the subject in relation to the background. When you use autofocus, first focus on your subject by half-pressing the shutter button, and then, while still keeping the shutter button half-pressed, recompose your frame as you see fit, finally fully pressing the shutter button once you have your desired composition. Your camera will remember where you focused as long as you keep the shutter button half-pressed, even if that subject isn't in the center of the frame anymore.

(It is worth noting that many cameras, including most DSLRs, allow you to customize various buttons in order to facilitate this focus-and-recompose method in different ways. For instance, sometimes you can press the AEL/AFL button to acquire focus, and half-pressing the shutter button has no immediate effect. Consult your particular camera's manual for details.)

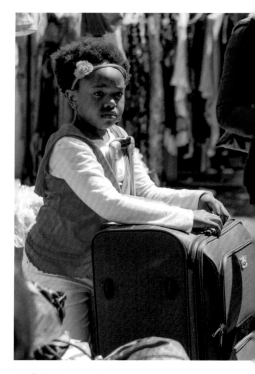

↖ ↖ ↑ Three scenes in one
Across these three photographs, we can see the way that getting closer to your subject changes the feel of the resulting image. Farthest away, the scene feels busy and eventful. The girl is probably the subject—or is it the woman beside her? Zooming in tight on the little girl makes the subject obvious, and invites an interpretation of her emotional state. The above photo is a happy medium—close enough to clearly indicate the subject, but still providing enough clues for the viewer to understand the surrounding scene.

Horizontal & Vertical

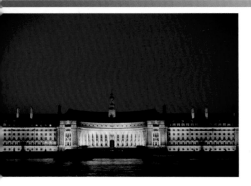

← → **Subject-dictated orientation**
London County Hall is considerably wider than it is high, so the horizontal orientation was the best means of capturing this straightforward shot. Likewise, the vertical orientation was the best means of capturing the tension from top to bottom of the shot on the right, as this woman looks down attentively at her tea.

Human vision is binocular, meaning that we have two eyes positioned adjacent to rather than on top of each other. As a consequence of this, our eyes are predisposed to scanning things along a horizontal plane rather than a vertical one. It's no surprise then that we're more inclined to capture horizontally oriented pictures. The vast majority of cameras have been designed around this fact, and have a default horizontal orientation. And as part of that design, simply rotating the camera into a vertical position can be slightly uncomfortable, such that it's easy to stick to the horizontal during casual shooting or when dealing with rapidly developing action.

Often the orientation is dictated by the subject—landscapes and portraits being such obvious examples that they have lent their names to the horizontal and vertical formats, respectively. In a typical landscape, the stretch of the horizon is such a powerful element that it begs to maintain as much length as possible. Plus, when surveying a scene, there is typically more to see and capture by scanning from left to right than from top to bottom. The horizontal orientation may be the default, but it is also the most natural and effective means of portraying the landscape subject.

Likewise, human subjects are taller than they are wide, and their figures are naturally suited to a vertical format. This isn't only a matter of fitting whole bodies or faces into frame—there's also the fact that the subject of their attention is often at arm or waist level, which can create an effective tension between the face's expression at the top and the action occurring at the bottom of the frame.

A CREATIVE CHOICE

While much of the time it will feel obvious when you're taking a photograph whether you should be using portrait

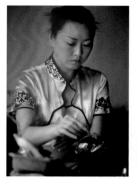
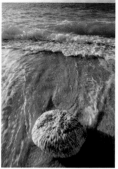
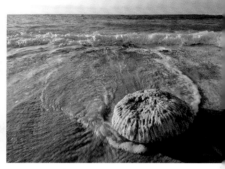

or landscape format, other times your subject will present you with a compositional dilemma. For instance: In a landscape with a clear mountain range extending horizontally, but with towering trees reaching up vertically in the foreground, which is the more dominant element? Which orientation best accommodates the elements you find to be important, and displays them for maximum effect?

Going beyond, your creative choices regarding orientation do not always need to take a problem-solving approach. It is well worth challenging your natural inclinations as to how a given shot should be framed simply for the sake of experimentation. This isn't to say you should start chopping off essential elements of your subject. Rather, you should allow yourself to take the time to fully consider all your options. Move around, rotate your camera, tilt it at a

↑ **Two takes**
Of these two seascapes, the horizontal format is probably the more traditional approach, as the wide horizon is allowed to stretch across from left to right. While the subject is the same in both shots, the vertical shot resists a traditional approach and introduces a stronger graphic quality, with greater tension between the upper and lower parts of the frame. What is important to recognize here is that one is not particular or objectively better than the other, but rather that they appear quite distinct and have different effects as a result of their framing, regardless of their common subject.

stronger angle or position yourself so the light or shadows are falling differently. Look for other elements that might make a vertical orientation purposeful in a landscape—they may be dominant (like a mountain) or subtle (like a lone bird occupying the corner of the frame against an otherwise empty sky). In any case, the point is to make sure you're not missing out on any novel or captivating compositions.

Subject Placement

Combining off-center framing with the inclusion of environment and context in your frame presents you with the question of subject placement: If dead-center is flat and dull, then where else should the subject be? The answer is not simply "anywhere else." The subject needs a dynamic and engaging position within the frame, but more importantly, it needs a meaningful one. Position without purpose comes off as confused and unfocused. If every shot in your portfolio has the subject far in the corner of the frame, the effect will be just as monotonous as if they were all centrally framed. Viewers respond well to thought-out, well justified compositions, which can in fact give you much greater leeway for extreme or eccentric compositions than if you sought them out just for eccentricity's sake.

A number of factors will come into play as you choose where to position your subject. The subject's size is significant,

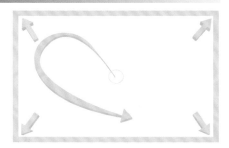

↑ **Wandering eye**
Confronted by a static rectangle, the eye doesn't just fixate in the middle—it tends to explore the edges and wrap around the space. A centrally placed subject won't hold the eye's attention completely; it will be more interesting if there are other elements to investigate.

↙ ↓ **Head-on vs off-center**
The photo on the left is a straightforward shot—and quite uninspired. It feels static and obvious. But moving the boat to the bottom right of the frame invites the viewer to think about the open water stretching across the rest of the frame—all the way to the edges, which suggests it continues on interminably. Suddenly this lone dinghy has a relationship to its surroundings, all by moving the camera slightly up and left.

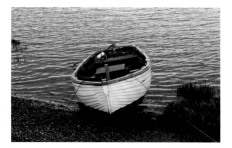

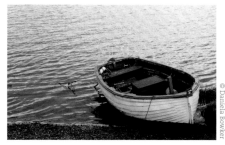

© Daniela Bowker

insofar as larger subjects do not have nearly the room for dramatic off-center positioning as do smaller ones.

You should also keep an eye out for secondary points of interest nearby. Perhaps a flock of birds in the sky or a tall tree positioned on the opposite side or corner of the frame from the main subject, inviting some degree of tension between them. In some cases, this secondary point of interest need not even be visible in the frame at all. If your subject is in motion, or even simply staring off in a certain direction at something out of frame, you can compose them so that they are looking or moving across the frame, into open space. Besides giving meaning and purpose to that empty space, it is also more traditional to have your subject moving or looking into the frame rather than out of it.

HORIZON PLACEMENT

It is also all too easy to allow the horizon to cut directly across the middle of the image, splitting it into two obvious parts and diffusing the composition of any sense of movement or tension. Having the horizon on the lower third will often feel more dynamic as it will give the image a sense of being grounded. However, you shouldn't feel that you can't place a horizon on the upper third. If the most significant element of your landscape is below the skyline then it makes sense for it to dominate the image. You can create some dramatic pictures by placing the horizon higher in the composition.

↓↓ Beware obvious bisections
Here you can see how the shot with the horizon running across the middle of the image looks flatter and less inspiring than the picture where the horizon is lower in the frame. The latter is also more effective at showing off the eerie yellow sky with the buildings silhouetted against it.

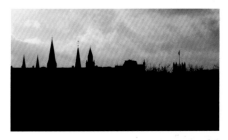

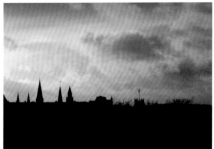

© Daniela Bowker

The Golden Ratio

While it may seem like you have some serious decisions to make regarding subject placement, there are a variety of helpful guides have been invented throughout the ages to help to choose how to arrange and distribute elements throughout the frame.

Perhaps most famous of these guides is the Golden Ratio, also called the Golden Section, the Golden Mean, Phi, or Divine Proportion. It is similar to, but mathematically different from, the rule of thirds. It has been used by architects and artists for millennia (the Parthenon was built on the principles of the Golden Ratio), so photographers following suit shouldn't be a surprise.

The Golden Ratio is an irrational number equal to approximately 1.618, denoted by φ—the Greek letter Phi (hence the rule also being called "Phi"). If you divide a line unevenly into two sections—(a), a longer part, and (b), a shorter part—the ratio of those two sections will conform to the Golden Ratio if (a) divided by (b) is equal to the sum of (a) plus (b) divided by (a).

Of course, it's all very well knowing the math behind the Golden Ratio, but the basis is that the ratio of the smaller to the larger is the same as the larger to the whole. This means the various elements, if properly arranged, relate to each other harmoniously, without battling each other for dominance. The whole ends up being more than the sum of its parts.

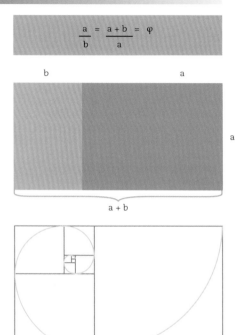

$$\frac{a}{b} = \frac{a+b}{a} = \varphi$$

b   a

a

a + b

↑ **Classical elegance**
The compositional guidelines of the rectangle function regardless of their specific orientation—you can flip it or rotate it to suit your subject.

THE GOLDEN SPIRAL

Another aesthetic principle that you can use to place your subjects is the Golden Spiral. It is based on the Fibonacci series of numbers, but is probably easiest to understand if you think of it as a series of joined-up quarter circles that have been drawn inside decreasingly smaller squares that have themselves been drawn inside a rectangle that conforms to the Golden Ratio. The center of the spiral is where your photograph's subject should be and if you allow the spiral to dictate the rest of your composition, you'll find that you have a strong image. There are many different ways of dividing up your frame so that your picture conforms to various sets of theories that we find proportionally comfortable. Where the key elements of the image are placed is proportionally the same, whatever the size or shape of the frame. And of course, they're not dead center.

All that said, keep in mind that this is just one method of dividing the frame into proportions and not a strict rule in any meaningful sense. It is also most useful when you have time to compose carefully, such as with a landscape and a tripod rather than a street scene.

↓ **Proportional arrangement**
This could have been a straight-on frame-within-frame composition, as the window composes the exterior well enough. But a slight shift in the composition to align the window with the golden rectangle makes the scene more dynamic.

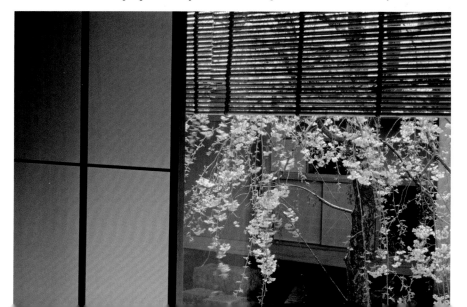

Using Lines to Pull Attention

Lines—horizontal, vertical, diagonal, curved, or imaginary—are an important tool in your compositional arsenal. We already touched on horizons when we looked at subject placement, and we covered lines that draw the eye across the image and give it a sense of movement in the section on organizing your frame. There are also lines that are referred to as "leading lines," which act as pointers and direct the viewer's eyes to the subject of the image. Different types of line have different properties that they will lend to your composition.

It's worth remembering that a single line or a series of lines doesn't necessarily have to be formed by solid objects running through the image. A series of points that the eye naturally links together can create the perception of a line, while light and shadow also produce beautiful and subtle lines in photographs. Similarly, even if you don't set out to deliberately photograph an image composed of lines, you need to remember their potential impact on your composition, keeping in mind how they will influence viewers later on.

Horizontal lines tend feel solid and stable, which is no surprise given their association with the ground and gravity.

They're also expansive, and will broaden the feeling of your scene as well as make it appear deeper. Where horizontal lines feel calming and restful, vertical lines are pretty much the opposite. They will elongate the frame and can give an impression of energy as they work against gravity; but they can also feel imposing and confrontational, especially if they run as a uniform series across the frame. Imagine the strength and power exhibited by a regiment of soldiers in battle lines, for example. Whether your photograph features horizontal or vertical lines, it is key that they are aligned with the frame. A wonky line is instantly noticeable.

In the section on frame orientation, we looked at how the subject of your photograph may suggest whether you shoot horizontally or vertically. Scenes featuring horizontal lines can be framed horizontally to allow the lines to work with the longer side of the frame; likewise, photographs with strong vertical lines usually translate well in portrait compositions. This isn't always the case, though. Sometimes, you can actually reinforce strong horizontal or vertical lines by using a portrait or landscape format, respectively.

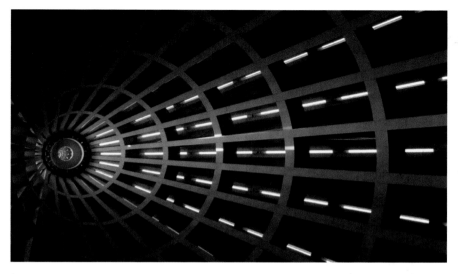

↑ Architectural abstract
Isolating segments of architecture is a great way to exploit strong lines, such as here, where the eye is both pulled toward the focal point on the left, and guided outward along the lines radiating out to the right.

↓ Connect the columns
This colonnade in Prague is full of strong vertical lines and diagonal movement.

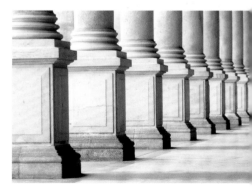

LEADING LINES

Lines can give your image an overall feeling or they can direct the eye across the photograph and out of the frame. However, they can also draw your eye toward your subject. A good leading line is just as effective as, and definitely more attractive than, a flashing neon sign screaming "The subject is here!"

Diagonal, Curved & Imaginary Lines

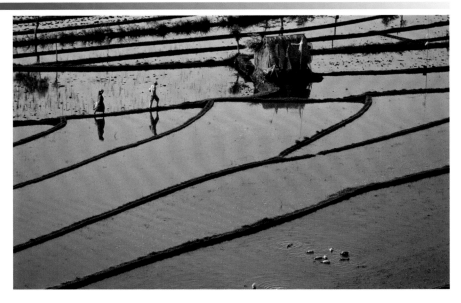

Whereas vertical or horizontal lines provide a sense of solidity or order, diagonal lines are far more dynamic. This means that they're great at giving a sense of implied movement and at accentuating actual movement in an image. However, there are some points you should be aware of when you use diagonal lines. Too many conflicting diagonal lines in an image can feel chaotic. Your subject can then get lost amid the chaos. Diagonals also have a wonderful potential to introduce a sense of instability to an image, as their direction conflicts with the more natural

↑ **Follow the tracks**
The human subjects are quite tiny, but their walking action is just recognizable enough to give meaning to the other, dominant elements in the frame: the levees stretching diagonally across the frame. These lines carry the movement of the human figures across the full expanse of the frame, while also providing valuable context as to their environment.

stability of horizontal and vertical lines. While this can be highly effective, it can also be disorientating and uncomfortable. In some cases, this could be just what you are looking for; but at other times, it might work against your composition.

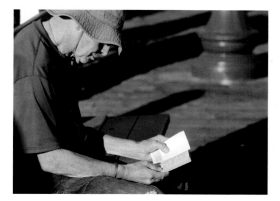

← **Real vs imaginary**
The eye-line between the man and the book runs perpendicular to the diagonal shadows. The resulting tension adds interest. In addition, the head, arm, and book make an implied curve.

It's also worth remembering that parallel lines shot at eye-level and running off into the distance will appear to converge and therefore become diagonal lines. This is the result of perspective, but it's another thing to think about introducing when diagonal lines into your photos.

IMPLIED LINES

So far, most of the examples of lines that we have looked at have been actual lines. What we haven't considered yet are implied lines, which we can sense in the image even if they aren't there physically. One of the most obvious implied lines is an eye-line. We're curious by nature, so when we see a face in an image, we're likely to follow where it's looking. This may be a single subject looking out of frame, or a large group of people all oriented toward a common point, drawing the eye toward that apparently significant object or element.

And it's not just human subjects—the way wildlife interacts with its environment can likewise lead a viewer's eye toward some other element in or out of frame. Eye-lines are powerful components of composition, as they work entirely by implication without having to have a physical presence.

CURVES

Whereas vertical and horizontal lines suggest stability and diagonal lines lend dynamism to an image, curved lines are far more sensual. They are smooth, inviting, and elegant. Just imagine the undulations of gently rolling hills or the silky curvature of a lover's neck. By using curved lines in your images, you'll lend them a softer, almost seductive appeal. They can also feel graceful and elegant, which you can use to play off otherwise stiff and rigid straight lines elsewhere.

Lead with Lines

Challenge

Your challenge for this section is to take a photograph that uses leading lines to draw your eye straight to your subject. Think about your point of focus and the narrative of the photograph. Where are you going to place your subject; how will you divide the frame; and what orientation will work best with your composition? What sort of aperture will you need to use to get the right effect for your shot?

↓ **Lines to eyelines**
Here, the window sill leads the viewer's eye to the child's eye, which then directs attention outward through the window, occupying the otherwise-empty left half of the frame.

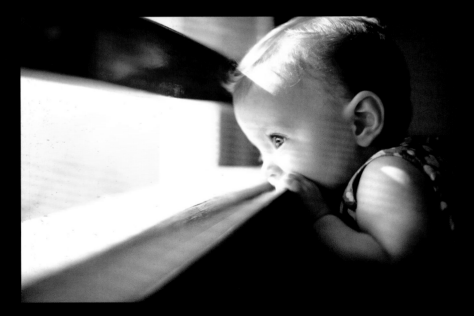

© Daniela Bowker

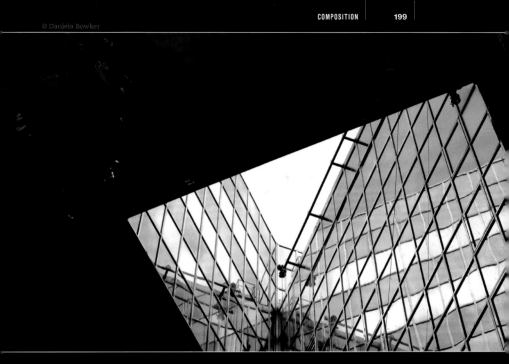

Challenge Checklist

→ Identify your point of focus.

→ Use one or more lines to draw the eye to the subject.

→ Ensure that the lines are working to emphasize the subject and not overwhelm it.

↑ **Framing a triangle**
Lines can also wrap around and give form to otherwise empty space, giving your eye something to follow and trace across the frame in the process.

Seeking a Balance

A fundamental part of composition, balance is arranging the elements of the frame such that tension is both created and resolved. Balance is not only about things being exactly the same in some scientific sense—that is veering into the idea of symmetry, discussed later. You're not necessarily aiming for perfect and literal equality in every section of the frame; balance is much more suggestive than that, less exact and more implied.

One way of approaching balance is finding an image's "visual center of gravity" and proceeding to organize its compositional elements around that point. That visual center can be a mass of color, a high-contrast area, an arrangement of shapes with particular directions, the list goes on. What's important is that you compose your images so that the eye wants to move across all of the frame. Although it might be directed to the subject, no part of the image feels under-used or superfluous.

The vital element governing the sense of balance in an image is the interaction between the subject and the background. By creating a subtle tension between them, the scene will have a point of focus, a feeling of movement, and a sense of direction. Even if the subject comprises only a small portion of the overall image, by ensuring that there's a strong relationship between it and the background, the subject won't look overwhelmed and the composition won't be lopsided. In a portrait, if you choose a placement that puts the model far over to one side of the image and leaves the other side a blur of background, it could be easy for that photograph to become unbalanced. The portrait can still work, however, if the model's eye-line or positioning directs you across the empty portion of the frame. The gaze or orientation creates a tension, which in turn creates a feeling of balance. Similarly, by not having such a blurred background and leaving some object to complement the model in the emptier side, the image will balance out.

If you're photographing in strong light, try using a shadow to give balance to the composition. A shadow that falls so that it replicates the shape of the subject can add an interesting dimension. Alternately, shadows can be used to elongate or widen the subject, drawing the eye down or across the frame. Don't feel as if you must balance your images only between left and right or horizontal and vertical. We've looked at how diagonal lines provide a strong sense of movement in a composition, and balance works just as effectively on a diagonal, too. Balance can come in many different forms. You might want to counterpoint contrasting colors. By being certain of what you're trying to communicate, thinking about your subject placement, and having a feel for movement and direction, you'll find the right elements to create balanced and satisfying images.

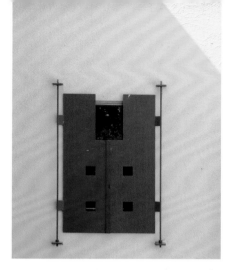

→ Diagonal distribution

This window, with its decorative shutters, could have been captured head-on for a symmetrical, but static shot. Shifting the subject slightly down and to the left livened up the composition, but it would feel slightly lopsided were it not balanced out by the strip of highlights forming a triangle at the upper right.

↓ Not-so-empty space

In this clear presentation of compositional balance, the elements at the top left and bottom right of the frame complement each other and are pulled into harmony by the diagonal lines in the background.

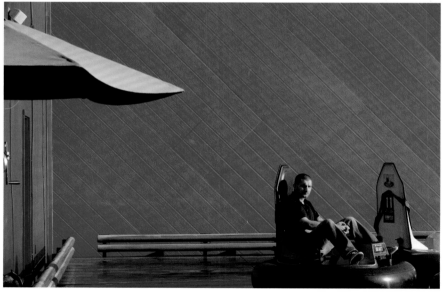

Symmetry

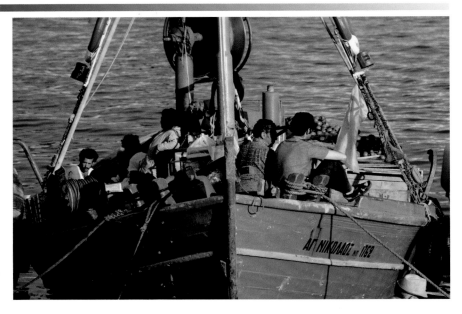

A particular kind of balance, symmetry takes the principles of balance to the extreme. Whereas more dynamic sorts of balance are an art of creative positioning of abstract weights and shapes, symmetry is much more of an exact science, with all the demand for perfection that a scientific approach suggests. It's a powerful effect in its own right, one that flouts the off-center approach to create punchy, graphic images. Of course, it isn't always possible, as some subjects simply aren't symmetrical. Man-made objects

↑ **Head on**
A close crop coupled with bilateral symmetry (which is further emphasized by directional light casting the left side in shadow) makes this boat feel like it's about to splash through the page.

are often well suited to this compositional approach, as the design of their construction often embraces symmetry as a guiding principle. But keep an eye out for natural subjects that can be captured this way as well, as their organic structure makes the symmetry all the more impactful.

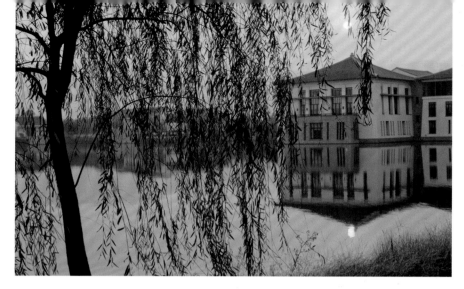

If you're aiming for a symmetrical image, in the vast majority of cases it's important that it's perfectly symmetrical. The human eye has an ability to recognize and finely evaluate geometric organizations, and an out-of-place element can become the focus of the image. It will take time to align all the elements and place them properly in the frame. Keep a close eye on the edges of the frame, and make sure that lines and elements are falling evenly.

There is a particular beauty to something that is a perfect mirror-image; it can feel restful, ordered, and simple. This is, of course, in contrast to asymmetric images, which feel dynamic and complex, and sometimes even chaotic. And it's why symmetry should be used sparingly, as it grows boring and inert quickly.

↑ **Through the trees**
Lake reflections are so idyllic as to often be a cliché—but that can be avoided by including additional elements, like this tree in the foreground.

NATURAL REFLECTIONS

The line of symmetry in a reflection usually runs along the horizontal plane. As we're naturally disposed to read images horizontally, we aren't immediately struck by the symmetry and we'll be inclined to look for the movement in the asymmetry of the left and right halves. In addition to lakes, portraits can work a treat if composed symmetrically, and some architecture can make strikingly symmetrical images.

Strengthening with Triangles

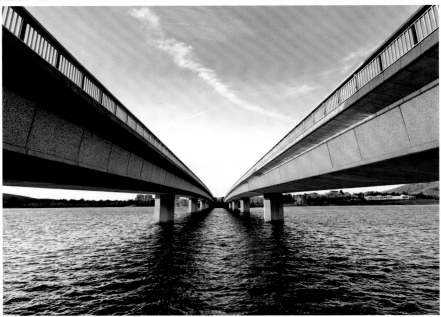

© Daniela Bowker

So far, we have concentrated on images that have one particular point of interest, for example a person, an insect, or the sunset. But not all pictures are going to be simple constructions of solitary portrait subjects or gorgeous vistas with an obvious point of focus. When the subject is interacting with other elements of the scene, making sure that the various points of interest have a definite shape and are somehow ordered within the frame will prevent the

↑ **Imaginary triangles**
Constructing a triangle is simple: It requires only three points and three lines between them. They can be configured in almost any format and the lines don't even have to be tangible—they can be implied or imagined, like an eye-line. This makes them easy to introduce into your compositions, and as a consequence bring order to your frame.

photograph from appearing disorganized. One of the most simple and effective means of doing this is to use a triangle. Triangles also have the advantage of being simultaneously stable and dynamic: Their edges can bring a sense of solidity to a composition, while the convergence of their points brings a natural sense of movement. Triangles also have leading lines. And unlike circles or rectangles, which require exact ordering and straight lines, triangles are much easier to create out of constituent elements, and more forgiving in their configuration (they achieve their strengthening effect regardless of their orientation, and their sides need not be of equal length).

↓ **Group portraits**
When photographing three people, one option is to arrange them so their faces become the points of a triangle. This will give the image a sense of structure and avoid the predictability of having three faces in a row. With more than three people, try placing them so that they create either one large or several smaller triangles.

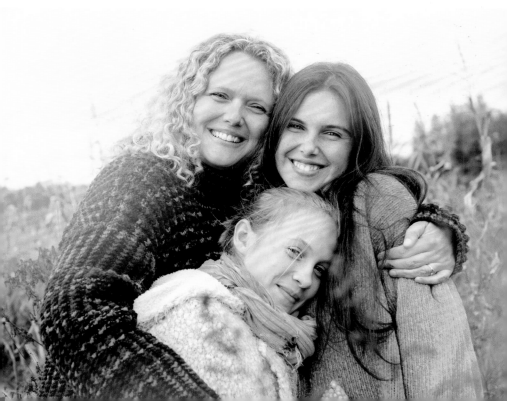

GIVING A SENSE OF MOVEMENT

A tall building photographed from below will give the impression of creating a triangle—it's a natural result of perspective as the vertical lines converge (see page 237 for more details). This sort of pyramid structure is very stable, and because it encourages the eye to move along the building, from bottom to top, it's also dynamic and offers a different perspective on an otherwise rigid structure. An inverted triangle won't have the same sense of stability as a pyramidal one, but it does still have a strong sense of direction and movement. By using its intrinsic leading lines, it will serve to direct focus toward something that is small or doesn't necessarily catch the eye immediately.

DIVIDING THE FRAME

As well as arranging three subject points into a triangle, you can also divide your frame into triangles to give it a sense of order. If your composition involves multiple objects—for example a bouquet or bed of flowers—this technique can work to encourage the eye to look toward the point of focus. You can also use triangles to bring a sense of balance to an image by emphasizing contrasts within it. Your triangles can consist of different colors, textures, shades of light, or any other distinguishing characteristic. This can work very well in bringing order to an otherwise busy and cluttered scene. Dividing the frame in this way is simple. You need only three lines to build a triangle, and one or two of those lines can be the edges of your frame.

THE GOLDEN TRIANGLE

There is also a more rigid division of the frame into triangles that is based on the law of the Golden Ratio, which we looked at earlier. This is, perhaps unsurprisingly, called the Golden Triangle. The idea behind it divides the frame into two right-angled triangles along the frame's diagonal. These two triangles are then subdivided again, by lines running from the other corners and each intersecting with the original diagonal line at right angles. Where the lines intersect, you have your points of interest.

If you're thinking of creating a triangularly oriented composition, then the Golden Triangle is something to bear in mind to help give it a sense of balance and a point of focus. And it is certainly something to be added to your collection of triangular shots.

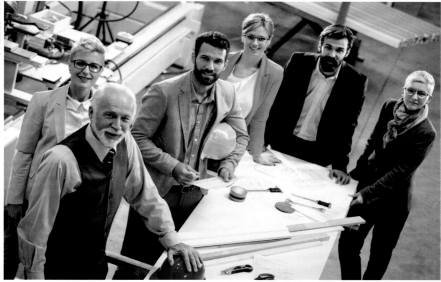

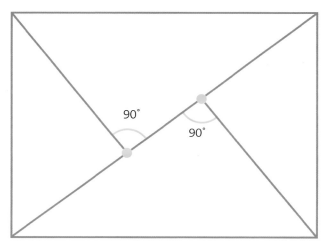

←↑ Off-kilter composition
The portrait works
because each of the
subjects falls along
the lines and points
of interest according
to the Golden Triangle.

90°

90°

© Daniela Bowker

Color

Colors elicit certain emotions. Red, being the strongest and densest, feels energetic, hot, and vital. Yellow, the brightest of all, feels cheerful and vigorous. Blue is quiet, contemplative, and subdued. Green, so abundant in nature, suggests growth and youth. Violet is quite rare in nature, and so has a mysterious quality to it. Orange, which coats every landscape during sunrise and sunset, is festive and inviting.

COLOR RELATIONSHIPS

Multiple colors can work together to contrast or harmonize and create a sense of balance in a photograph. Just as a large object at one end of the frame can create tension with a smaller one at the opposite end, complementary colors both create and resolve tension in a photograph, and can bring disparate elements together in a meaningful and satisfying way.

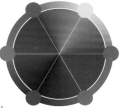

↗ **Endless possibilities**
This particular representation of the color wheel illustrates the almost infinite number of hues that exist under the broad categories of blue, green, yellow, orange, red, and purple.

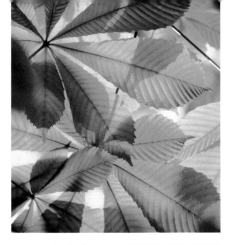

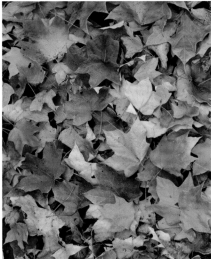

↑↑ **Two takes on nature**
These images are both nature subjects, but with their different color palettes, they create two completely different feelings.

THE CONSTRUCTION OF COLOR

Digital photography gives us exact terminology for both describing and manipulating color: hue, saturation, and brightness. Hue is what most people mean when they say "color," as it identifies the specific wavelength that corresponds to, say, blue, yellow, or green. Saturation is the strength, purity, or intensity of a particular hue (or lack thereof—as a completely desaturated color appears as a shade of gray). Brightness is simply how dark or light the hue appears. Of these three terms, hue is the most significant, with saturation and brightness being constituent parts. Hue can also be measured in 360 degrees as it moves around the color wheel, shown left. At any point, the color 180-degrees opposite on the color wheel is that hue's complementary color, which gives a naturally pleasing contrast that enhances the quality of both colors and creates harmony in the image. This is yet another role of balance in composition, which we began to discuss in the last chapter, except rather than discussing lines and weight, we now also have to consider the way in which color can create—or disrupt—harmony in your photography.

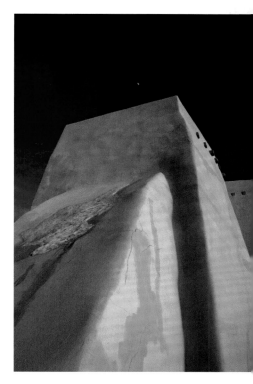

↑ **Nature's palette**
This image relies on the rich color of the adobe church, which complements the dark blue sky in such a way as to both accent the church's structure, and pull the lower and upper elements into harmony.

Rich & Restrained Color

Not every scene relies on color to communicate its themes. In fact, while we expect to see a variety of colors everywhere in our day-to-day life, the natural world offers far fewer bold colors than we may realize. Just try going out on a nature walk and capturing all six strong colors. If you come across some exotic flowers, you might luck out, but otherwise you're likely to find lots of soft greens and browns, some pastels and slate blues, and plenty of grays. This natural color palette is not necessarily something you should fight against. If you want to communicate the peaceful, pristine conditions of a babbling brook or a rolling countryside, adding color isn't going to suddenly achieve that for you. Rather, you will need to lean on your other compositional tools and techniques. If, on the other hand, you want to communicate the dynamism of a metropolis, vivid colors will be ideal,

↓ **Intense color**
Some subjects a naturally presented in all their rich colors; it's simply a matter of choosing when to highlight the colors, and when to hold back.

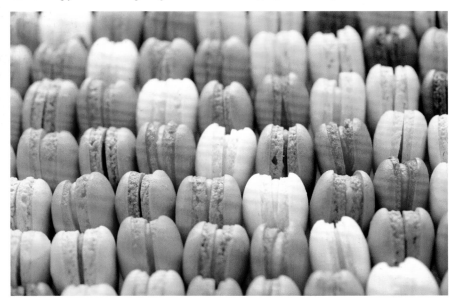

and you will have no trouble finding examples of them in man-made environments. Yet again, it is simply a matter of recognizing the right tools for the job, and implementing them in such a way as to both achieve your creative vision, and adequately (if not accurately) represent your subject.

COLOR INTENSITY AND LIGHT

If you're shooting in low light, colors from the blue and green family will appear brighter to your eye than reds and yellows. This is known as the Purkinje Shift, and is a result of the transition from using mostly cone-based color-sensitive vision during the day to rod-based light-sensitive vision at night. Cones detect yellow light better; rods pick up blue light more effectively, hence the eye finding blues and greens brighter at twilight. Of course, our cameras don't have rods and cones, which means that they'll detect the colors differently than our eyes. What you see at the time might not be quite the same as what your photograph shows later.

MULTIPLE COLORS

Just because too many colors can make an image chaotic, it doesn't mean that you can't use them. Flooding a picture with a host of different colors can be extremely effective. A lot of it depends on how it is done. You might find that in this situation it's the range of color itself that is the subject.

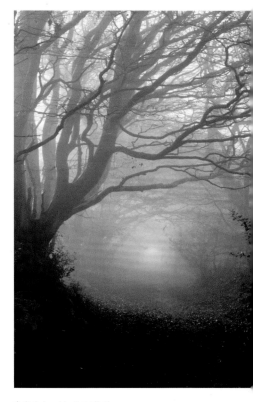

↑ **Subdued but realistic**
There's no point in trying to pull color out of a scene like this, where the low contrast and misty atmosphere is the engaging part of the photograph in the first place.

Compose with Color

Challenge

Color has the most dramatic potential for your images. It can change the entire mood of a photograph; it can bring life to an image; it can accentuate the subject in a way that simple placement can't; it can even form the subject of a photograph itself. So for this challenge, you need to go and experiment with capturing color. Make color the most significant aspect of your photograph—superseding the particular shapes and lines of the subject. Of course those elements will still be there, but what's important here is that you get a feel for the primary impact that color can have on your images.

Challenge Checklist

→ Train your eye to see color first and foremost, and compose around either one color, or the interplay of several.

→ Identify the contrasting and analogous colors in your scenes.

→ Use color to bring balance to your photos.

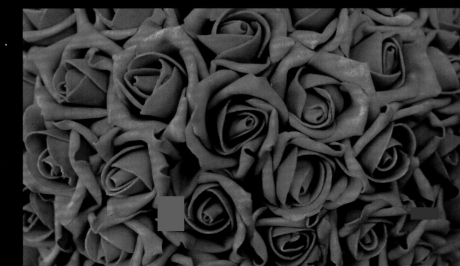

← **Dominant reds**
Letting one color consume the frame will give your photo a punch.

→ **Up, up, and away**
On the other hand, including multiple colors gives the eye some contrast and invites comparison among different parts of the frame.

Rhythm & Pattern

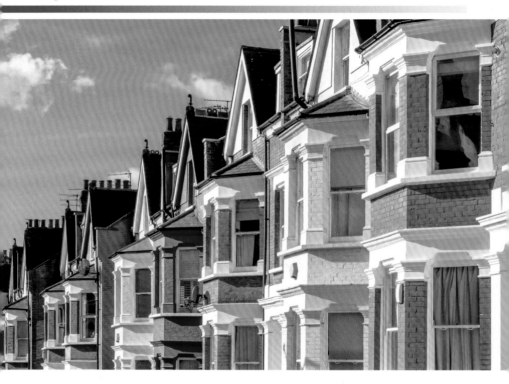

When multiple similar elements are set within a frame, their arrangement may set up a rhythmic structure—meaning the way the eye scans the picture will have certain beats, rather like a musical melody. This requires repetition, but that is not to say repetition will always create a rhythm. A photograph of 12 traffic cones in a line, all identical and shot

↑ **Establishing a rhythm**
This row of houses may look unextraordinary to the naked eye, but set a frame around a segment of the larger scene, and the viewer will naturally be struck by the repeated elements— the small architectural ornamentations, the reflections in the windows, the sharp, pointed roofs, the variations of color. The eye is drawn back and forth to compare one element to the other, and in doing so, establishes a rhythm as it scans the photo.

head-on, is unlikely to engage the viewer's eye. There needs to be enough elements of interest to give momentum to the act of scanning the photograph, and enough structure to guide that momentum. The eye and mind will naturally extend a sequence beyond what is visible, particularly when the frame is filled edge to edge with the repeating elements. For this reason, telephoto focal lengths are often easier to use when creating a rhythmic photo, as the can crop out extraneous elements that would otherwise hault the eye's movement across the frame.

↓ **Elevating repetition to a larger theme**
A basic line (or queue) of taxis isn't particularly engaging, but when they're iconic London black cabs, coupled with union flags repeating into the distance, the subjects combine to elevate simple repetition into a thematic statement, one that represents something larger than the framed scene (in this case, the larger concept of "Britishness."

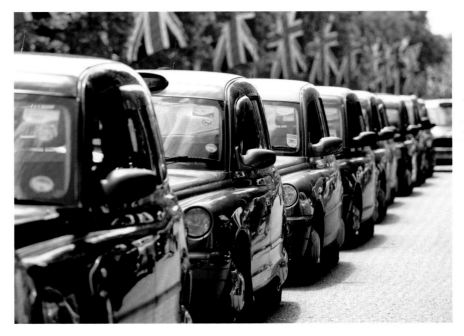

Pattern is also built on repetition, but it doesn't direct the eye across the image the way rhythm—rather, it presents the entire area of the frame at once, and invite the eye to roam freely across, evaluating small details without any particular momentum. The larger the number of elements contained in the frame, the stronger the sense of pattern, as opposed to a group of individual objects. Again, this is reinforced by letting the repeating elements stretch past the edge of the frame, allowing the viewer to mentally extend the subject beyond what may even be physically possible.

→ **Perusing the details**
For all the viewer knows, this is a vast marina that stretches on for miles. And yet, each boat is unique, and invites a closer look. With over 70 repeating-yet-individual elements to evaluate (plus the two people walking at the top right), the act of viewing the image is elongated and the viewer is free to explore at their own pace.

↓ **Establishing a rhythm**
Here, one zebra is basically indistinguishable from the next, and so, quite the opposite from the marina photo on the right, close scrutiny of each individual element gives way to an overall appreciation of the visual texture and strong graphic qualities of the image.

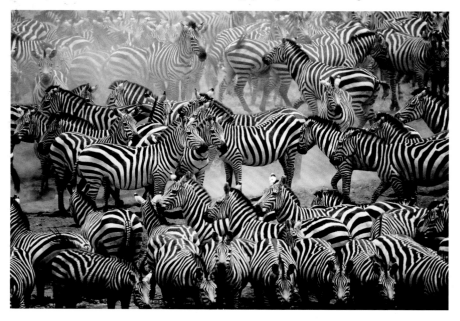

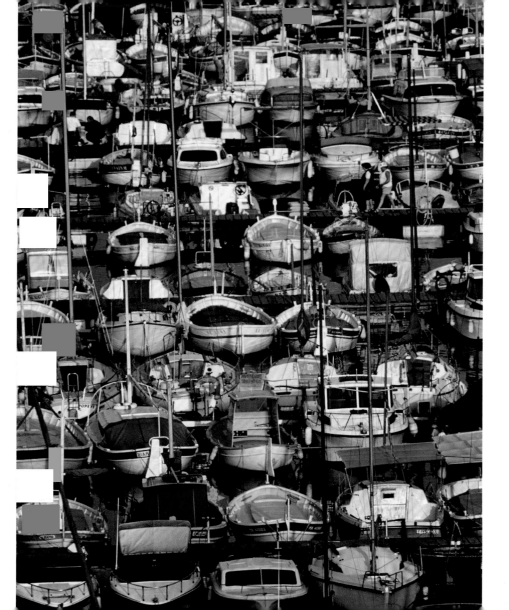

Frames within the Frame

Viewfinders aren't the only things that can frame a scene. Far from it. If you keep an eye out for them, you will find innumerable "internal frames" that you can capitalize on to aid in your composition. They serve as great compositional tools to direct the eye straight to the subject of the photograph. They're also valuable because they can bring perspective and a sense of three-dimensionality to an image. It's as if you're looking through one layer of the image and on to another. We also tend to find images that use internal frames attractive because it brings order, in the same way that using triangles helps to organize scenes with multiple subjects. A frame puts a limit on the scene and provides it with some boundaries.

Almost anything can serve as an internal frame: windows, doorways, and arches are obvious choices, but trees, fences, and cave openings work as well. They don't have to be complete frames, either. You might find that the trunk and over-hanging branches of a tree create a frame on only two sides of an image, but it is enough to create a feeling of depth in the photograph and direct the focus to the subject.

When you're composing a photograph using an existing internal frame, it's important to think about how the frame is going to interact with and affect both with the subject it's containing and also the photographic frame of the image itself. You'll need to pay attention to the lines that the image is creating, and how they are going to emphasize the subject and maintain a sense of dynamism.

Just because the image has an internal frame that is bringing focus to the subject, you shouldn't ignore other compositional principles—for example, the Golden Ratio.

Think carefully about depth of field, too. If your subject is at a different distance than the frame, and you intend for both frame and subject to be sharp, then you will need a small enough aperture to give you adequate depth of field. Sometimes an internal frame can still serve its purpose without being in sharp focus, and you can isolate only the subject in a shallow depth of field. In the portrait opposite, for instance, the dark shadow of the tree does the job of framing the little boy while being nothing but a blurry amorphous shape. Indeed, details in the branches or trunk likely would have only distracted the viewer.

If you're inside a cave or tunnel, shooting out through its opening to capture a subject that is brightly lit by exterior light, you might find that you have to

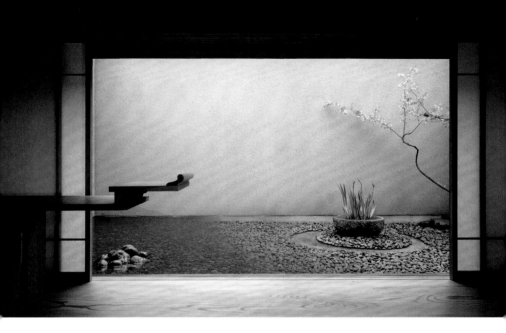

compensate the exposure in order to use the opening as an internal frame. If you are using a matrix metering mode, you can ensure the exterior is not overexposed by some negative exposure compensation. Another approach is to use spot metering to measure only the light falling in the exterior. On the other hand, if you want to capture the full dynamic range of both the interior frame and the exterior subject, you can take two shots—one for the shadows, one for the bright outside subject—and combine them in post-production.

↑ **Doorway frames**
Architectural design often takes into consideration how certain views will be framed as one moves through a building, so keep an eye out for these cues and take advantage of them.

Finally, a note of caution: Using frames within frames is so effective that it can be easy to try to use them to solve all your compositional problems. Just because a potential internal frame exists doesn't mean it is the best way to compose the shot—ideally it should still bear some relationship to the main subject.

Negative Space

It might seem counter-intuitive to talk about "filling your frame" and "negative space" in the same sentence, but it's more helpful to think of them as two sides of the same coin. If you have a complex subject, contrasting it against a blank area will bring some balance to the composition. It helps the eye to find a point of focus. The negative space itself, however, needs to be absolutely barren and as uniform as possible in order to maximize its effectiveness. Consistency of tone and color can support the main subjects without offering any distracting elements. Heavy fog can achieve this very well, as can blank architectural walls. The negative space may be a complementary color, but most often it's a simple neutral.

A SENSE OF SPACE

We've already looked at how to create the illusion of the infinite by filling your frame with a pattern or repeating subject and denying any sense of a boundary. You can create a similar feeling of infinity by surrounding a solitary subject with negative space. For example, you could photograph a sailboat on a lake and include the shoreline, but that limits the feeling of space and gives a boundary to the water. By composing your image so that you capture just the sailboat on a negative space of water, it is suddenly sailing on an infinite sea.

↓ **Placid water, empty frame**
Because the majority of this frame is empty, the few elements that remain are further emphasized and given greater focus.

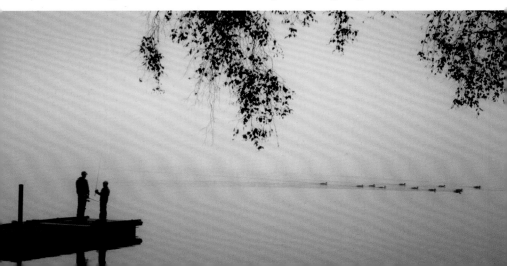

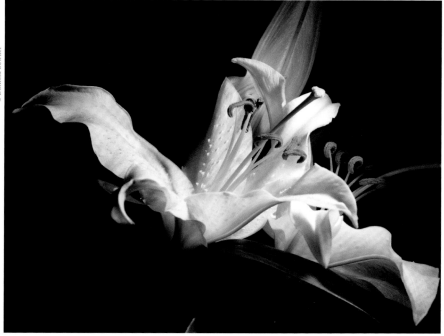

© Daniela Bowker

© Daniela Bowker

CREATING ATMOSPHERE

Negative space can contribute to the atmosphere that you want to create in your photographs. Negative space in certain colors can lend a particular feeling to an image; blue is calming, for example, while yellow is uplifting. Light-colored areas of negative space work toward a feeling of airy positivity, something we explored in high-key photography.

↑ **Spotlit lily**
By draping a black cloth behind this beautiful flower and using the sun as a strong spotlight, the flower takes on a kind of elegance, with its soft, white petals, and then with its delicate but radiant-orange stamens. The negative space is just as much a part of the finished photograph as the subject itself.

Of Light & Shadow

Light itself can often be the main subject of your photograph. Perhaps the light streaming through a window is casting beautiful shadows of a row of bottles sitting on the windowsill across the wall. Or maybe it's the interplay of light and shadow falling through a tree canopy that is creating an image that deserves to be captured.

A silhouette can work as a main subject as well, though it isn't strictly a shadow. Rather, it's the outline of something unlit in the foreground against a more brightly lit background. If you have a beautiful, burning red sunset sky, it can make a stunning background for the twisted shapes of tree branches, or of a couple walking hand-in-hand on a beach.

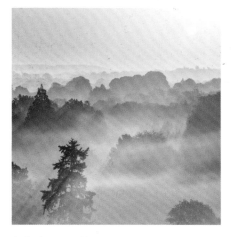

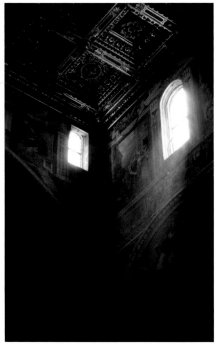

↑ **Shadow as subject**
The light and shadows stretching across this scene are accentuated by a monochrome conversion.

→ **The light comes first**
In this shadowy Italian cathedral, it was the contrast of the shafts of light slicing through the shadows that caught my eye. The ornate architecture is really just a backdrop (granted, a very nice one).

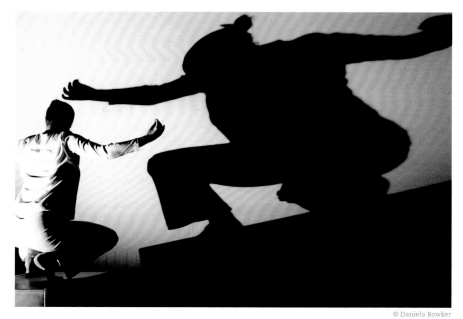

SHADOWS THAT CONCEAL

↑ Shadow performance
Strong directional lighting always casts obvious, defined shadows.

Occasionally, what a photograph doesn't show can be just as effective or telling as what it does show. By letting the shadows dominate your frame and inserting an abundance of negative space, you can create something moody, atmospheric, and evocative. If dark tones are the prevailing feeling from your photo, then it's known as a low-key shot (think "low" on the histogram). These sorts of low-key images that are full of shadows don't have to be sinister and brooding; they can be enticing and intriguing, too. It will all depend on what it is that you're photographing and what you place in the shadows. The light cast into a shadowed room by a door left ajar can evoke a feeling of intrigue; light coming through shuttered windows might make an image feel more constrained. A half-lit face with a coy smile is potentially seductive; a half-lit face with a glare can suggest menace, and this effect can be emphasized depending on the angle from which you photograph your subject, too.

People

Just about everything that we have looked at so far can be applied to photographing people. In most cases, we have explored how much of an impact a particular technique, whether it's the rule of thirds or high-key lighting, can have on a portrait. But photographing people is very special and it deserves a closer look.

It doesn't matter if you're having a go at street photography, capturing a spontaneous moment at an event, or working more formally, there will always be something that you are trying to convey. Maybe it's the mischievous glint in someone's eye, the hunch of their exhausted shoulders, or their gesture while walking down the street; it's all a story—a personal and individual one.

EYES FIRST

For nine photos out of ten, the most crucial element will be getting the eyes in focus. Even if the subject isn't looking at you, which is going to be the case for a good many spontaneous photographs as well as some posed ones, the eyes still need to be pin-sharp. Good presenters always make eye-contact in order to build a connection between them and their audience or conversation partner, and that's applicable to photography as much as verbal communication.

CANDID AND MOMENTARY

People can be naturally nervous around cameras; it's not that they object to having their portraits taken— which is an entirely different situation— but that they simply find it uncomfortable. If you're taking photos at a party or among a group of people, you can reassure them that they don't need to pose or even look at the camera. They can have a good time and you can concentrate on documenting it. This sort of candid photography has the advantage of putting people at ease as well as presenting you with plenty of opportunities It's also the sort of photography to practice out on the street or when you're traveling, capturing the fleeting instant when something catches your eye. As you practice more, you'll find that your eye will become attuned to seeing things that make excellent photographs—people's reactions and expressions, the effects of light, shadow, color, and shapes—and that you will be able to compose on the fly. The vital factors to remember are to get the eyes in focus, to orient the frame to support the image, and to get in as close as you can. The more pictures that you take, the better you'll become.

→ **A candid moment**
Anticipating a relaxed moment required setting the aperture (wide) and focus in advance, then releasing the shutter at just the right moment.

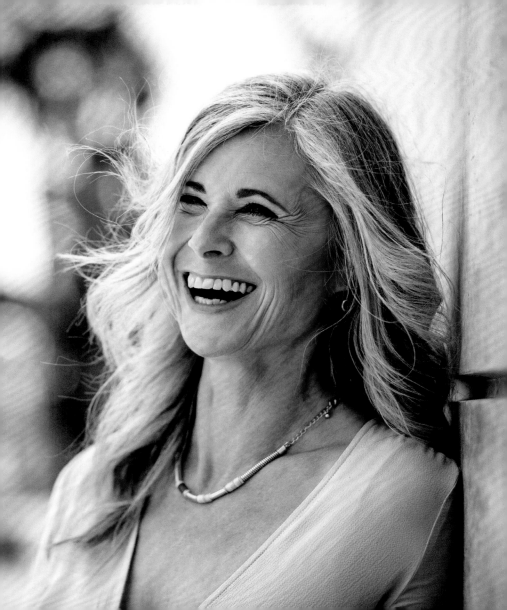

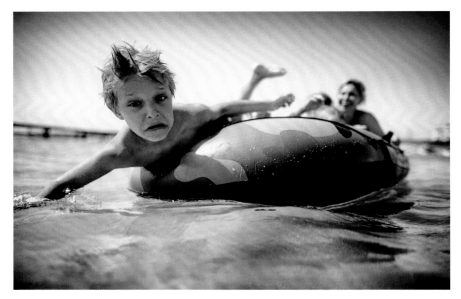

FORMAL VS POSED

Asking someone at a party to move slightly because you want to catch them against a complementary background isn't formal, but you are still posing them. A holiday snap can become something so much better if you take a moment to ask your subject to move into the shade or turn their face into the light. Indeed, you may be surprised how often a subject will welcome a bit of instruction—it takes the burden of proper posing off their shoulders and puts them at ease.

A photo shoot in your garden doesn't have to be formal, but it can certainly be posed. This sort of directed portraiture will help give you the opportunity to compose your shots more completely, taking into consideration the light, subject placement, lines, color, and shape. Just remember to give plenty of feedback to your model, showing them what you've done and explaining to them what it is that you are trying to achieve.

← ↓ Look for their eccentricities

There is a time and place for stiff portraits, with makeup and hair styling and all the trimmings. But candid portraits often do a better job of telling a story and giving a sense of time and place. Keep an eye out for hand gestures, facial reactions, or funny and energetic movements in your subjects. Anticipating such actions will give you time to angle and compose other elements in the shot.

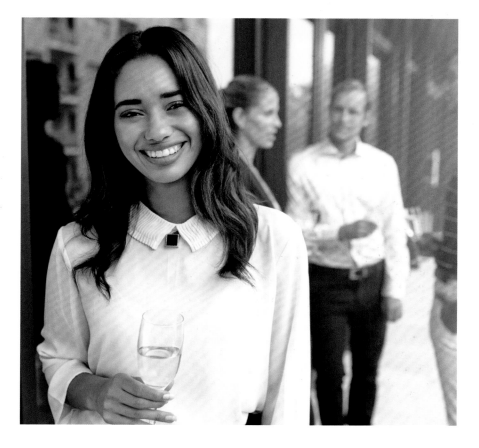

Capturing Couples

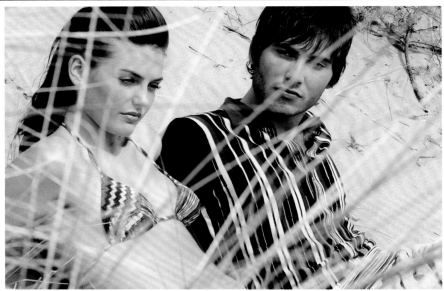

© Daniela Bowker

When you're taking spontaneous or candid photographs, you have to be on the lookout for the moment of interaction between two people. When you're starting out, you'll be more inclined to focus on capturing the moment—the quiet look, the raucous laugh, the gentle touch—than anything else. After all, this is what makes the photograph special and meaningful.

If you've only a split-second to take the photograph, spending too much time worrying about composition will

↑ The eyes tell it all
Talking to your subjects will always set them at ease, and with couples, their conversation will eventually take off on its own, giving you time to work and observe their interactions. This was shot during a split-second pause as the woman reacted to her boyfriend's comment.

doubtless mean that you'll miss what it is that you want to capture. The more photographs that you take, the more naturally composition will come to you. Keep in the back of your mind the fundamentals of eyes-in-focus, frame orientation, off-centering the subject, and getting in close, and you'll be fine.

If you have the opportunity to photograph two people in a more structured way, you'll benefit from having more time to compose every shot, but you will need to be careful that you don't lose the intimacy between your subjects as you direct them. Whatever their relationship may be—lovers, siblings, parent and child, friends—each photograph will still be about their interaction, so think about what it is that you're trying to convey first, then set about achieving it.

Portraiture often uses a wide aperture to create a shallow depth of field with the subject popping out of a soft background, but this can be tricky with multiple subjects. You'll need to either carefully line them up next to each other—which can look static and rigid—or stop down the aperture to increase the depth of field and ensure both subjects are sharp.

↓ Just enough depth of field
This shot, taken at a slight angle and with the subjects at slightly different distances from the camera, required stopping down the lens slightly, but by getting close enough, the background is still out of focus.

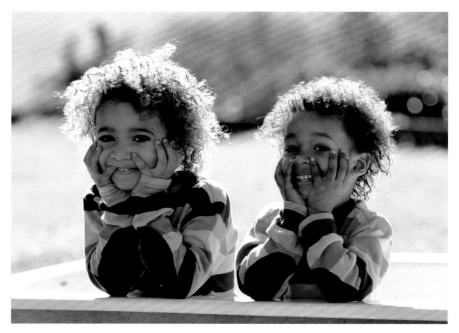

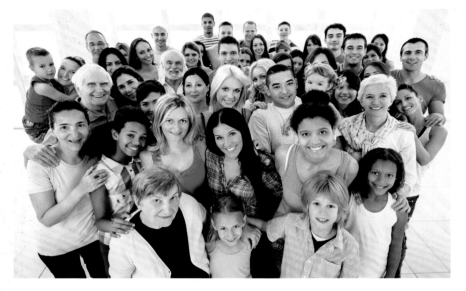

GROUPS

As with couples, photographing small groups of people is going to be about capturing the relationships among them, and you'll want to approach it in the same way. Photographing large groups of people can easily become a logistical challenge rather than something fun. Someone is always reluctant, there's always at least one person playing the clown, and it can feel as if you're attempting to herd cats. There are a few things you can do to make life easier. Try photographing them from an elevated position, whether up a step-ladder, from a balcony, or even leaning out of a window—this makes it

↑ Looking up
Arranging everyone by height can take time, and doesn't always result in the most dynamic portraits. A simple footstool gives the viewer a welcome change in perspective.

easier to direct your subjects. Alternatively, have the group stand on a staircase with you at the bottom of it. Arranging taller people at the back and shorter people at the front is an obvious one, as is staggering the arrangement of rows, giving everyone an individual space for their head. Taking many, many photos will increase your chances of having at least one where all your subjects are smiling, looking in the right direction, and have their eyes open.

A Couple's Portrait

Seeing as you might already have photographed one person for earlier challenges, and large groups of people willing to have their pictures taken aren't readily available, this challenge will focus on capturing the interaction between two people in a photograph. Whether you would like to try a more directed shoot or something spontaneous is up to you; the important thing is to clearly identify the relationship between the two subjects and bring it to life in a meaningful and flattering way.

Challenge Checklist

→ Capture a moment between two people.

→ Think about the aperture you will need to use to ensure that both sets of eyes are in focus.

→ Use the right frame orientation and get in close to bring out the best in your subjects.

Challenge

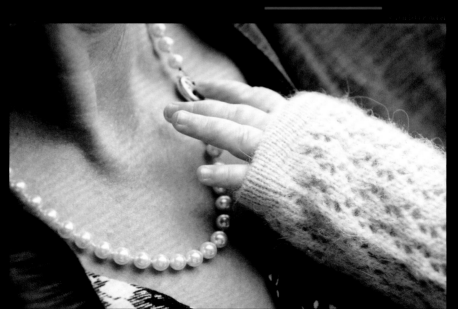

Focal Length

Your camera's lens works by refracting the available light from a scene and converging it at a single focal plane on your sensor to create an image. How much of a scene a lens is able to bring into view depends on its focal length.

All the discussions of focal lengths here are referring to the angle of view that such a lens would have on a traditional, 35mm camera. If your camera has a 1.5x crop (i.e., an APS-C sensor), just divide the focal lengths given here by 1.5, and you'll have your camera's equivalent figures.

PRIME AND ZOOM LENSES

Cameras are often sold with a 28–85mm kit lens (or something in that wide-to-short-telephoto range). It has a variable focal length, and is therefore a "zoom" lens. You can change the focal length between 28 and 85 millimeters, which alters the angle of view. Another popular, but very different kind of lens would be a 50mm "prime" lens, meaning that it has a fixed focal length and its angle of view doesn't alter. If you want to change the size of the subject in the frame, you have to move physically closer to or farther away from them.

Prime lenses exist for almost every practical focal length, and they induce their own specific method of shooting. Closer attention is paid to the edges of the frame and with a keener eye for potential compositions. There's nothing inherent in the design of a fixed-focal-length lens that makes a photographer act differently, and a zoom lens can facilitate precisely the same degree of contemplation. It's simply a matter of restriction breeding creativity.

Another advantage of using fixed-focal-length lenses is that you learn to gain appreciation for the differences particular focal lengths have on your shot. Zoom lenses tend to make wide angles function simply as means to "get it all in," whereas telephoto lenses end up being a means of bringing faraway objects closer. These are indeed benefits, but they do not take into consideration the dramatic differences in perspective that changes in focal length will create. For instance, wide angles can stretch images toward the edges of the frame, which may or may not be intended. Regardless of whether you use a zoom or a prime, you should always be sensitive to the effect of the focal length on your scene.

**Longer focal length /
Narrower angle of view**

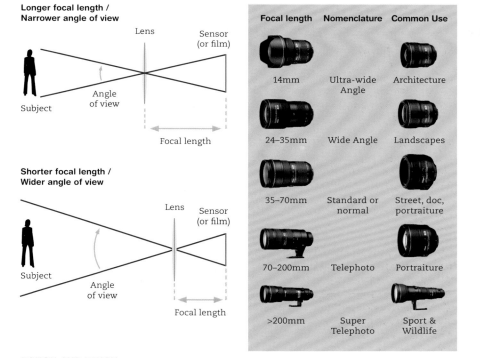

**Shorter focal length /
Wider angle of view**

Focal length	Nomenclature	Common Use
14mm	Ultra-wide Angle	Architecture
24–35mm	Wide Angle	Landscapes
35–70mm	Standard or normal	Street, doc, portraiture
70–200mm	Telephoto	Portraiture
>200mm	Super Telephoto	Sport & Wildlife

ROUGH-AND-READY
GUIDE TO FOCAL LENGTHS

The exact focal length you use will depend on your personal preference. Still, this rough-and-ready guide (above) to what you might want in different situations is useful. Note that the examples of lenses shown here are just that—examples. They by no means cover the full range of available lenses from all manufacturers. For each focal length range, a zoom is pictured on the left, while a prime is on the right—you can see there is a significant size difference.

Wide-Angle Lenses & Perspective

Wide-angle lenses greatly affect our perception of depth in an image— which is essentially a visual illusion. So while the viewer is not able to physically reach into a scene and explore its depth and dimensionality, you can use an exaggerating perspective to draw them in visually by capturing a wide angle of view. So the question is, what is responsible for the exaggerated perspective? And how does one use that exaggeration to maximum effect?

Technically speaking, the emphasis on depth is a matter of spatial distortion, in that the apparent distance between close and far objects is greater as your angle of view widens. Of course, this depends on your viewpoint and what is in the frame. If you are shooting the edge of a cliff without including any foreground elements, all the elements of the composition will be far away and there will be hardly any effect on the perspective. But if you include some object closer to the camera, the space between it and the distant landscape features will seem immense. Additionally, the size of that foreground element will appear quite large comparatively, as it will take up much more of the frame compared to more distant elements. It simply suggests that the scene extends beyond the frame, giving the viewer a sense of

"being there," in the middle of the scene or amid the action of the moment. For this reason, wide angles are commonly used in photojournalism, in which it is critical for the viewer to feel a connection to the scene, and to give them a sense of participation. Shooting a crowd with a telephoto from across the street gives a cooler, less involved feeling—you won't be able to include as many elements, and they won't extend around the edges of the frame in the way a wide angle lens does when it is thrust into a middle of the action.

UNFLATTERING FOREGROUNDS

Portraits shot with a wide-angle lens tend to make the subject's nose looks comically large and their chin juts out. This is because by the time you fill up a wide-angle frame with a face, you are mere inches away from it, and as objects get closer to the frame, their size becomes exponentially exaggerated. Relative to the rest of the face, the nose and chin are going to look huge, and the ears will be tiny specks on either side. This same effect will be responsible for making the base of a building appear absurdly large and the entire structure look ridiculously tall if you shoot it up close and from a low angle. Being so close emphasizes the foreground, while the increased angle of

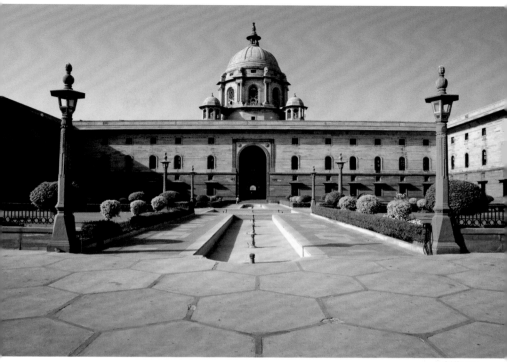

↑ Step right in

Although the lamposts nearest the camera are only a few feet away, the stonework foreground manages to constitute a full third of the complete frame. The effect is such that you can very much imagine yourself standing there in the courtyard, with the building continuing along the right and left of the scene. Additionally, note how far apart the first pair lamposts seem from the second, which themselves are about midway between the camera and the archway at the far end of the courtyard. Although the second pair bisects the distance almost exactly, it appears as if they are much closer to the archway because the foreground distance is so heavily exaggerated.

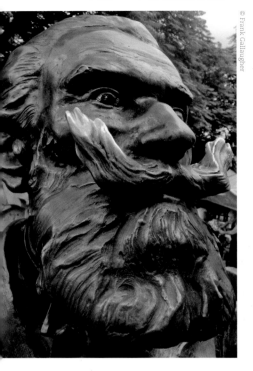

© Frank Gallaugher

view brings more of the building into the scene. But what works well for buildings doesn't necessarily translate into a successful portrait, so it's wise to keep a safe distance when photographing people with a wide-angle lens, and make it an environmental portrait.

ENCLOSED SPACES

If you're taking photographs in an enclosed space, using a wide-angle lens will ensure that you can fit everything or everyone into your scene without having to resort to demolishing walls, which you'd have to do if you were using a normal or telephoto lens. It also makes interiors appear spacious and comfortable, and as such they are well suited for indoor events and real-estate shots.

CONVERGING VERTICALS

Owing to perspective, parallel lines will gradually appear to converge toward a vanishing point as they approach the horizon, regardless of the lens you use. However, this effect is far more noticeable with a wide-angle lens as it takes only a very small adjustment of the camera to move the vanishing point significantly. One solution is to aim your camera perpendicularly to the front of the building, and crop out the bottom later.

↑ **Unflattering portraits**
Granted, this statue already had a fairly large beard, but the wide angle further exaggerated its jaw, making it appear almost twice the size as the rest of his head.

→ **Keystone correction**
This shot on the top shows how strong the converging verticals (an effect also called keystoning) appear if the upward angle is too sharp. On the bottom, the same photograph has been adjusted in post-production (using the Filter > Lens Correction > Vertical Perspective tool in Photoshop) so that the verticals are all parallel, but it required cropping out extensive areas on the side and at the top.

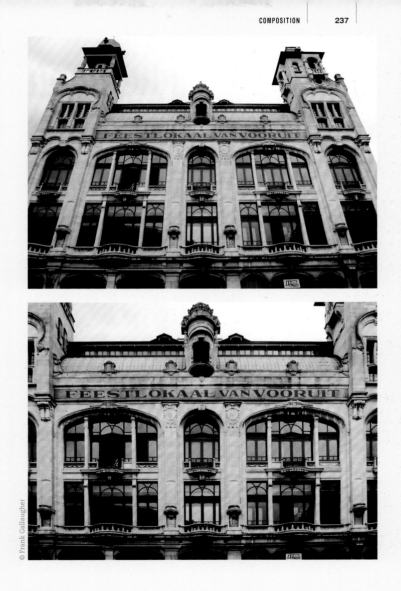

Telephoto Lenses

Roughly speaking, telephoto lenses (also called long lenses) have focal lengths beginning at around 70mm, and going as high as 600mm. This is an immense range that exhibits diminishing returns the higher you go—not in image quality, but in visible effect. Whereas the 10mm difference between a 28mm and an 18mm wide-angle lens is extremely noticeable, the difference between 300mm and 310mm is barely perceptible (such that no 310mm lens exists—instead, manufacturers tend to make leaps from 300mm to 400mm to 500mm, etc.). When people think of telephoto lenses, they automatically have visions of wildlife or sports photographers with long lenses, because they magnify distant objects and scenes. But that isn't their only function.

NORMALIZING

The narrow angle of view from a telephoto lens will create an impression of scenes being compressed and flattened, with distance between objects made less obvious. This is excellent for portraiture, ensuring that all parts of your subject's face are represented in equal proportion to each other. The narrow angle of view means that objects in the background of a scene take up proportionally more of the frame,

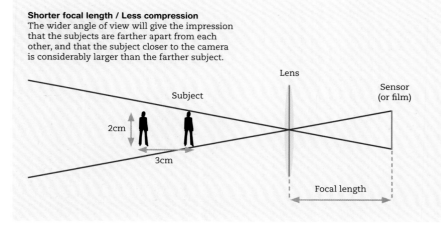

Shorter focal length / Less compression
The wider angle of view will give the impression that the subjects are farther apart from each other, and that the subject closer to the camera is considerably larger than the farther subject.

making them appear roughly the same size as things in the foreground, even if they should be considerably smaller. This is known as the "normalizing effect."

CAMERA SHAKE, MAGNIFIED

When you use a telephoto lens, be aware that even the slightest movement of the camera will be magnified massively. This makes it easy for your point of focus to be a blurry smudge instead of a crisp image, especially as telephoto lenses tend to be heavy and fairly unwieldy. The easiest solution is to use a tripod, but if that isn't practical, keep your shutter speed as fast as you can manage. The general rule for finding the slowest shutter speed for a given lens is to divide 1 by the focal length. So a 200mm lens should use a minimum shutter speed of 1/200 second, and a 500mm lens shouldn't venture below 1/500 second. That said, your telephoto lens may have a stabilizing feature (called Vibration Reduction, Image Stabilization, or other names depending on the manufacturer) that compensates for varying degrees of perceived motion. These features can be highly effective, but unless required by low lighting conditions, you should always try to keep your shutter speeds as high as possible. Also, be sure to deactivate the stabilizing feature if you use a tripod, as it can overcompensate and induce blur.

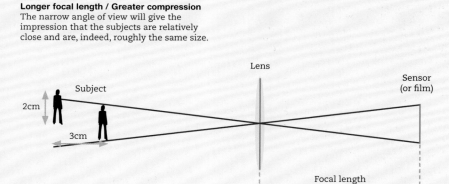

Longer focal length / Greater compression
The narrow angle of view will give the impression that the subjects are relatively close and are, indeed, roughly the same size.

Lens

Sensor (or film)

Subject

2cm

3cm

Focal length

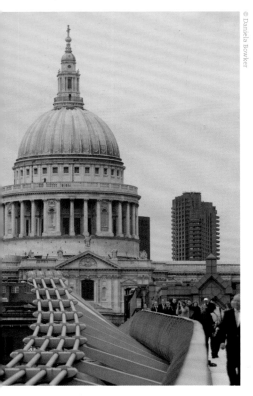

© Daniela Bowker

↑ St. Paul's to scale
A short telephoto perspective retained the sense of scale: The people in the foreground are small, the cathedral in the background is huge.

→ Dense down below
Shooting this city street from far above with a very long telephoto pulls all the elements of the scene into a very tight, compressed composition that, coupled with the technique of letting the elements reach all the way to the edges of the frame, makes the scene feel crowded, busy, and energetic.

DENSITY

The impression that telephoto lenses give of compressing scenes and bringing subjects closer together as well as normalizing their relative sizes means that you can increase the apparent density of your subject, and make it look as if there is more happening in the frame. You could photograph a moderately busy high street with a telephoto lens and the compression effect will make it look bustling and full of people. A flower bed can look positively overwhelmed with flowers as you keep the relative sizes of the flowers approximately the same and the distances between them look as if they've been reduced.

LAYERING

A telephoto approach opens up many compositional possibilities for a landscape. Emphasizing the idea of different layers in a photograph, with clear foreground, mid-ground, and background elements, creates effective landscapes with strong graphic qualities that emphasize the shapes and textures of the various elements, giving them an opportunity to contrast with and play off of each other.

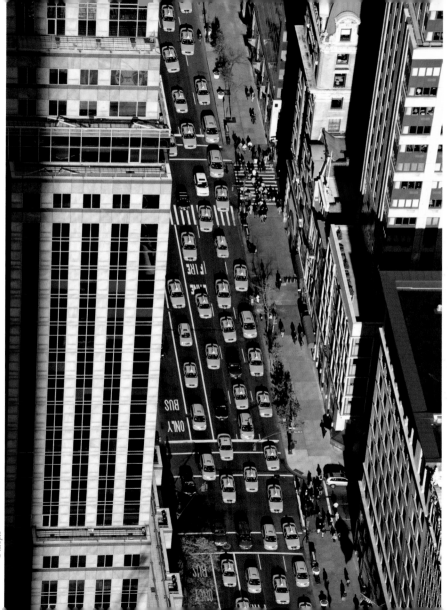

Panning

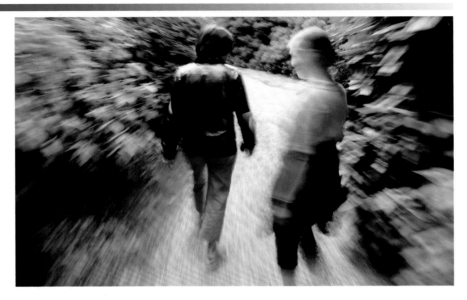

The trademark of a panned image is a subject in sharp focus, cast against a motion-blurred background (as opposed to a simple shallow depth-of-field shot in which the background communicates no sense of motion, and is blurred by being out of focus). The contrast makes the subject feel as if it is leaping off the page, as its orientation is in the opposite direction of the motion blur. The effect is achieved by tracking a moving subject across a plane, and using a shutter speed that is just low enough to blur out the background, but still fast enough to freeze the subject before it

↑ Forward panning
Once you master the panning technique, you can apply it to other scenes beyond those passing from left to right directly in front of you. It gets more difficult, of course, but you need only capture part of the subject sharply for the effect to be readily apparent.

moves too far out of frame. The subject has to be kept exactly in the same position within the frame—which is particularly difficult as the viewfinder will black out as soon as the exposure begins. It takes practice, anticipation, and steady hand-holding technique.

SHUTTER SPEED

Relatively slow shutter speeds are needed, as this will create the background blur that provides the sense of motion. Set the camera to Tv or S mode with a shutter speed around 1/30 second for sufficient blur. If 1/30 second is a little too slow at first, try something a bit faster until the technique becomes familiar. Continue to slow down the shutter speed, which will increase the blurriness of the background and make it look as if the subject is whizzing past.

SUBJECT

The faster the subject moves, the harder it will be to capture it; so planting yourself on a street corner and starting with bicycles or passing cars is ideal. When those are mastered, try motorcycles and cars, or dogs, horses, and runners.

STABILITY

Using a small, light lens, with elbows held tight against the torso, feet shoulder-width apart, and left hand underneath the lens for support, you should have the stability needed to capture a shake-free shot. Often this is even more useful than a tripod with a swivel head. If your lens or camera has an image stabilization feature, either deactivate it, or switch to one of its panning modes, so it doesn't interfere.

COMPOSITION

Aim to keep the subject in the center of the frame—at least at first as this will be easiest. The idea is to capture a sense of motion, and if you're successful, it will still feel dynamic regardless. You will, however, want to get in as close as you can so that you can photograph the detail of the subject but still have some background to give the feeling of movement. If your camera's autofocus is fast, you shouldn't have any problems focusing on the subject by half-pressing the shutter release button and allowing it to focus just before you take the shot. Otherwise, you will need to pre-focus manually on something that's the same distance away from you as your intended subject.

↓ **Bold subjects**
Some of the best panning subjects are vividly colored such that they pop out of the blurred background—the combination of saturation and sharpness works well.

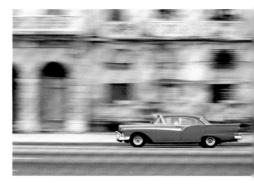

TECHNIQUE

Once chosen a position from which to track the subject, set all the camera settings, and braced for stability, you're ready to go. Position the subject in the center of the frame and track it with the camera, moving at the same speed by rotating your torso. Make sure to use the viewfinder rather than the LCD screen, so that there is no delay (however minuscule) between what the subject does and the shutter release. As the subject begins to pass in front, gently release the shutter and keep following it with the camera at the same speed. Follow through with the movement even after the shutter has closed again. The more you practice, the steadier you will be able to track your moving subjects.

→ **Street scene practice**
Make sure that you're able to move your camera in parallel to your subject and that nothing is going to obscure your view. You want to be able to track your subject smoothly as it approaches, passes in front of you, and then moves off. Even though your shutter won't be open for all of this motion, the fluidity and follow-through will help you to capture a better image.

© Daniela Bowker

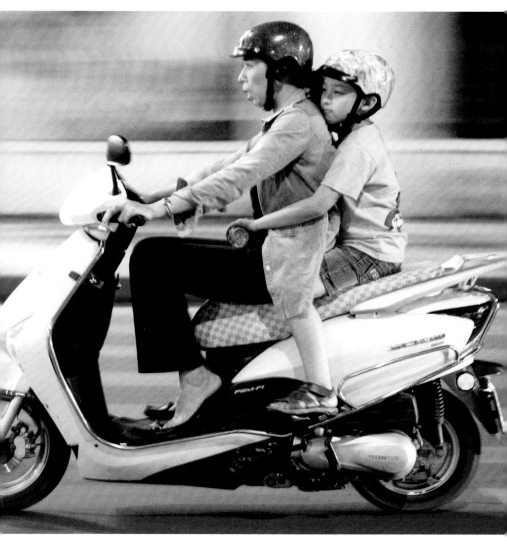

Motion Blur

While blur may be the enemy of sharpness, it is not necessarily the enemy of good photography. This may take some getting used to, as sharpness is typically seen as a sort of prerequisite for an acceptable shot. In most cases this is perfectly logical, but when it comes to communicating motion, the rules change a bit. No longer are you necessarily seeking to freeze a moment in time, because motion is an extension of that moment, and a sharp, frozen representation isn't necessarily an effective way to communicate that. Blur, on the other hand, can extend that moment and preserve a sense of time and motion within a single, still frame. Like so many other creative decisions in photography, whether or not this particular techniques is a success is a matter of intent. A viewer can easily tell the difference between a blurry shot resulting from sloppy handholding technique and one that uses that blur for a self-evidently creative purpose.

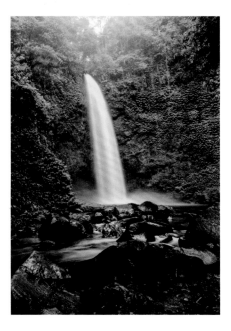

Moving water—waterfalls especially—is another commonly blurred subject, and one whose motion is easier to predict. The water takes on the appearance of a shimmering silver haze, and as the background doesn't move, its sharpness contrasts with the silky contours of fluid motion to great effect. The same principle applies to water splashing up against the shore. A tripod is usually essential for giving the greatest range of creative options.

← **The right shutter speed**
The longer the shutter speed, the more diffuse the appearance of the water will be. All the stray droplets of water will gradually combine and look misty or cloudy. Depending on the speed of the waterfall, between 2 seconds and 1/8 second will usually result in a blurred capture that still retains the shape of the falling water.

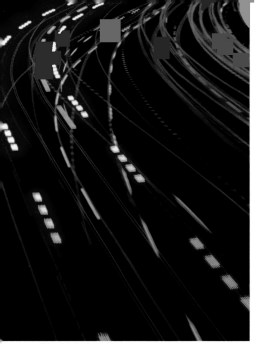

© Daniela Bowker

Dancers, musicians, and other performers all exhibit a vitality and spirit that lends itself very well to motion blur. The swish, sway, sparkle, and color of dancers in motion can look just as effective in motion blur as a shot that freezes the action and depicts their shapes. The key, as with many other motion subjects, is to still capture some sharp element off of which the blurred areas can contrast. This will also help ensure that the subject is identifiable, and keep it from descending into total abstraction.

← **30-second exposure**
The individual, separate dots of blue light are the results of an emergency vehicle passing beneath the bridge from which this was shot.

LONG EXPOSURE

Apart from the subject actually being in motion, the shutter speed will be the critical factor in achieving a photograph that captures motion blur. As a consequence, set your camera's exposure mode to either Manual or Shutter Priority (Tv or S, depending on the make of your camera).

There's no definite formula that dictates how long the shutter needs to remain open. The slower the shutter speed and the faster the moving subject, the more blur there will be. If you're aiming for any kind of motion blur from a snail, you might need a shutter speed of several times longer than you would from a moving car. The car's motion blur could probably be achieved within a few tenths of a second. Really, it will be a case of playing around to discover what works best in the situation.

If you're concerned that having the shutter open for a long period is going to overexpose the image before any blur can be captured, even with a small aperture, then you might want to consider using a neutral density filter. These filters work by reducing the

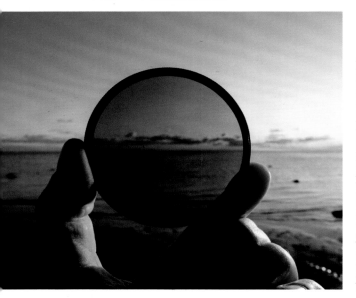

← ND filters
Neutral density (ND) filters come in a range of strengths, and can be stacked to combine their strengths and further reduce the amount of light reaching the sensor (though this will affect image quality, even with high-quality filters). Additionally, there are variable ND filters which rotate like a polarizer (see page 113) so you can dial in the precise strength needed. Finally, some cameras with built-in lenses also feature built-in ND filters, allowing use of wide apertures in bright sunlight.

intensity of all wavelengths of light equally as they pass into the lens, so that the colors aren't altered, but excessive brightness is reduced. A neutral-density filter can be incredibly useful on a bright day, even if long exposure work isn't something that you're thinking of doing, as it will allow you to use a larger aperture for creative purposes without having to use a super-fast shutter speed.

There is something of a difference between motion blur and a blurry photograph; one is creative and the other is, well, a blurry mess. Your shutter is going to be open for a relatively long period of time to allow you to capture

your subject in motion. This will, however, lead to the entire photograph being blurry owing to camera shake if you don't stabilize your camera. Using a tripod is probably the easiest way to ensure that you get the photograph that you want, but depending on where you are and what you're photographing, a beanbag or a flat surface can suffice, too.

→ Just a touch of blur
The motion blur is made all the more effective by contrasting against the sharply captured faces and other figures in this shot. The two elements reinforce each other to communicate the festive spirit of the occasion.

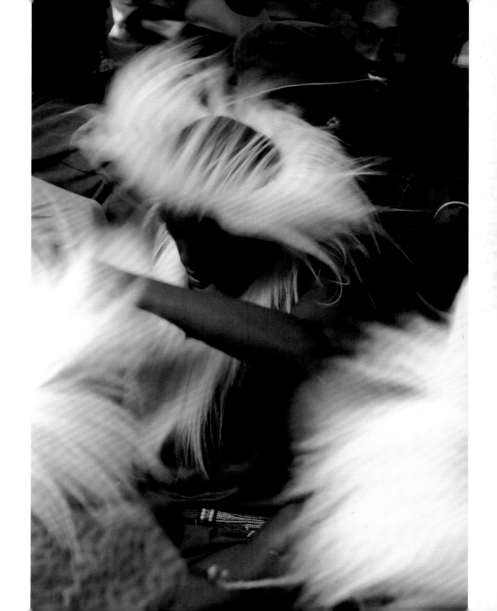

Communicate Movement through Blur

Challenge

Movement in a photograph can help to tell your story and give your image a feeling of dynamism. The key is to ensure that any instances of motion blur look deliberate. You want enough blur to give a sense of movement, but not so much that the image is just a mass of streaks with no obvious subject. As well as thinking about your shutter speed and ensuring a good exposure, you must consider the direction and flow of the blur and how that will impact on your composition. Primarily, think about leading lines and frame orientation.

↓ **Urban dynamics**
Street scenes are filled with motion, and benefit from a touch of motion blur here and there.

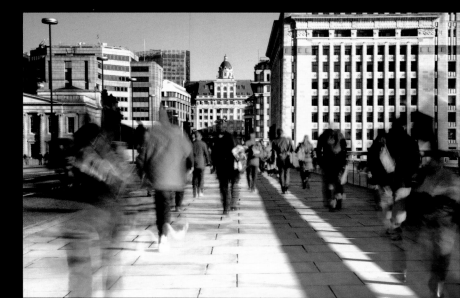

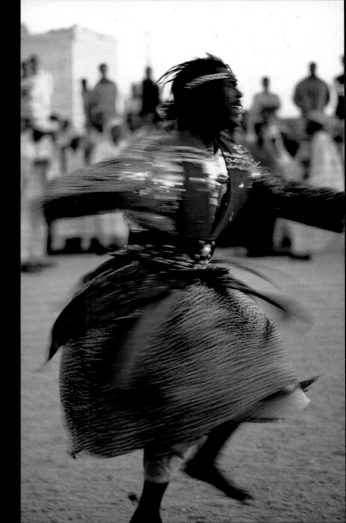

Energetic and spirited
Action, be it an athlete running across a field, or a dancer performing, is easily represented by some well controlled motion blur.

Challenge Checklist

→ Use a range of different shutter speeds to identify their effects on motion blur.

→ Take care not to over-expose your image.

→ Compose your frame carefully to make the most of the blur.

→ Use a tripod or other stabilization mechanism so that the only blur in your photograph is from the subject in motion, not camera shake.

CHAPTER 4 | **Processing & Post**

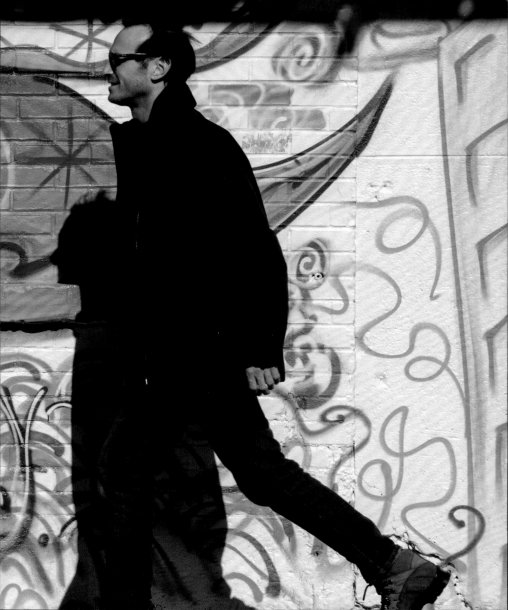

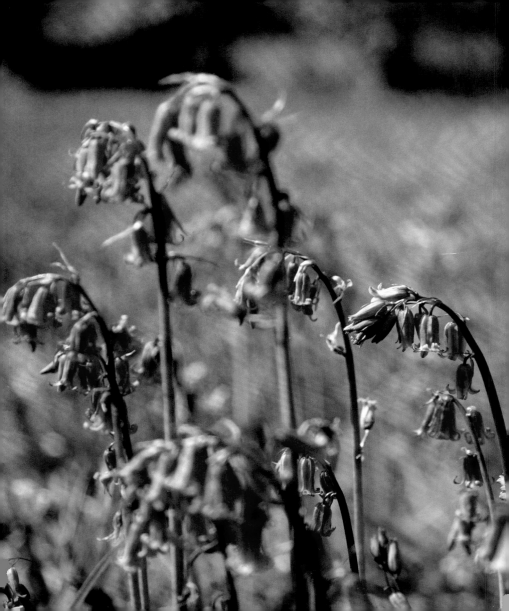

Introduction: Processing & Post

Processing and post-production work is often a polarizing part of digital photography. Everyone has an opinion: some say that any departure from a completely faithful and untouched reproduction of the original subject is fraudulent; others say the sky is the limit, and you can do whatever you like to any image. As usual, the truth lies somewhere in the middle. For one, there is no such thing as a completely faithful reproduction—the process of capturing photons, converting them into digital information, and displaying that information in a two-dimensional format requires various levels of creative interpretation at several steps along the way. And on the other hand, the more digital enhancement that goes into an image—particularly as you begin introducing special effects and adding elements that weren't in the original scene at all, such as with composites—the closer you get to crossing a line between a photograph and a work of digital art. This chapter will cover the space in between these extreme interpretations Starting with an overview of the post-processing programs available to today's photographer, we will cover your various options for image optimization—and that word is used quite intentionally; the methods covered concern themselves primarily with making the most out of the latent potential within each image. The chapter ends with more open-ended topics of processing, in which you'll be combining separate images into one composite, removing unwanted objects from the image, stitching together panoramas, and other techniques that delve deeper into the creative tools available.

Some of these techniques will resonate with your personal photographic style and workflow, others will likely not. However, for all the techniques discussed herein, whether or not you use them in your own photography is not nearly as important as the fact that you will be able to if needed or desired—that you recognize and are familiar with the various tools and options available, so that you can make the right decisions for each image that crosses your desktop.

The Digital Workflow

Before we begin to look in detail at the tools and practices of digital photo processing, it's worth spending just a brief moment or two discussing the concept of the digital photography workflow, as this will help you see where image processing fits within the broad scheme of creating a digital image. In the context of digital photography, "workflow" essentially describes the entire process of producing a digital image—from capture and importing, organizing and reviewing, through Raw processing and post-production, to distribution and backup. If you're unfamiliar with any of these terms: capture essentially means the action of taking the photograph; importing is simply transferring the image files to the computer; organizing and reviewing involve creating appropriate folders, ranking, and making a selection of your images; Raw processing and post-production (often grouped together) are concerned with optimizing the image so that it looks as good as it possibly can; distribution is primarily about preparing the image for either print or viewing on-screen; and finally, backup refers

to the process of safely archiving and storing your images. Although there's no single specific workflow for all photographs, there are definite considerations that must be taken before an image is ready for display.

Out of the workflow just described, the two areas that are of specific relevance to photo processing are Raw processing and post-production. For the purposes of this chapter we'll use the term Raw processing to describe all aspects of optimizing the Raw image file once it has been downloaded to the computer. The term post-production, on the other hand, we'll use to describe any aspect of optimization once the Raw file has been saved as a TIFF or JPEG. As you'll see later, this does have a bearing on the type of software you'll use for certain tasks.

THE RAW FORMAT

To understand Raw processing, you first need to be familiar with the Raw format. "Raw" is the generic term for the unprocessed file format available on all interchangeable-lens cameras and many

| A Digital Photograpy Workflow | CAPTURE | → | IMPORT | → | OPERATE & REVIEW | → |

advanced compacts—whether Nikon's NEF, Sony's SR2, or Canon's CR2 format, to name just three. The benefits of shooting Raw are well documented, but are essentially concerned with capturing the most amount of image data possible. This data, rather than being processed automatically and indiscriminately by the camera as a JPEG, can instead be downloaded onto the computer, where you can manually process it using more powerful processors and software than are available in-camera. The end result, particularly with images shot under challenging lighting conditions, is improved tonal quality, sharper detail, and more accurate colors. Of course, you can process JPEGs instead, and much of the time JPEGs will provide perfectly good results. But when things get tough, you want as much data as possible in order to get the optimum result.

Dramatic improvements in Raw-processing software in recent years have allowed more optimization to take place at this initial stage than at the post-production end of the workflow. The benefits of optimizing at the Raw stage are: you have the greatest amount of leeway when correcting aspects such as exposure or color; and Raw processing is nondestructive—i.e., although on the surface you're altering how the image looks, the alterations are being relayed by a series of instructions (or "parameters") that simply overlay the original image data, which itself is left untouched and can be accessed again whenever you want. Post-production software, on the other hand, such as Photoshop or PaintShop Pro, alters the tonal and color values of the image's pixels themselves, and while up to a point you can track back and undo changes, saving the files is permanent.

Increasingly, therefore, it's good practice to perform as much optimization as possible in Raw processors. However, as we shall go on to discover, there are certain things that Raw-processing software can't achieve, and that's when you have to turn to post-production software. Bearing in mind the distinction between these two optimization processes, the first section of the chapter deals with Raw processing, the tools and techniques, while later sections cover post-production, paying particular attention to what can be achieved only with post-production software.

RAW PROCESSING → POST-PRODUCTION → DISTRIBUTION → BACKUP

Optimizing & Enhancing

We can think of optimizing an image as bringing out its best qualities for a given purpose. An image file intended for use on a website, for example, should be optimized to be as small as possible without visual loss in quality. But if you plan to print a photo onto 13x19-inch canvas paper, frame it, and hang it on the wall, the most important attribute is image quality, and the depth of detail and color preserved. The size of this file is of little concern.

In either case, if you're starting with a Raw file from your camera, you'll want to turn to a Raw-processing software for this type of image processing. Or, if you only ever shoot JPEGs and perform basic optimization like adjusting color, saturation, and contrast, then most Raw processors will do the trick as well.

More creative interpretations, on the other hand, fall to post-processing programs like Photoshop. When you want to go beyond simply optimizing and outputting your photos, and dig into more artful pursuits, you'll most certainly require at least a basic post software. Cloning out unwanted elements, adding new elements, creating double exposures and composite images, and adding text are all examples of enhancement and are best achieved with post-processing products.

© Danilovi

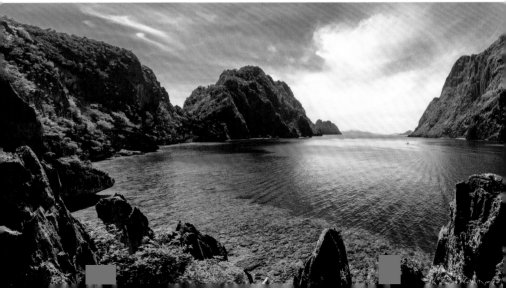

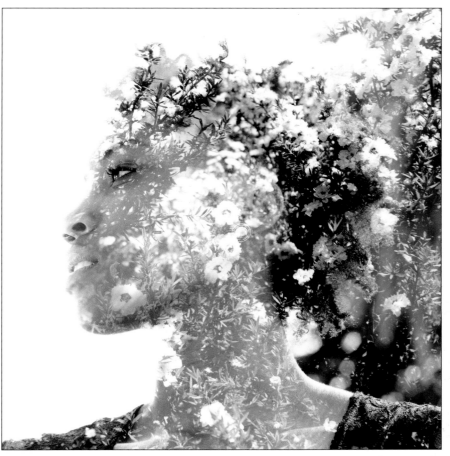

© Victor Tongdee

← **Optimized**
This image of a lagoon in El Nido, Phillipines was recorded by the camera as a Raw file and then optimized for print using Lightroom. The white balance was rendered just slightly on the cool side to enhance the blues and greens, and saturation turned up a hair.

↑ **Enhanced**
This "double exposure" was created in Photoshop by layering two JPEG photos together and experimenting with Blending Modes to make an entirely new, artistic image.

Raw-Processing Software

Along with the development of more efficient image sensors and the ability to shoot video on DSLRs, another of the more significant advances in digital photography—certainly for those photographers who enjoy the editing process—is the development of Raw-processing software.

Early examples of Raw processors, such as the first releases of Adobe Camera Raw (ACR)—a plugin that became available in 2002 with Photoshop 7.0.1—did not offer a great deal of freedom when it came to the adjustments that could be made to Raw files. Exposure, white balance, and color adjustments were well catered for; but other features, such as sharpening, noise reduction, and fixing chromatic aberration were in their infancy, while yet more features such as lens correction, adjustment brushes, and spot removal didn't even exist.

As the true value of Raw processing became increasingly apparent in terms of the image quality it provided, software developers, such as Adobe, Apple, and Phase One, to name just a few, worked hard at developing Raw-processing software that was capable of an ever-broader range of adjustment. Camera manufacturers like Nikon and Canon also developed their own Raw processors that were designed specifically to work with their proprietary Raw formats. This

was often bundled on CD-Rom with the purchase of the manufacturers' cameras.

Today's Raw-processing software has come a long way since these early examples. As the software has evolved, it's become possible to undertake more and more image-processing tasks at the Raw-processing stage of the workflow. Processes such as sharpening, noise reduction, and fixing lens distortion are now performed by powerful algorithms that are capable of producing excellent results. These developments, together with the advent of localized adjustment in the form of spot removal, editable adjustment brushes, and control points have almost rendered post-production software obsolete for certain types of photography. Many professionals today who shoot and process large numbers of images, such as wedding or sports photographers, will often use only Raw-processing software to optimize their images. However, as we shall discover later, for other types of photography or for certain specific tasks, using post-production software like Photoshop or PaintShop Pro is the only option.

Along with increasing the functionality of Raw processors, software developers have also taken the opportunity to develop programs that mirror the digital workflow. Taking the example

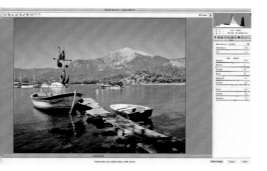

← **Adobe Camera Raw (ACR)**
This processor ships as a plugin with Photoshop and Photoshop Elements, and is an extremely powerful Raw-processing package in its own right. It features an almost identical toolset to Lightroom (in fact, it shares the same processing engine), only arranged and presented in a different way. As a plugin, it works seamlessly with the rest of Photoshop or Elements.

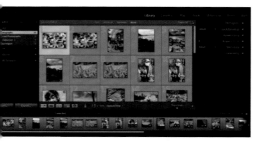

← **Lightroom's Library module**
This module behaves like a dedicated image database. Here you can view, compare, rank, organize, and add captions and keywords to your images. It's also possible to view the EXIF data embedded in the image.

of wedding or sports photographers again: everything they need for their images, from importing and selecting, to optimizing and distributing, can all be achieved within the same program.

Adobe's Lightroom illustrates this perfectly. The program features seven discrete modules—Library, Develop, Map, Book, Slideshow, Print, and Web. Images are imported and organized in the Library. Optimization takes place in the Develop module. Using the Map tab, you can tag a geographical location to a photo. You can create and order an on-demand photo book using the Book module. Slideshow mode allows you to create presentations, incorporating watermarks and music and making JPEG, PDF, or video slideshows. In the Print and Web sections, you can prepare your images for either delivery method. This setup isn't unique to Lightroom; other Raw processors have similar modes and they are often referred to as "workflow software."

With workflow being crucial to Raw-processing software, it comes as no surprise to discover that most Raw processors feature modules to walk users through the process. Lightroom, for example, has seven, while Phase One's Capture One—another popular Raw processor—has a similar environment but fewer modules. Regardless of these details, the broad approach of all these programs is to organize, edit, and share.

The digital photography workflow begins with importing, and with most Raw processors, simply attaching the camera or memory card to the computer and launching the software will prompt an import routine. At this stage, you can create a folder in which to place the images, add keywords that are common to all the images, apply preset or customized picture settings, and embed metadata—which may include information about the photographer, any copyright notices, the date and location of the shoot, and so on. Getting into the habit of organizing your photos into folders and embedding keywords and other metadata during the import routine will help you maintain a coherent image library later down the line. Once the images have downloaded to the Library, you can quickly go through the collection ranking or deleting images, and making an initial selection of your favorites. With the selection made, you can add keywords that are specific to the individual images. If your intention

is to sell your images via any of the numerous micro picture libraries available, keywords are essential, as they help people search for your images.

DEVELOP

Lightroom's Develop module is where all the image processing takes place. The Develop mode is arranged into four main areas. Running down the left-hand side, you'll find an extensive list of Lightroom preset photo styles, including a variety of black-and-white, cross-processed, and sepia-toned options, to name a small selection. These can be applied to an image simply by clicking on the preset name. Beneath these presets are Snapshots. This allows you to record the actions you've undertaken on one image and apply them to another. The History tab details the actions applied to the selected image. You can use History to retrace your steps and return to an earlier phase of the sequence. The main image view located in the center of the screen shows a preview of the image. Naturally, this updates as you apply different commands. You can toggle through the appearance of the preview using the icon found directly under the main view.

The right-hand panel is home to Lightroom's extensive range of tools. We'll look at these in greater detail later, but it's worth noting here that the tools are grouped together and organized into discrete palettes. Each palette relates to a

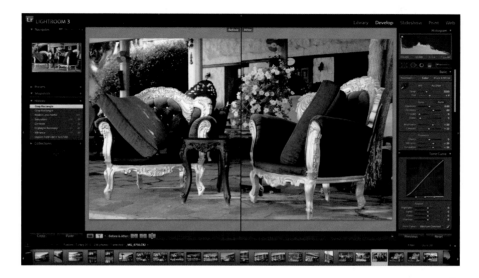

specific area of processing, whether
dealing with tone, color, or sharpening,
for example. Like most of Lightroom's
controls, the palettes can be expanded
and collapsed by clicking the small
triangle next to its name.

Beneath the main preview runs the
filmstrip. This shows thumbnails of all
the images in the selected folder. The
filmstrip appears in all seven modules
and provides a way of accessing images
without having to return to the Library
each time. The Map, Book, Slideshow,
Print, and Web modules all have a
similar arrangement, with control panels
on either side of the main view, and the
filmstrip running below. Although we've

↑ **Before and after**
By clicking on the icons underneath the
image preview, you can call up a Before &
After viewscreen, which gives you excellent
perspective on the degree of adjustment you
are making to the original image.

described in some detail the Lightroom
setup, as suggested earlier, other Raw
processors share a similar structure.

Raw-Processing Tools

The similarity between the tool panels of much Raw-processing software is clear from the two examples shown opposite. Individual palettes or panels, each with readily identifiable names such as Exposure, Detail, Highlights & Shadows, and Lens Correction, feature a number of labeled sliders that can be accessed by clicking on the arrow that expands the palette. It's mostly clear what each of the sliders does—Brightness and Contrast, for example, are self-explanatory; and in less obvious cases, a slider's functionality is quickly learned by experimentation and observation. Because Raw processors, unlike post-processing programs, have been designed with photographers in mind, the palettes and sliders are all closely associated with specific digital photography issues, and that's one of the things that helps make Raw processors so intuitive.

With most Raw processors, the sliders make adjustments in real time. In other words, the image will change in correspondence to the movement of the slider, as opposed to the adjustment being made once you release the slider. This allows you to achieve the exact look you want, rather than by trial and error. Although real-time adjustment is not unique to Raw processors, it reinforces such software's user-friendliness. As well as making adjustments using the sliders, it's also usually possible to input

specific numeric values in boxes next to the sliders. Although you're unlikely to make many adjustments this way initially, it can be useful if you're attempting to replicate specific settings between two different images.

As you progress through this chapter, you'll become familiar with what each control slider does, when you'll use it. And over time, you'll discover that there are some panels, palettes, and controls that you'll use frequently, while others you'll barely use at all.

KEYBOARD SHORTCUTS

Nearly all computer programs have keyboard shortcuts that you can use instead of clicking on menus and commands with the cursor—Raw processors are no exception. As you become more familiar with the program you're using, you'll find that you'll begin to learn the more common shortcuts. It really pays remember these—they increase the speed of your workflow considerably. For the time being, however, the most important shortcut to remember now is Ctrl/Cmd + Z. If you're not already familiar with this life-saver, it's "Undo" in most programs. So if you make a mistake, hit these keys to take a step back.

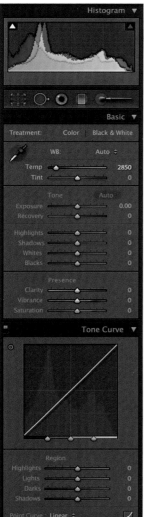

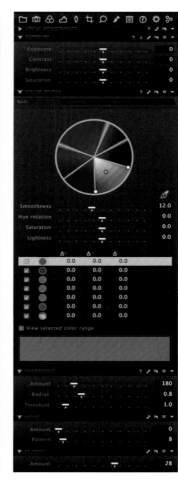

← Capture One
While Phase One is primarily a high-end, medium-format camera manufacturer, they have also developed an impressive Raw processor called Capture One that is in most cases just as robust as other options.

←Lightroom
It's easy to see the common tools that exist across various Raw processors—some even appear in the same order. Here is Lightroom's toolbar. Each palette can be collapsed, making it easy to scroll through all the various tools and sliders.

Post-Production Software

Post-production software started with Adobe Photoshop. Photoshop, and the programs that followed, were initially general graphics packages. Photoshop's ability to create and manipulate vector graphics using features such as Paths and the Pen and Shape tools, together with the Text tool, reveals its identity as a graphics program. However, it also supports pixel-based, or raster, graphics, and as digital photography developed, software companies began creating tools that are useful to photographers, such as Healing and Spot Removal brushes.

However, unlike Raw processors that are aimed at photographers, Photoshop has a much broader audience. In fact, there are vast sections of Photoshop that are of limited use to photographers. But we can't be dismissive of the program that most professionals and many amateurs have embraced; and, of course, it's not just Photoshop. Photoshop Elements, PaintShop Pro, and the myriad other post-production programs are extremely powerful, versatile tools. The ability to manually change each individual pixel in an image provides an unparalleled level of control. This powerful versatility, coupled with features such as layers, adjustment layers, masks, channels, and filters, ensures that, given enough time and with sufficient skills, you can make an image appear pretty much however you want. For professional photographers,

notably in fashion or advertising, the ability to process at this level is essential. For such professionals, Raw-processing software simply won't provide the comprehensive tools they need.

In terms of workflow, complex programs such as Photoshop cannot compete with Raw workflow software. Photoshop does, however, ship with a dedicated browser—Bridge—which is a perfectly adequate image organizer, and from which you can access Photoshop directly. Less complex post-production software, such as Elements and PaintShop Pro, have been redesigned over time to take into account the workflow approach. Elements, for example, has discrete modules: Organize, Fix, Create, and Share, while PaintShop Pro takes a similar approach with its Manage, Adjust, and Edit modules.

WHICH SOFTWARE DO YOU NEED?

So, which type of software do you need? That depends largely on what you shoot, the amount you shoot, and what your intended use is. Most professionals will have both Raw processing and post-production software—and this will be the case if you choose Adobe products, since subscribing to either Photoshop or Lightroom gives you access to both. That said, for most amateurs, it probably isn't necessary to have both. If you shoot a lot

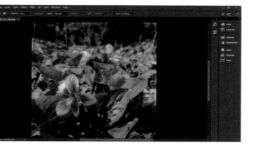

↑ Adobe Photoshop
Photoshop has evolved from a primarily graphics-intensive program into a comprehensive post-processing workhorse.

↗ Corel PaintShop Pro
While Adobe certainly dominates the field of post-processing software, alternatives do exist. PaintShop Pro is a fully competent option, and one that has been around almost as long as Photoshop itself. Here, the workflow is divided among Manage, Adjust, and Edit modules.

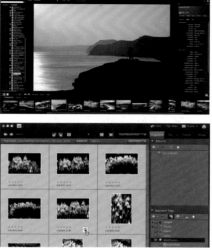

↑ Elements import window
Elements, while not quite as comprehensive as the full version of Photoshop, offers most of the features more commonly used by photographers, and also offers a complete workflow setup—beginning with this Import window.

of images, but don't want to spend hours retouching them, and don't need to add text or special effects, then a Raw processor is likely to be most appropriate. These programs are generally quicker and more intuitive to use than post-processing programs, and they're better at creating image libraries. And remember, although they're called Raw processors, you can process JPEGs and TIFFs using the same nondestructive methods—the only difference is you won't have the the extra data you get

from Raw files. If, however, you enjoy manipulating images, such as merging elements from different photographs, and adding text or other special effects, then you'll need post-production software, as Raw processors simply can't perform such tasks. And just as Raw processors will allow you to work with JPEGs or TIFFs, most post-processing software will allow you to process Raw files to a lesser or greater degree, before you convert to a TIFF or JPEG.

Photoshop is the undisputed king of the post-production programs. It was the first one to have a truly global impact, and as such, most other programs have emulated it in regards to its tools, functions, menus, architecture, and commands. For this reason, most of the terminology in the post-production sections of this book will have a bias toward Photoshop—although for the reasons stated on the previous pages, it should be clear to users of other programs which tools or menus are being referred to. It's probably also fair to say that if you've mastered Photoshop, it won't take you long to master other similar programs.

Despite being the heavyweight, Photoshop is certainly not a big-hitter when it comes to efficient workflow (of course, it was never intended to be). Before the arrival of the Bridge plugin, Photoshop had no form of browser or image organizer at all. And even now, in comparison with Raw-processing software, jumping between Bridge and Photoshop is still slow and rather cumbersome.

In terms of workflow, the less powerful, but often perfectly satisfactory programs such as Photoshop Elements or PaintShop Pro are more useful, certainly for the amateur photographer.

These emulate the environment of Raw processors, such as Lightroom, by having discrete modules in which you can organize, edit, and share your images. Although switching between the various modules is not as seamless as it can be with Raw processors, you do at least have all the tools you need to create, edit, and share images from an image library.

Turning to the main processing screen of post-production software, what is immediately obvious is that there's a great deal to take on. While with many Raw processors, you can find your way around on your own in a relatively short space of time, with programs like Photoshop, delving into them without prior instruction is likely to result in mental meltdown. It's exactly for this reason that consumer versions such as Photoshop Elements have readily accessible tutorials to help you learn your way. Photoshop has also added the Tooltips feature—short tutorial videos that pop up when you hover over a tool. Photoshop's main workspace is relatively clutter-free. However, this belies the sophisticated toolset that accompanies the software. Shown opposite are images of Photoshop's and PaintShop Pro's Edit workspace, showing how similar they are.

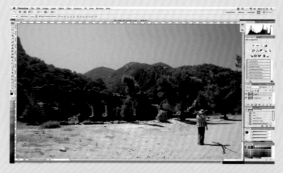

← **Photoshop vs PaintShop Pro**
There are quite a few commonalities to be seen between these two programs. The main toolbars are both arranged along the left side, while the right side is dominated by a series of palettes, with Layers being the most significant feature.

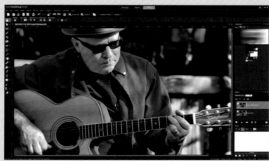

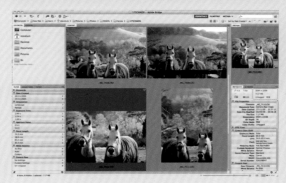

← **Adobe Bridge**
You can customize this main screen to offer a wide variety of additional information, or clear it of everything but your image thumbnails to get a light-table appearance.

Rotating & Cropping

One of the first assessments you're likely to make before progressing with other processing tasks is whether or not an image is straight. Depending on the shot, this may not be too critical, but if there are distinctive horizontals or a horizon visible in the shot, you'll want to ensure that the frame is properly aligned with these linear elements contained within it.

Cropping an image—essentially, removing any unwanted part of a composition—is another simple task, and yet potentially one of the most

effective ways of ensuring a photo has the greatest possible impact.

Naturally, we should always be thinking of composition when we're framing our photos, but often we're shooting at speed or grabbing a shot under rapidly hanging

↓ Grid options
Above we've selected the Thirds grid, but other options include Golden Ratio, Triangle, or Golden Spiral, all of which are intended to help with composition (though they are all doubtful formulas to apply without careful thought.)

✓	Grid	
	Thirds	
	Diagonal	
	Triangle	
	Golden Ratio	
	Golden Spiral	
	Cycle Grid Overlay	O
	Cycle Grid Overlay Orientation	⇧ O

↓ Lightroom's Crop palette
This palette is found near the top of the Develop module under the histogram. To reveal the various tools associated with the Crop Overlay mode, click the dotted rectangle (or press R).

Crop Overlay mode button

Crop Frame tool

Straighten tool

Straighten Slider control

→ Grid overlay
Having selected the Crop mode, a grid will be displayed over the image. At the corners of the image and in the center of each side are bounding box handles.

lighting conditions, and it's not until later, when we have time to fully assess an image on a computer monitor, that we can see how the composition of the image can be improved. It may also be the case that there are some alternative crops we'd like to try to see which works best.

Another reason for cropping is that the image size and shape is dictated by something outside of our control. Perhaps the final image requirement is for a square shot, in which case you'll need to crop a landscape or portrait format to suit.

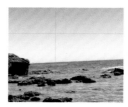

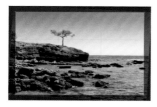

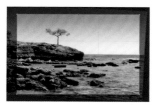

↑ ↗ → Rotate options
There are a number of ways to rotate an image. If you place the cursor near a corner box handle it will turn into a double-headed arrow. Move the cursor up or down and the image will rotate. However, a more accurate method is to select the Straighten tool. On the image draw a line along the horizon or horizontal line that you're using as a point of reference. As soon as you've drawn the line and released the mouse button, the image will automatically rotate. Notice also, that the image is automatically cropped to accommodate the rotation.

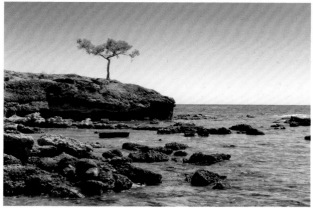

↑ Cut out distractions
To tidy up the image and improve the crop, using the Thirds grid the left-hand control point was dragged to the right so that the slightly distracting tree at the edge of the frame is cropped out, and so that the remaining solitary tree sits on a rule of thirds line. The top handle was then dragged down so that the ocean horizon is in the middle of the frame, giving the final image a better sense of balance.

© Steve Luck

Choosing White Balance

We're all aware that daylight can change color during the course of the day, from an orange hue just after sunrise, through the purer, almost blue white light of midday, and then warming up again as the sun sets. But the color temperature of light is also affected by atmospheric conditions such as clouds, or more dramatically by artificial light sources such as streetlamps or even lightbulbs.

↓ Not quite blue enough
Although the lighting (daylight) in this shot of a Greek monastery was neutral, the Auto setting has produced a slightly orange image. The sky isn't as blue as it should be and the overall effect is a muddy appearance.

To ensure that white objects always appear white, no matter what the ambient color temperature, your camera has a variety of white balance settings—these usually have names such as Daylight, Cloud, Shady, Tungsten, Incandescent, Flash, and so on. And, in fact, most cameras will perform adequately if left on the Auto setting. However, every now and again you may come across a shooting situation that has the camera fooled—a mixture of natural and artificial light, for example, which results in an image that exhibits some odd-looking color casts.

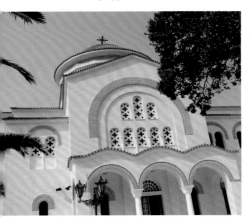

→ A neutral target
With the Eyedropper tool selected, click on a neutral gray pixel—try to get the red, green, and blue values as close as possible.

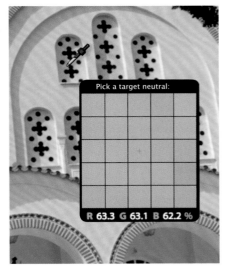

Pick a target neutral:

R 63.3 G 63.1 B 62.2 %

↓ ↘ Creative white balance

You can use white balance sliders in a creative rather than purely prescriptive way. White balance can be subjective, with no actual right or wrong result, so use the sliders to cool down or warm up the image for very different results.

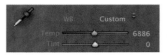

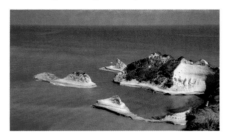

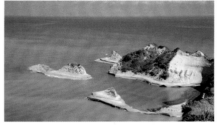

Shooting Raw is the best way to ensure that you can freely adjust the color balance when processing your images. If you shoot Raw, no matter what the camera's white balance setting at the time of shooting, you can alter this to give a more (or less, if you want a creative interpretation) neutral result without impacting on image quality in any way.

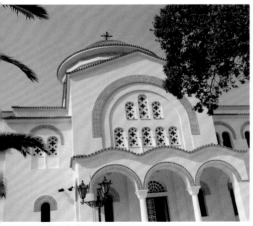

© Steve Luck

← Blue sky restored

As soon as you select a neutral-gray area, the software automatically balances the colors in the image, and the result is a photo free from the orange color cast.

Avoid clicking on an area that's too white or bright, as one of the color channels may be clipped (exhibiting only the maximum intensity of the color with no detail), resulting in an inaccurate white balance measurement, which in turn could produce an inaccurate color adjustment.

If for some reason using the Eyedropper doesn't produce a result you're happy with, use the Raw processor's Temperature and Tint sliders to manually adjust the white balance. Raw processors even have some presets that might provide you with the result you want.

Adjusting Exposure & Contrast

Of all the benefits of shooting and processing in the Raw format, perhaps the greatest is the level of adjustment that can be made to exposure long after you've pressed the shutter release. In most cases, it's possible to increase or decrease the exposure by around two stops—making a total possible adjustment of up to four stops—without affecting the quality of the image. This is done easily in Raw processors with a quick movement of the Exposure slider. Furthermore, thanks to tools like Lightroom's Adjustment Brush, exposure adjustment doesn't necessarily have to be global. It's possible to make only certain areas brighter while holding (or even reducing) the exposure in other areas.

There are some nuances to exposure, however, meant to ensure that the image

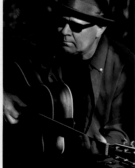
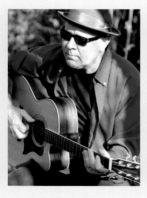
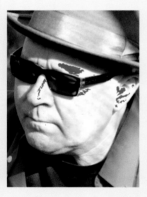

© Steve Luck

↑ **Mostly underexposed**
Shot outside in dappled, contrasty lighting, a spot-meter reading from the guitarist's face has ensured the most important element of the image is not over-exposed, but has left the rest of the image too dark.

↑ **Global exposure increase**
Using the Raw processor's exposure controls, we can globally increase the exposure by a couple of stops. This has improved the overall exposure, but the face now looks overexposed.

↑ **Highlight clipping warning**
Activating this feature shows that parts of the musician's face are in fact blowing out—they've become pure white and have lost detail altogether. It's essential that we fix this if the image is to be successful.

has the fullest possible range of tones while maintaining the maximum amount of detail. (Naturally, these nuances are provided for in any Raw processor or post-processing software.) For starters, you'll want to avoid overly clipped highlights (bright areas of the image where detail is lost). When highlights are not bright enough, however, the image can appear dull and flat. Shadows work similarly: Too dark, and you lose detail; not dark enough, and the image can appear flat.

But before you enter the nebulous land of highlights and shadows, let's first explore black point and white point. You can have most processing programs set black and white points automatically, or you can do it manually, either by sight, or by going just to the edge of where things start to get clipped (see the images below).

It's important to set defined values for black point and white point when you process an image, because it tells the software which values to establish as

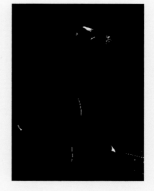

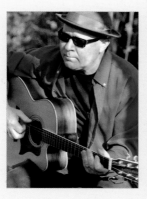

↑ **Setting the white point**
Using the Whites slider in Lightroom, and holding down the Alt/Option key, move the slider until you begin to see some parts of the image appear. These are the areas where highlights are just beginning to clip, and they will be established as "true white."

↑ **Setting the black point**
Using the Blacks slider, and holding down the Alt/Option key, move the slider until you begin to see some parts of the image appear. These are the areas where shadows are just beginning to clip, and they will be established as "true black."

↑ **Automatic white/black point**
By holding down the Shift key and double clicking on the white- and black-point sliders, both points were set automatically to create an image with a natural-looking range of tones and to preserve a good amount of detail in both dark and bright areas.

"true black" and "true white." This creates parameters for the Shadows and Highlights sliders once you start to adjust them, so it's wise to do this first. This practice also produces a richer image with better contrast.

Highlights, then, can be thought of as the tonal space between true white and a theoretical, perfectly exposed, perfectly detail-rendered area of the image. And the same, of course, goes for shadows and true black.

Once black- and white-point values are established, you can tinker with highlights and shadows without having to worry about going too far off the deep end in either direction. You've already set the whitest white and the blackest black—your highlights and shadows won't go past the limits you've set. Now we're talking about what happens in those areas between perfect exposure and true white or true black.

Set a positive value on the Highlights slider (to the right), and you'll see less detail in the brighter areas. Slide Highlights left, and you'll see more detail. It may seem counterintuitive that you'd set a positive value to see less detail and a negative value to see more, but that's because a positive value increases exposure in highlight areas, while a negative value reduces it. On the Shadows slider, move right to increase exposure in the image's darker areas, revealing more detail; and move left to make the shadows darker and less detailed.

You may notice, depending upon how you adjust Highlights and Shadows, that the image starts to lose some of its "pop." Brightening shadows and darkening highlights to reveal more detail can severely impact the visual depth of an image. It can begin to look flat or dull. A small contrast adjustment is the perfect revival. Sliding contrast up, even just a hair, will better define the boundaries between light and dark areas and bring some pizzazz back to your photo.

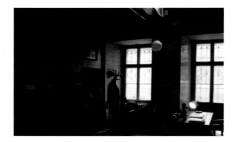

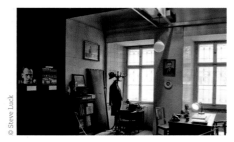

© Steve Luck

→ Highlights slider

This slider tool will darken highlights and add back some lost detail. Holding down the Alt or Option key while moving the slider will reveal the elements of the image that are clipping against a black background. Here, the blown highlights on the subject's face have been recovered, and the only ones now clipping are the specular highlights of the guitar's white edge. These are acceptable. Returning to the preview, we can see that no details are lost in the bright regions of the image.

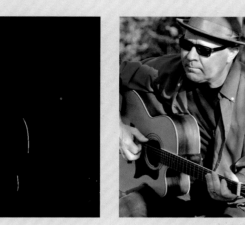

← Shadow fill

The ability to open up shadows in an image without affecting the highlights is another relatively new aspect of Raw processing. Lightroom's Shadows slider (sometimes called the Fill Light slider in other programs) performs the task exceptionally well.

Here, we've used a Raw processor to lighten the interior of a room in the Communist museum in Prague without losing detail around and outside the windows.

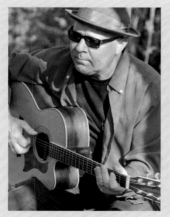

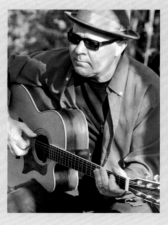

↑ ↗ Shadows and Contrast sliders

This image was looking pretty good, but we used the Shadows slider tool to bring out just a little bit more detail from the shadow areas. By setting a positive value (moving the slider to the right), we lightened the image just enough to accomplish that. As you can see in the image on the left, this did in fact cause a loss of depth, which we recovered by adding some contrast using the Contrast slider.

Clarity, Vibrance & Saturation

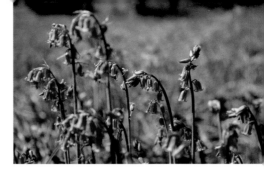

Like Contrast, Clarity adjusts tone—the range of tones rendered, and the differentiation between them. The difference between the two is that Contrast applies to every tone; Clarity only adjusts the differentiation of middle tones, leaving shadow and highlight areas alone. Turn Clarity down, and the image gets softer. Saturation is a global adjustment that turns up the colors in an image, making them more vibrant. Saturation's broad-spectrum application is perfect for some images, a green landscape with a blue sky for example, but it can wreak havoc on skin tones. It may also be the case that you have an image with some colors already looking plenty vibrant but others that you'd like to intensify. Adding saturation could make those already-vibrant colors appear unrealistic. As for saturation's subtractive quality, setting a negative value on the Saturation slider will "turn down" the color; and since it applies to the full range of color in the image's RGB histogram, setting Saturation all the way to the left will make a black-and-white photo. Desaturating an image partway can be a compelling artistic interpretation.

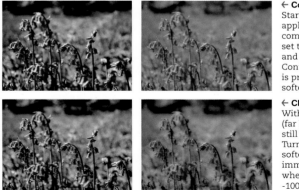

← **Contrast**
Starting with the original above, we applied Contrast adjustment for comparison. At far left, Contrast is set to +100. The shadows are harsh, and detail is lost. At immediate left, Contrast is at -100. Plenty of detail is preserved, but the whole image is softer and less dynamic.

← **Clarity**
With Clarity set all the way to +100 (far left), you can see the image is still "contrasty," but not as harsh. Turning Clarity down begins to soften the image, and the example at immediate left shows what happens when Clarity is set all the way to -100, a surreal, fairyland look.

Vibrance is the answer to Saturation's indiscriminate nature. When you don't want to "punch up" the whole image but only portions of it, Vibrance is the tool for the job. Like Clarity, it only applies to the middles. In this case, we're dealing with color instead of tone—so, Vibrance affects the middle colors, making a more moderate change to those at the ends of the histogram. The brightest and most subdued colors in the photo are affected drastically less; this would include skin tones, earthy colors, and on the other end, those colors that are already vibrant enough. Like Saturation, setting Vibrance to a negative value can give an interesting artistic effect. Turning it all the way down leaves some subtle color behind, rendering a soft, vintage look.

↘ Saturation
This comparison shows clearly what a difference it makes to increase color globally (Saturation) vs just in mid-tones (Vibrance). Skin tones no longer look natural, and the strange intensity of the colors is distracting. The middle example shows Saturation set to -50; we get a nice, soft, almost-filtered effect. And finally, at -100, a completely monochrome image.

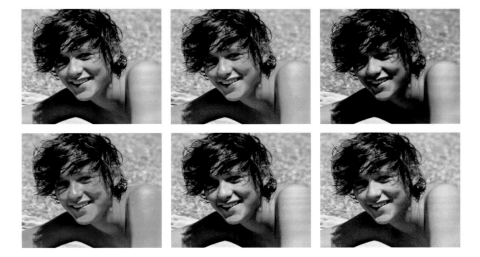

Local-Area Adjustments

Raw processors and post-processing software indeed offer powerful tools for improving images globally, but you don't always want to adjust an entire image. There are a few tools meant to help you easily and precisely apply changes to portions of an image; these changes are known as local-area adjustments. Again, we will focus on Lightroom, but all processors will include some variation on these tools.

One such tool, the Adjustment Brush, allows you to make changes like exposure, color temperature, contrast, highlights, shadows, clarity, saturation, and more, to specific portions of an image, instead of the whole thing. Adjustments can be painted on and then tweaked or erased after the fact. This is a handy helper for evening out color temperature in a shot where there was mixed lighting, or changing exposure in an over- or underexposed portion of the image, a technique known as "dodging and burning." Or, maybe you want to add contrast or clarity to make the clouds in the sky stand out better; you might use it to reduce contrast on a portrait subject's face if there are harsh shadows; or you can even add and enhance specific colors within the image.

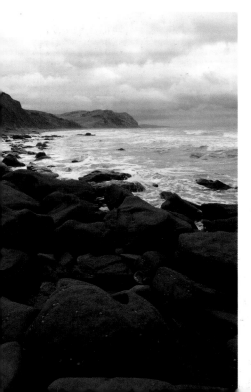

← → Adjustment Brush / Graduated Filter
We used the Graduated Filter to darken the sky without darkening the foreground, and selectively applied the Adjustment Brush to bring up the shadows between the rocks in the foreground, just enough to retrieve a bit of detail.

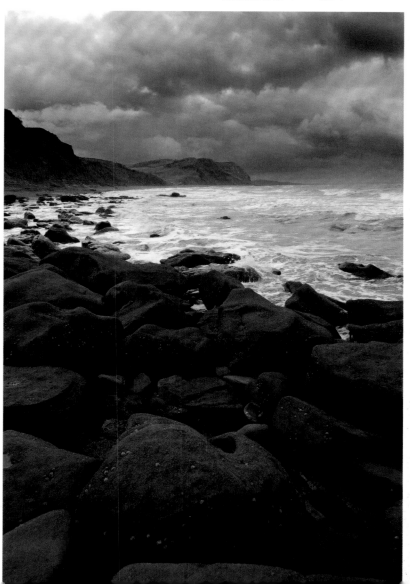

Two other tools offering the same variety of adjustments as the Adjustment Brush are the filter tools—Graduated Filter and Radial Filter. They apply your changes in broader ways than the brush, but still in a controlled way, over just a selected portion of the image.

The Graduated Filter allows you to adjust regions of an image—changing exposure to draw the viewer's attention to a particular part of an image, for example—though the possibilities are endless. You can simply click and drag to darken a linear area of the image, leaving the rest alone; and the filter is graduated, so the effect tapers off to create a smooth transition between where the change is applied and where it isn't. The Radial Filter works similarly, except rather than the adjustment being along a straight line, the change is made in a circular or oval shape. Contrary to what you might expect, the adjustment(s) you select on the sliders will be applied outside the area of the circle you draw, not inside, unless you check the "Invert" box. So, a +1 exposure adjustment will make the area outside the circle brighter, with the effect tapering in toward the middle of the circle, where the exposure is unchanged.

←↗→ **Graduated / Radial Filters**
Here, starting with the original image (at left), we used a Graduated Filter to reduce exposure in the upper left and lower right corners of the image in order to draw more attention to the second row of spices. Next, we used separate inverted Radial Filters to increase saturation, contrast, and clarity in the three bright-colored spices in that row without increasing the same values in the burlap sacks, as that would appear unnatural.

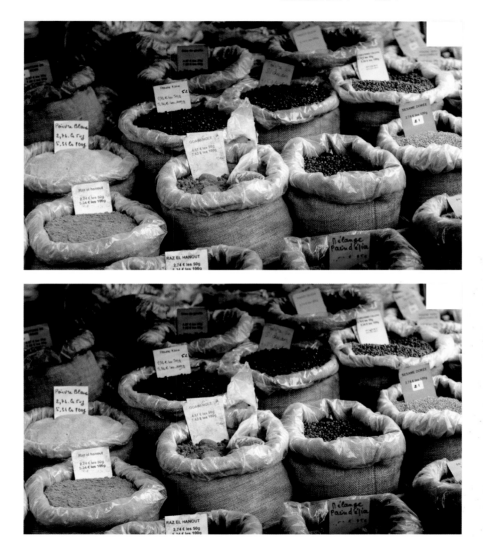

Removing Spots & Blemishes

Many of the spots you see on digital photographs are caused by dust on the image sensor. This primarily affects DSLRs, and occurs when dust enters the camera body—when a lens is being changed for example—and settles on the sensor's surface. Fortunately, such spots are only really noticeable in areas of flat color, such as blue skies. Getting rid of most spots is quick and easy, although with others, you may have to work a bit harder to remove them.

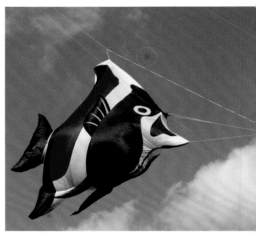

© Steve Luck

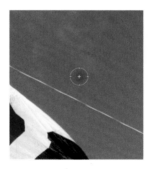

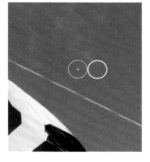

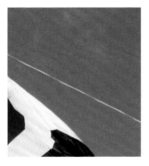

↑ Select the dust spot
Select the Spot Removal tool or Retouch brush. Check that the tool is in Heal mode. Adjust the size of the tool or brush so that it fits neatly over the dust spot. There are usually keys you can use to adjust the brush size— it's quicker and more accurate than using the slider.

↑ Sample a separate area
With the tool fitting neatly over the dust spot simply click the mouse. The Raw processor will automatically choose a sample area (usually adjacent to the target area) that it uses to blend with the pixels from the target area, so removing the spot.

↑ A clear sky regained
In a matter of moments, the ugly dust spot has disappeared, and we're ready to move on to the next problem area.

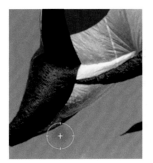

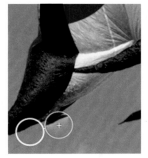

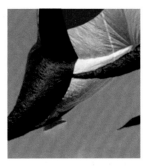

↑ Trickier edges
Here, the dust spot is located close to a dark edge of the kite. Let's see what happens if we use Spot Removal or Retouch brush in Heal mode, and simply click the mouse button.

As before, the Raw processor automatically selects a sample area to blend with the target area.

However, here the result is unsatisfactory. First, because the sample circle hasn't aligned with the target circle. Second, because in Heal mode the Removal tool uses pixels from the edge of the target circle when blending with the sample.

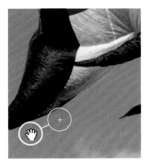

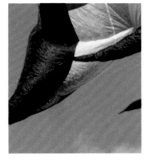

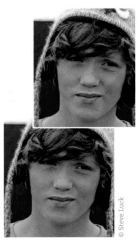

↑ A case for cloning
Where the spot is near an edge, change to Clone mode, in which the Spot Removal tool doesn't attempt to blend the surrounding pixels. This gives a more clearly defined blending edge. Here, we've selected the sample and dragged it to a cleaner position. Moving the sample area to a more

appropriate position has resulted in a better alignment, while the Clone mode creates a cleaner result.

↗ Applied to a portrait
The Spot Removal tool or Retouch brush, when in Heal mode, is an ideal way to remove skin and other blemishes.

© Steve Luck

Sharpening

We've learned a lot about sharpening digital images over the last few years—and software manufacturers have too. Recently, distinctions have been made between capture sharpening and output sharpening. Output sharpening takes place at the end of all other post-production tasks to prepare an image for specific display purposes. It is mostly automated, and we won't go in-depth about it here.

Capture sharpening, on the other hand, is applied during Raw processing. When shooting Raw, no in-camera sharpening is applied as it is with JPEGs, therefore you may well need to sharpen an image so that it looks crisp on-screen; and that is what we're going to cover here.

The aim of capture sharpening is to get the image to look pleasingly sharp on-screen. Oversharpened images can exhibit halos or visible noise, so proceed conservatively.

The aim of capture sharpening is to get the image to look pleasingly sharp on-screen. Oversharpened images can exhibit halos or visible noise, so proceed conservatively. To help you make adjustments carefully, in Lightroom, you can use the Alt/Option key to display a monochrome preview as you move the sliders, which more clearly shows the effects, as they can be hard to see in the full-color image.

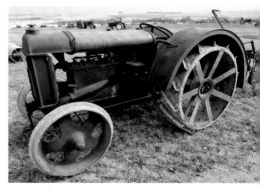

↑← **Straight from the camera**
This image of an old tractor has been reproduced straight from the Raw file, and although optimized for color and tone, no capture sharpening has been applied aside from the small amount automatically applied by Lightroom. You can see from the close-up view that the image is soft, and the texture of the metal is not rendered as sharply as it could be.

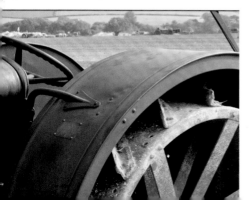

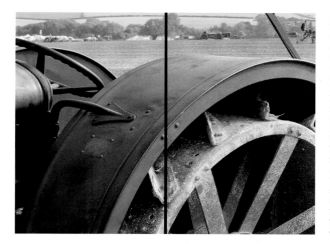

← **Amount**
Most Raw processors have one main sharpening slider that applies an overall sharpening effect. In the side-by-side comparison shown at left, Lightroom's Amount slider has been increased from its defaalt of 25, to 70 (left), and the maximum, 150 (on the right). It's clear that the maximum setting has oversharpened the image, as there are visible artifacts. At a setting of 70, the image is visibly sharper, and although the artifacts are less obvious, there is still some noise visible in the flatter areas of the image.

Here are some simple tips to help you make the proper adjustments:

Amount: Some images will require more or less, as this is certainly a case-by-case proposition, but you'll likely want to stay around 50 in most instances.

Radius: Set this too high, and edges will appear shadowy. You will rarely need to go above 1.5.

Detail: This sets the threshold of the size of detail to which sharpening is applied. Images can easily appear oversharpened if Detail is set too high, so it's best to keep this below 50.

Masking: Particularly with images containing areas of even tones, like a sky or a beach, hold down the Alt/Option key and adjust until those even-toned areas appear black. This will minimize any noise introduced with sharpening.

↓ **Sharpening complete**
The final image following capture sharpening is much crisper and shows more textural detail without the introduction of halos, noise, or other sharpening artifacts. This image is now ready for further post-production work, if necessary.

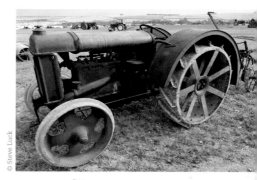

Noise Reduction

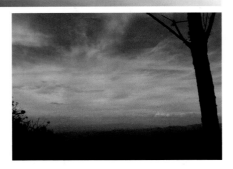

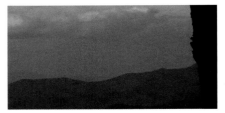

↑ Too small to notice
Printed at this small size, the noise in this image may not be particularly visible (and it's worth bearing in mind that some print processes are very forgiving). However, the detail shown above clearly reveals there is significant luminance and color noise present.

Noise manifests itself as ugly-looking clumps of pixels and a graininess that is particularly apparent in larger areas of a single, flat tone. It's also more prevalent in shadow regions, and the problem is exacerbated at high ISOs. There are two principal types of noise: luminance and chroma (or color). Luminance noise is likened to the static you see on an old television station with poor reception—it is grainy and, if particularly bad, may appear as vertical or horizontal stripes (or bands) across darker areas of the frame. Chroma noise, on the other hand, appears as discolored blotches, and is usually more unnatural looking (and therefore more important to reduce).

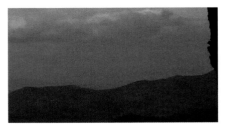

↑ Chroma vs luminance
With Lightroom and Capture One, you have the option of tackling either the luminance or color noise individually, using the relevant sliders. Other Raw processors reduce both types of noise at once. If you have the option, you may find dealing with color noise first makes it easier to judge the more subjective task of luminance noise reduction. Here, the Lightroom Noise Reduction Color slider was set to 50.

With many Raw processors the noise controls are located near the sharpening commands. This makes perfect sense, as the more you sharpen an image, the noisier it becomes. As with sharpening, noise reduction has become increasingly sophisticated and effective as software algorithms have evolved. Even with the noisiest images, today you can often expect to end up with a usable image, depending on the size of your final output.

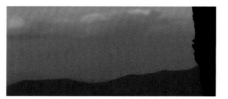

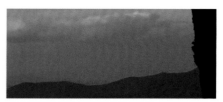

↑ **Not-so-fantastic plastic**
Having dealt with the chroma noise, it's time to look at reducing the luminance noise. It's tempting when reviewing an image at 100% to set a noise reduction value that eradicates the noise altogether. However, this will result in an unrealistic, plastic-looking image (seen above).

↑ **A touch of texture**
You want to retain some of the luminance noise as it gives the image an essential photographic textural quality. Here, the Luminance slider was set to 27, and the Detail to 85. The Detail slider provides a good way of fine-tuning the amount of noise left in the image.

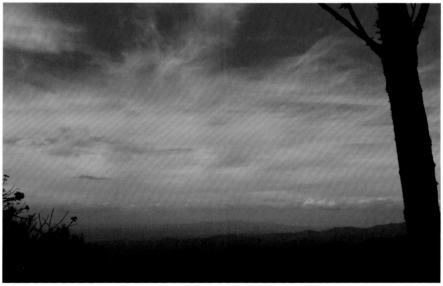

© Rebecca Shipkosky

↑ **Ready for output**
The finished image retains enough detail without including any obvious or distracting areas of noise, and can be printed at a much larger size as a result.

Tone Curves

A tone curve is a visual representation of the relationship between the highlights, mid-tones, and shadows in an image. Tone curves appear in the form of a graph, in which the horizontal X-axis represents the original tonal values (or input), while the vertical Y-axis represents the adjustments made to the original values (or output).

Tone-curve commands are found in a number of applications, both in Raw processors such as Lightroom and in post-production programs such as Photoshop, Photoshop Elements, and PaintShop Pro.

Tone curves provide a powerful and versatile means of adjusting the entire range of tones present in an image by dragging points on the tone-curve line. Broadly speaking, the lower third of the line represents the shadows, the middle third reflects the mid-tones, and the upper third stands for the highlights. By default, the tone curve forms a straight diagonal line (because no adjustments have yet been made, so each input value on the X-axis corresponds exactly to its equivalent on the Y-axis). Adjusting the shape of the curve alters the relationship between the various tones in the image.

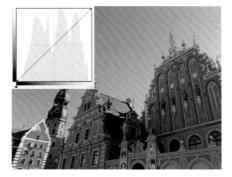

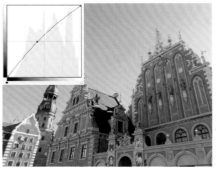

© Steve Luck

↑ **Histogram overlay**
This example of a default tone curve overlays the image's histogram—a graph representing the image's distribution of tonal values. Like the tone curve, the histogram moves along the horizontal X-axis from shadows, to mid-tones, to highlights.

↑ **Mid-tone brightening**
Clicking on the central point of the line and dragging it upward will brighten the entire image, but primarily the mid-tones. You pull up not only that particular segment of the curve, but also the rest of the curve, which is to say, Curves adjustments are global, affecting the entire image.

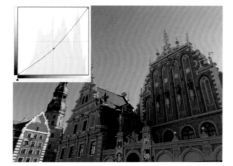

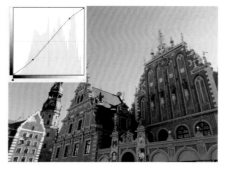

↑ **Mid-tone darkening**
Clicking on the central point of the line and dragging it down will darken the entire image. Again, it is primarily affecting the mid-tones, but all other areas are also affected, with the adjustment gradually becoming less significant as you move away from the mid-tone areas.

↑ **The S-curve**
A common curve adjustment is the "S-shape" curve. This is formed by clicking in the highlight region and moving the point up, while at the same time selecting a shadow point and moving it down. The resulting high-contrast image adds greater detail in the mid-tones, but loses detail in the highlights and shadows, which become brighter and darker, respectively.

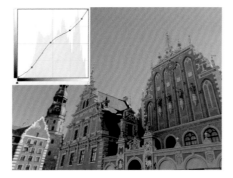

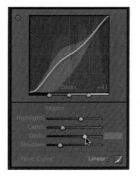

↑ **Multiple adjustments**
Here, a highlight point has been selected to darken the highlights in the top right of the image, while other points have been added to create extra contrast in the rest of the scene.

↑ **Lightroom's Tone Curve**
Here, this command also features sliders that can be used to alter the shape of the tone curve. This is helpful for users who aren't familiar with making adjustments via points on the tone curve.

Black & White Conversion

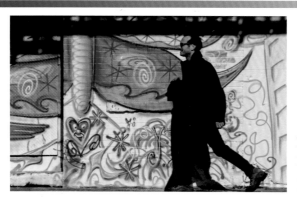

← **An appropriate subject for B&W**
This street shot of a man in profile passing in front of a colorful mural has an interesting composition, strong graphic qualities, and lots of different tones to play with.

Another positive aspect of shooting digitally, and in particular when using the Raw format, is that when reviewing your images you're likely to find a few that potentially lend themselves well to a monochrome treatment.

Raw processors utilize color sliders that allow you to adjust the tones in the black-and-white image once the basic conversion has been made.

Lightroom offers seemingly endless manual adjustments for making your new black-and-white photo pop. PaintShop Pro, on the other hand, has a wide variety of preset filters and film simulators for black-and-white conversion. Lightroom does include a few B&W presets, and you can purchase more, but PaintShop Pro wins out when it comes to its fun Instant Effects.

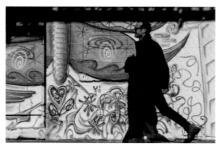

↑ **Initial conversion**
When you select the B&W mode in the Raw processor, the program uses the grayscale information in the red, green, and blue channels to create the black-and-white version. The Auto conversion is an accurate version of the color image, and is fine as such; but we can make more of an impact with some quick adjustments.

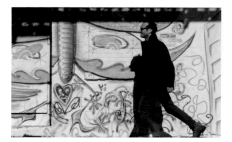

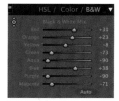

↑ Selective luminance adjustments
Between his dark coat, his shadow, and the
bold blue and red-orange on the mural behind
him, the main figure is getting a bit lost in the
dark. To enhance the contrast and make him
stand out more, we can selectively brighten
the colors behind him by using the Target
Adjustment (upper left corner of the B&W
panel above). Simply click on the colored area
and, while keeping the mouse button pressed,
move the mouse up slightly to brighten that
particular color (or balance of several colors).

↓ Conversion complete
With the main figure now adequately
pronounced, the rest of the colors are
darkened to add interest throughout the
rest of the frame. The finished shot has
a classic street-photography feel to it, and makes
an excellent graphic statement.

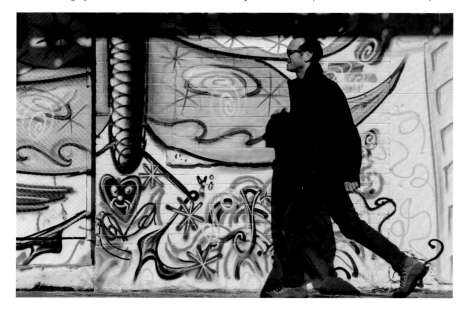

Convert to Black & White

Challenge

This challenge begins with finding a shot that has lots of potential for a black-and-white conversion. You're looking for something with contrasting colors—too much of the same tone, and all you'll end up with is a gray image. Once you make your selection, you still have a lot of options in terms of how to render your subject in grayscale. If it's a portrait, you probably don't want to push your contrast too hard, and you'll want to keep your color sliders relatively close to each other. On the other hand, if you're going for a more dramatic look, see how far apart you can spread your tones in various parts of the frame for a final image that delivers a big impact.

↓ **Mountain vista**
The bold, blue sky cast against the white snow, with foreground shadows in the river, all come together to make this a color shot with great B&W potential. The initial conversion, set to Auto, is quite conservative, resulting in a mostly gray image that doesn't really inspire. To add drama, the tones are pushed farther apart, upping the contrast considerably.

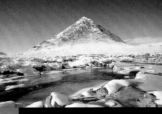

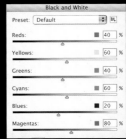

Black and White		
Preset: Default		
Reds:	■	40 %
Yellows:		60 %
Greens:	■	40 %
Cyans:	■	60 %
Blues:	■	20 %
Magentas:	■	80 %

Challenge Checklist

→ Start by using your processing program's automatic conversion, just to set a baseline from which to explore other possibilities. You may also experiment with some of the presets.

→ Contrast is the name of the game, and you will have to decide not only how much or how little, but also where you want your contrast, and which tones best play off each other in grayscale.

→ Remember that you can specify colors to adjust by clicking and holding on that area of the frame, then sliding your mouse up or down to make your luminance adjustments.

↓ **Dark skies, bright snow** The high-contrast final image, with the blue skies pulled into almost pure black, contrasting strongly with the bright whites of the landscape but complementing the foreground shadows, is bold, impactful, and effective.

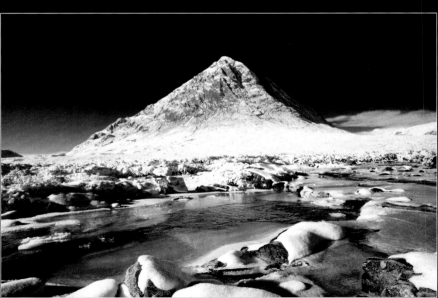

Levels in Post-Production

Levels is one of the key ways to adjust overall tone. Although it isn't as versatile as Curves, the Levels dialog is still one of the first places to go when post-processing an image (particularly if it hasn't been through Raw-processing).

The Levels command is centered around the histogram. Histograms are graphical representations of the tones in the image. Running along the horizontal (X) axis are the tonal variations ranging from black at the left to white at the right, while the vertical (Y) axis represents the number of pixels with a specific tone. This is an excellent way to quickly judge an image's tonal distribution, which is why histograms are available to view on almost all digital cameras, and why they are a key reference in processing. The main function of an initial Levels adjustment is to set the black and white points, in other words to ensure that there are a good number of both true black and true white pixels. This, in turn, ensures that there are a full range of tones in the image. This can also be done in Raw processing using the Blacks and Whites sliders.

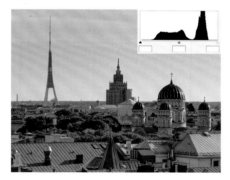

↑ **Low-contrast original**
This image was shot under diffused natural lighting and the overall tones are flat and gray. The lack of contrast is clear to see in the accompanying histogram, which is displayed when you call up the Levels command. There are almost no pixels recorded at either the dark shadows (left) or bright highlights (right).

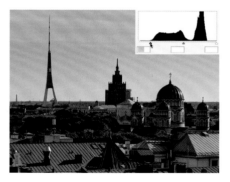

↑ **Setting the black point**
Here we've clicked on the Black Point slider and moved it right to align with the left-hand group of pixels, darkening the image. Notice that the central Gray Point slider moves relative to the black slider. This indicates that the mid-tones are adjusting in proportion. If you notice a color cast in the deep shadows, go to the channel of that color in Levels. If the pixels are not closed up to the left, dragging in the Black Point slider for that channel only will neutralize the cast.

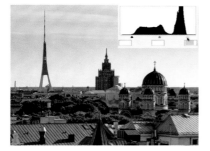

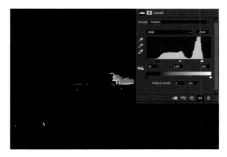

↑ Setting the white point
The next step is to repeat the process, but this time with the White Point slider at the right of the histogram. Drag the slider left until it sits under the group of pixels at the right of the histogram.

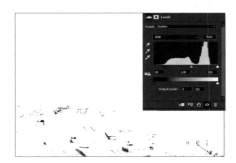

↗ → Show clipping
Pressing the Alt or Option key while you slide the histogram sliders will display the portions of the image where highlights (top) and shadows (bottom) are clipping.

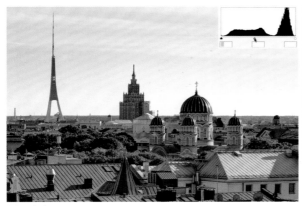

← Mid-tone adjustment
Although the image now has a full range of tones from white to black, the mid-tones are a little dark. This is easily addressed by moving the midpoint or gray slider left toward the black point so that more of the mid-toned pixels are grouped at the white end of the scale. This has the effect of brightening the image. Moving the midpoint slider to the right would have the effect of darkening the mid-tones in the image.

Color Adjustment in Post-Production

Color changes in post-production are made in much the same way as they are in Raw processors, in that colors are specified by their hue and saturation, as well as lightness (although this is called luminance in Raw processors). In addition to being able to adjust all the colors at once (for, say, an overall saturation increase), post-production programs also allow you to adjust individual colors.

Where Raw processors and post-processing software can differ is that the former use a Luminance slider while the latter a Lightness slider. This may sound a trivial difference, but it is important. Reducing the Lightness value of a specific color in Photoshop, for example, will also desaturate the color rather than just darken it. To darken a color in Photoshop without desaturating it you may need to experiment with all three sliders to get the result you want—for example, decreasing Lightness while compensating with a saturation boost.

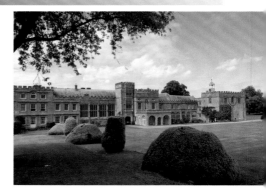

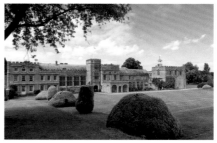

↗ Fresh from Levels, but lacking in color
This image of a former medieval monastery, Forde Abbey, England, has been tonally optimized using the black and white points in the Levels dialog, but the colors still look dull.

→ Global saturation boost
Using the Hue/Saturation command to increase all the colors (Master) has definitely given the image a color boost, but the sky still appears a little washed out.

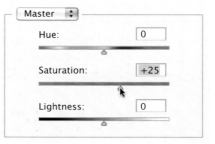

Master	
Hue:	0
Saturation:	+25
Lightness:	0

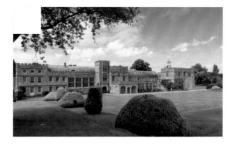

Blues

Hue: 0

Saturation: +52

Lightness: −62

Yellows

Hue: 0

Saturation: +17

Lightness: 0

↑ Selective saturation boost
To increase saturation in the sky only, select Blues from the pull-down menu and bump up the saturation until you're happy. It's easy to overdo blue skies, so use preview to switch between the original and adjusted preview to gauge its effect.

← Add a touch of sunshine
Although this image was shot at the height of summer, that isn't particularly apparent. To add some warmth to the image, try increasing saturation levels in the Yellows.

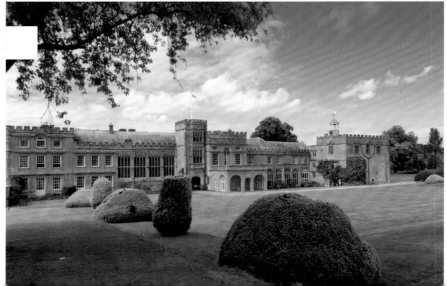

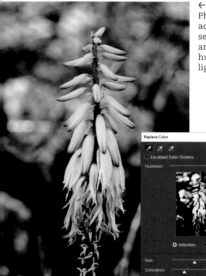

← Replace Color

Photoshop's Replace Color adjustment allows you to select a color in an image and change it to a different hue, saturation, and lightness.

↙↓ Fuzziness

Fuzziness sets the threshold for the Replace color mask; or to put it another way, how wide a range around the original hue you want to replace. You can see in the mask preview that Photoshop detected some similar tones in the background, and compared to the original, the new photo's background is a little cooler as a result of having replaced some of the background yellow with the new green hue.

↗ Replace Color droppers

The first dropper allows you to select one hue, and it will locate that hue throughout the image, selecting it to be replaced. You can use the dropper with the + symbol to add more hues to your selection, and subtract using the one with the - symbol.

↗ → Replace Color sliders

Move the Hue slider to select a new color. Here, we selected a value of +13 to achieve the green you see in the new version of the image. Saturation controls the intensity of the new color. We set a negative value here, because the default of 0 was very unnatural-looking. And, Lightness determines the luminance, which we set to a slight negative value in order to get a pastel, springtime color.

© Rebecca Shipkosky

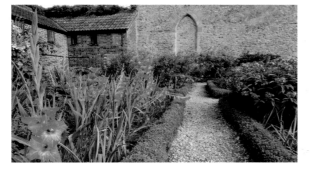

← Changing specific colors
As well as the Hue/Saturation control, which allows you to adjust all colors together or the primary colors individually, a number of programs have a Color Range or Color Changer control that allows you to be much more selective about the colors you want to adjust.

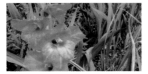

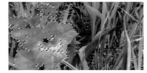

↑ Select a color
Find the Color Range/Color Changer command in your processing program, then use the Eyedropper tool to select the color you want to adjust. The dialog box allows you to set a higher or lower threshold to determine the extent of the selected color range. Only what appears white in the preview panel will be selected—the remaining black areas are left untouched. Above, you can see the dotted outline around the flowers, indicating the selection of that particular shade of red/orange.

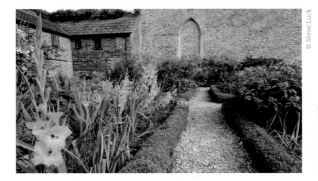

© Steve Luck

← Red-to-yellow shift
With the gladioli flowers on the left selected via the Color Range command, I then opened the Hue/Saturation window and shifted only their color from red to yellow.

Layers

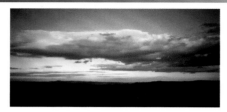

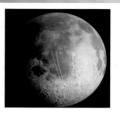

Layers have been a feature of post-processing programs since 1994. These powerful tools allow you to create composite images made up of individual elements held on layers that can be "stacked" on top of each other, and which
can be moved, resized, tonally amended, and so on—independently of one another, but also merged when necessary. You can also use Layers to enhance a single image, with adjustments applied to duplicate layers of the original. In this way you can optimize an image while leaving the original untouched—though this function has largely been replaced by Adjustment Layers.

As nondestructive Raw-processing controls have grown increasingly more versatile, particularly in terms of the localized adjustments that you can now make with them, in some ways Layers have become less significant, at least in terms of "standard" photographic image processing. However, if you're looking to combine images to create

↑ **Beginning with two distinct images**
Using these two shots—one skyscape of dusk over the Catskill mountains, the other a NASA model of the moon—we can make a simple layer-based montage to show how layers work and interact with one another.

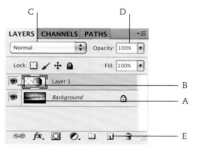

A   Layer thumbnail and name
B   Visibility eye
C   Blending mode
D   Opacity slider
E   Controls for adding new layers, deleting layers, adding effects, and creating layers masks

a montage, for example, or replace one element of a photo with that from another, or add text or special effects, it's essential that you know how Layers work.

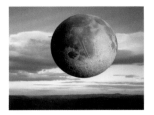 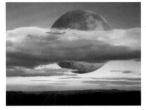 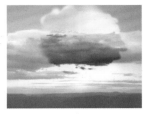

↑ **Place moon on top**
The first step is to make a selection of only the moon (dropping out the surrounding black) and place it in its own layer on top of the background. Then the moon is resized and positioned over the clouds at the right spot. The skyscape is also flipped horizontally for better composition.

↑ **Layer reversal**
Next, switch the layers to bring the clouds forward, and blend the two layers to weaken the moon.

↑ **Touch-up**
The cloud background is then duplicated and selectively brushed to strengthen the clouds until they appear to overlap perfectly.

↓ **Massive moon**
By combining these shots using layers, we're able to achieve a surrealistic shot of an enormous moon on the horizon. These same blending techniques are applicable to a wide range of potential composites.

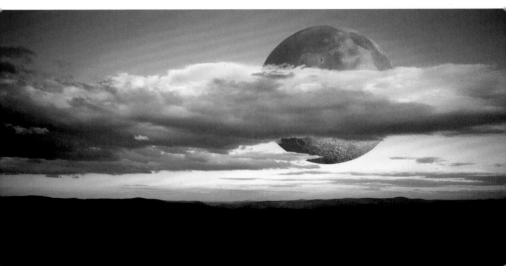

Adjustment Layers

Just as layers can be thought of as comprising individual image components that combine together to make up the composite image, so adjustment layers can be considered as comprising individual image adjustments that together create the finished image. And just as layers are independent of one another and can be amended at any time during the creation of the composite image, so too are adjustment layers.

Although there are many similarities between layers and adjustment layers, they differ in one important respect: Layers contain image objects made up of actual pixels, just as in any digital image, whereas adjustment layers don't contain any pixels; instead they comprise the information that shows how the image will look when the adjustment is applied. The adjustment can be anything from a Levels or Curves command, to a Hue/Saturation boost, to a Dodge or Burn. This means that you can make and view any number of adjustments to the original image without altering the image itself. In this respect, adjustment layers are comparable to the nondestructive adjustments made during Raw processing.

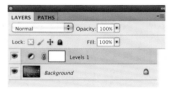

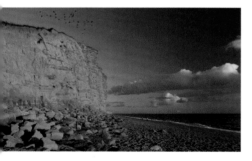

↑ **Sandstone cliffs**
This image of a coast in southern England has potentially strong colors, an attractive sky, and some pleasing graphic qualities. However, it's underexposed, lacks contrast, and the colors are initially a little dull.

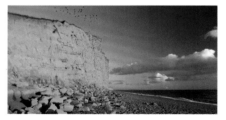

↑ **Levels adjustment with an adjustment layer**
When you create a new adjustment layer (Layer > New Adjustment Layer) you'll be presented with the corresponding dialog. Here, we've created a new Levels adjustment layer to set the black and white points; the Levels adjustment layer will appear as a new layer in the Layers palette (above top).

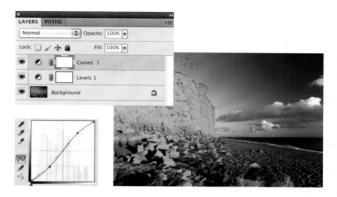

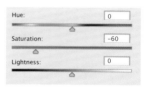

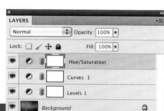

← **A second layer for contrast**

The next step is to add contrast by creating a Curves adjustment layer, and setting a characteristic "S" curve. Adjustment layers behave just like normal layers; you can use the visibility eye to gauge its effect, and even use the Opacity slider to alter the strength of the adjustment.

← **Finishing touches**

In our example, the last adjustment layer added was Hue/Saturation. In the Hue/Saturation dialog, I selected Red and reduced the Saturation setting; I then increased the Blue saturation. To finish, I double-clicked the Levels layer to bring up that dialog, and moved the midpoint slider to the left to brighten the mid-tones.

© Steve Luck

Blending

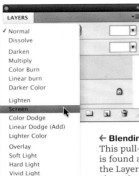

Blending modes are another powerful feature associated with layers. They offer numerous ways layers can interact with one another based on the color and luminance values present in the images.

There are a variety of blending modes, and they have a vast number of photographic uses, too many to go into detail here; but the most useful are those that help to control and amend exposure and contrast. It's certainly worth spending time applying each blending mode to a couple of images to get a feel for what each does.

← **Blending mode**
This pull-down menu is found at the top of the Layers palette in Photoshop.

⊻ Uneven underexposure
This image is underexposed, but more so at the bottom than the lighter sky at the top—a common photographic scenario. Increasing overall brightness using a Levels command would improve the exposure at ground level but result in a washed out or even overexposed sky.

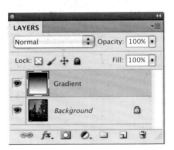

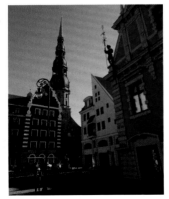

↑ **Gradient layer**
To address the exposure issue, create a new layer and apply a black/white gradient from top to bottom. With the blending mode set to the default Normal mode in the Layers palette, all you'll see on screen is the gradient.

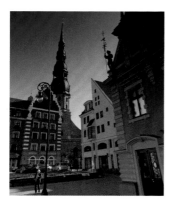

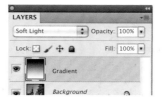

← Blend in the gradient

If, however, you change the blending mode to Soft Light, the background image will appear, but you'll see that it has been altered by the gradient layer. The black of the gradient renders the top of the image darker, while the whiter area of the gradient renders the bottom of the image lighter—basically mimicking the look of a graduated neutral density filter.

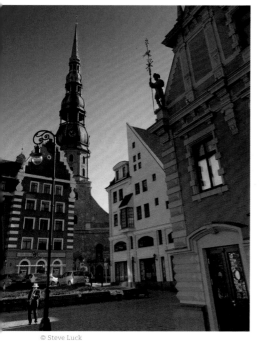

© Steve Luck

← Fine adjustment

Although the street level is now much lighter and the sky is darker, there are elements at the top of the image, the building and spire, for example, that need to revert to the original exposure. To do this, add a layer mask to the Gradient layer and paint out the dark gradient. We can also reduce the effect of the gradient by reducing its opacity using the Opacity slider.

Removing Unwanted Objects

Along with making selections and cut-outs, removing unwanted objects from photos is another common post-production task.

There are innumerable reasons why you might want to delete objects from a photo, whether it's a sign emerging from someone's head or, as is the case here, cables running in front of a building.

Although there are ever-more sophisticated cloning tools and algorithms available, such as Photoshop's Content-Aware option (which is certainly worth trying), you're still likely to have to turn to manual cloning at some point to get the precise result you want.

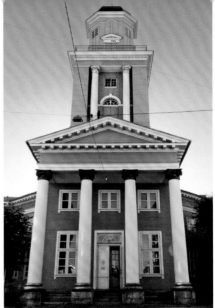

© Steve Luck

↑ Cluttered with cables
In this example, we're going to use a variety of tools to remove the cables and lamp from this otherwise attractive image of a church.

← Healing brushes
If you have a healing brush option, it's certainly worth trying it where you can. Photoshop has two healing brushes: the Spot Healing Brush, which automatically attempts to replace the selected object with pixels of a similar color and brightness value located nearby; and the standard Healing Brush. With the latter you have to sample a source before the tool works.

← Spot Healing Brush
With Content-Aware set in the Options bar, this has done a good job of replacing the cables in the sky, but look closely at the side of the building and you'll see that the tool has created two darkly colored blurred areas, where the cables pass in front of the building.

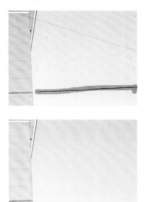

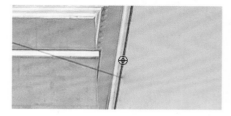 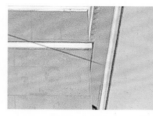

↑ Clone Stamp

As the area that we need to fix is uniformly patterned, we can't use any auto healing options. Instead, we turn to the Clone Stamp tool, and sample the edge of the building by holding down the Alt/Opt key.

↑ Follow the edge

With the area sampled, simply click on the affected region, ensure it's aligned accurately, and replace it with the unaffected area that we cloned earlier. The Clone Stamp tool works best with a soft brush—a hard brush may result in visible edges. It's also worth experimenting with the Opacity setting in the Tool Options bar. A setting of around 50% means you have to click a few times for the cloning to complete, but it does afford a level of control.

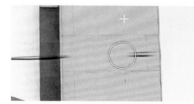

← Keep it aligned

Keep the Clone tool on the default Aligned option. This ensures the source point moves with the brush as you clone over affected areas.

← Easy cleanup

If you're cloning straight objects, such as this cable, select a source point as usual, click to clone away the cable, but hold down the Shift key. Click at the end of the cable and the tool will automatically replace the entire length of cable.

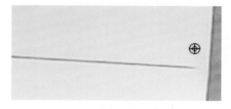

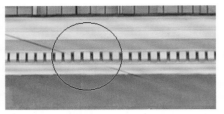

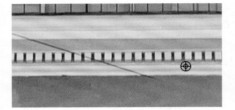

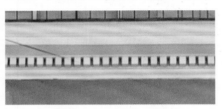

↑ Larger brushes for faster work
Don't be afraid to increase the size of the
Clone Stamp tool brush when cloning regularly
patterned areas. As long as the alignment
is true, the cloning will look natural.

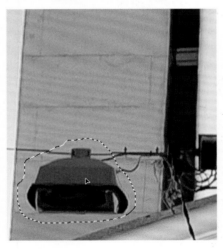

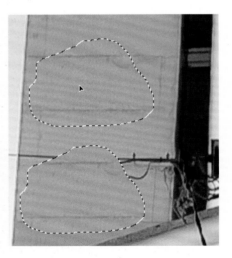

↑ The Patch tool
There are number of ways you could remove
this lamp. Photoshop's Content-Aware Fill option
would do a good job, but here we're using the
Patch tool. In Source mode, make a selection of

the lamp, then move the selection to a source
area and release the mouse. The tool will
automatically use the source area to replace the
lamp. When replacing a large object in one go,
you'll need to tidy up after with the Clone Stamp.

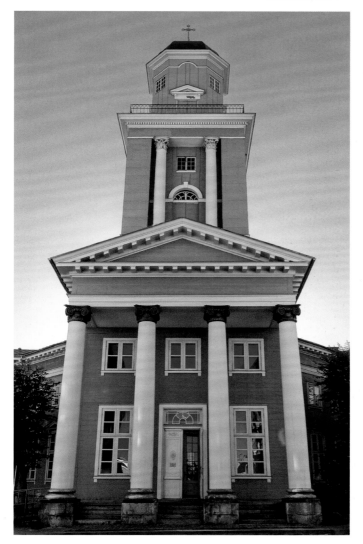

← **Uncluttered**
The finished image,
free of distracting
and ugly cables.

Panoramas & Stitching

Creating panoramas has never been so straightforward as it is today. In fact, with the sophisticated stitching software that's now available, pretty much the whole process is taken care of automatically once you have the source images. There are, however, some important rules to remember when shooting panoramas. First, use manual exposure when shooting your source images to ensure consistent exposure throughout the series. Second, it pays to focus manually, so that the camera doesn't inadvertently autofocus on some close-up object as you're panning round. Finally, to be safe, use the most appropriate white balance preset for the conditions under which you're shooting rather than relying on auto white balance. Again, this ensures consistency. (Yes, this is adjustable as long as you're shooting Raw, but it does simplify the process.) If your camera has a Panorama shooting mode, it may implement these settings on its own.

Using a tripod will help you ensure the individual source images align, but most of today's software is powerful enough to identify features to create an accurate alignment even if the source images aren't perfectly aligned.

→ Photomerge

In Lightroom and Photoshop's Photomerge screen, you're given six layout options: Auto is almost always the best choice, and will analyze the constituent photos to select either Perspective, Cylindrical, or Spherical. Perspective select one photo as the center of the image, then stretches the other images around it. Cylindrical evenly skews the images as if they were lining the inside of a cylinder—best for very wide panos. Spherical maps the images inside a sphere for 360-degree photography. Collage and reposition do not stretch or skew the images at all—Collage changes only rotation or scale, and Reposition only the alignment.

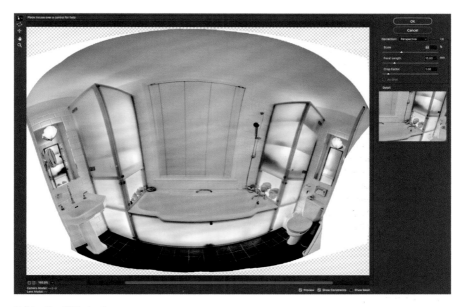

↑ **Adaptive Wide Angle**

Photoshop's algorithms cope very well when the camera-to-subject distance of your constituent shots is relatively high, but in close quarters— as in this hotel bathroom—it can succeed in stitching the content together but completely loses the perspective. This is when the Adaptive Wide Angle tool comes into play: At the top left, you'll find the regular constraint tool. Draw a line across your photo with this while holding shift down, and the photo will morph in order to pull other elements in the frame to make that a straight line. You can draw as many of these contraint lines as you need. You can also build a more complex shape using the Polygon Contraint Tool, second from the top on the left.

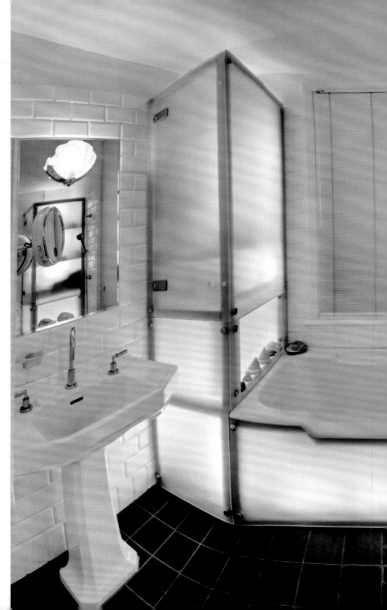

→ Finished result
Setting all the various constraints can be quite time-consuming, based on the complexity of the distortion, but fortunately you can use a trial-and-error approach, as you're given an immediate preview of each effect as you apply it. As you can see from the final image here, extreme panoramas like this will still have distortion evident—just look at the tiles curving away toward the edges. It's a natural effect of transposing a three-dimensional space onto two dimensions. But as long as distortion is minimized in the key elements of the photo, the eye accepts the representation.

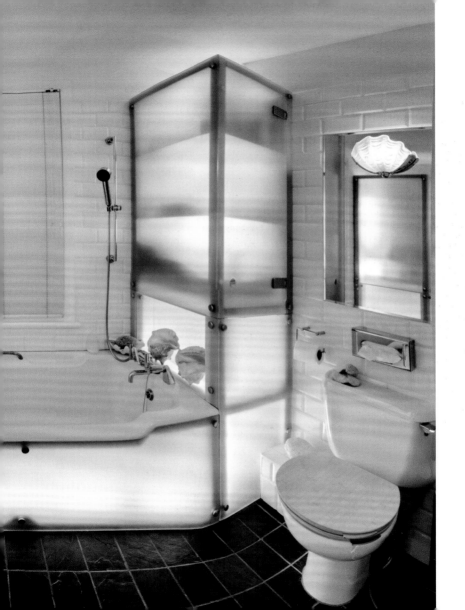

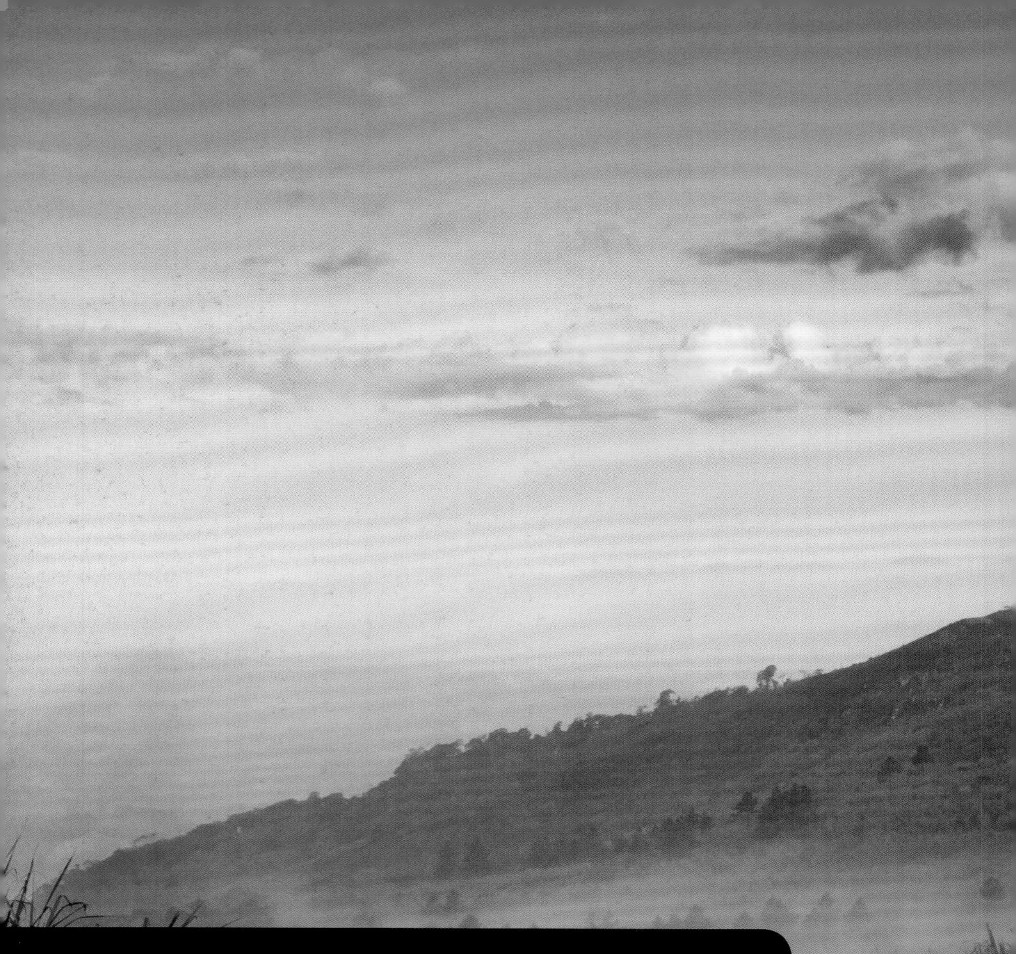

REFERENCES | Glossary & Index

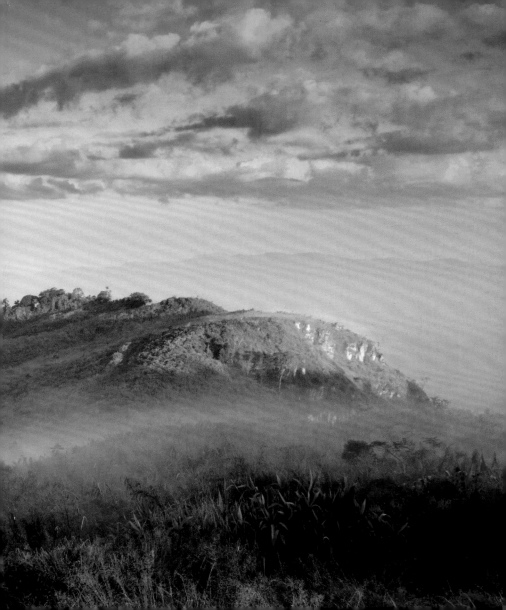

Glossary

A Aperture priority mode, as indicated by some camera manufacturers.

additive primary colors The three colors red, blue, and green, which can be combined to create any other color. When superimposed on each other they produce white.

algorithm Mathematical procedure that allows the step-by-step solution of a problem.

aliasing The jagged appearance of diagonal lines in an image, caused by the square shape of pixels.

ambient light Environmental light, for example daylight and light from normal domestic fittings.

angle of view Essentially what your camera is able to "see," from wide to telephoto.

anti-aliasing The smoothing of jagged edges on diagonal lines created in an imaging program, by giving intermediate values to pixels between the steps.

aperture The opening behind your lens that allows light to pass through it and reach the sensor.

Aperture priority A camera setting that allows you to choose the aperture while the camera selects the appropriate shutter speed to ensure a good exposure. Some camera manufacturers indicate it with A, others with Av.

application (program) Software designed to make the computer perform a specific task. So, image-processing is an application, as is word-processing. System software, however, is not an application, as it controls the running of the computer.

artifact A flaw in a digital image.

artificial light Photographer-supplied light, usually from a flash.

aspect ratio The ratio of the height to the width of an image, screen, or page.

autofocus When the camera lens adjusts the focus to ensure a sharp image.

Av Aperture value, the term used to indicate aperture priority mode on some cameras.

axis lighting Light aimed at the subject from close to the camera's lens.

background The part of the scene behind the subject.

backlighting The result of shooting with a light source, natural or artificial, behind the subject to create a silhouette or edge-light effect.

backup A copy of either a file or a program, for safety reasons, in case the original becomes damaged or lost. The correct procedure for making backups is on a regular basis, while spending less time making each one than it would take to redo the work lost.

Balance What you want to achieve with your composition: A sense of equilibrium in an image achieved by the considered placement or use of color, light, and subject matter.

ballast The power pack unit for an HMI light which provides a high initial voltage.

banding Unwanted effect in a tone or color gradient in which bands appear instead of a smooth transition. It can be corrected by higher resolution and more steps, and by adding noise to confuse that part of the image.

barn doors The adjustable flaps on studio lighting equipment which can be used to control the beam emitted.

Barrel distortion The effect when straight lines appear to curve, as if they've been stretched over a sphere or barrel, seen with wide-angle and fish-eye lenses.

Bézier curve A curve described by a mathematical formula. In practice, it is produced by manipulating control handles on a line that is partly held in place by anchor points.

bit (binary digit) The basic data unit of binary computing. See also byte

bit depth The number of bits of color data for each pixel in a digital image. A photographic-quality image needs eight bits for each of the red, green, and blue channels, making for a bit depth of 24.

bitmap (bitmapped image) Image composed of a pattern of pixels, as opposed to a mathematically defined object (an object-oriented image). The more pixels used for one image, the higher its resolution. This is the normal form of a scanned photograph.

Blown-out Areas of white in an image where it has been overexposed.

BMP Image file format for bitmapped images used in Windows. Supports RGB, indexed color, grayscale and bitmap.

boom A support arm for attaching and assembling studio lighting setups.

bracketing A method of ensuring a correctly exposed photograph by taking three shots; one with the supposed correct exposure, one slightly underexposed, and one slightly overexposed.

brightness The level of light intensity. One of the three dimensions of color. See also hue and saturation

buffer An area of temporary data storage, normally used to absorb differences in the speed of operation between devices. For instance, a file can usually be sent to an output device, such as a printer, faster than that device can work. A buffer stores the data so that the main program can continue operating.

byte Eight bits—the basic data unit of desktop computing. 1,024 bytes equals one kilobyte (KB), 1,024 kilobytes equals one megabyte (MB), and 1,024 megabytes equals one gigabyte (GB). See also bit

cache An area of information storage set aside to keep frequently needed data readily available. This allocation speeds up operation.

calibration The process of adjusting a device, such as a monitor, so that it works consistently with others, such as scanners or printers.

candela Measure of the brightness of a light source itself.

channel Part of an image as stored in the computer; similar to a layer. Commonly, a color image will have a channel allocated to each primary color (e.g. RGB) and sometimes one or more for a mask or other effects.

Chiaroscuro Literally "light/dark," the interplay of light and shadow to create an image.

clipboard Part of the memory used to store an item temporarily when being copied or moved. See also cut-and-paste

cloning In an image-processing program, the process of duplicating pixels from one part of an image to another.

CMYK (Cyan, Magenta, Yellow, Key) The four process colors used for printing, including black (key).

color depth See *bit depth*

color gamut The range of color that can be produced by an output device, such as a printer, a monitor, or a film recorder.

color model A system for describing the color gamut, such as RGB, CMYK, HSB, and lab.

color temperature A way of describing the color differences in light, measured in Kelvins and using a scale that ranges from dull red (1900 K), through orange, to yellow, white, and blue (10,000 K).

color separation The process of separating an image into the process colors cyan, magenta, yellow, and black (CMYK), in preparation for printing.

color space A model for plotting the hue, brightness, and saturation of color.

color wheel A diagram that shows the relationships between different colors.

Complementary color Colors that sit opposite each other on the color wheel, for example green and red.

compression Technique for reducing the amount of space that a file occupies, by removing redundant data.

compression Technique for reducing the amount of space that a file occupies, by removing redundant data. There are two kinds of compression: standard and lossy. While the first simply uses different, more processor-intensive routines to store data than the standard file formats (see LZW), the latter actually discards some data from the image. The best known lossy compression system is JPEG, which allows the user to choose how much data is lost as the file is saved.

contrast The range of tones across an image, from bright highlights to dark shadows.

crop The framing of a scene, either through the viewfinder or in post-production.

cropping The process of removing unwanted areas of an image, leaving behind the most significant elements.

cursor Symbol with which the user selects and draws on-screen.

cut-and-paste Procedure in graphics for deleting part of one image and copying it into another.

default The standard setting or action used by a computer unless deliberately changed by the operator.

depth of field The distance in front of and behind the point of focus in a photograph, in which the scene remains in acceptable sharp focus.

desktop The background area of the computer screen on which icons and windows appear.

desktop computer Computer small enough to fit on a normal desk. The two most common types are the PC and Macintosh.

dialog box An on-screen window, part of a program, for entering settings to complete a procedure.

diffusion The scattering of light by a material, resulting in a softening of the light and of any shadows cast. Diffusion occurs in nature through mist and cloud cover, and can also be simulated using diffusion sheets and soft-boxes.

digital A way of representing data as a number of distinct units. A digital image needs a very large number of units so that it appears as a continuous-tone image to the eye; when it is displayed these are in the form of pixels.

digital zoom Many cheaper cameras offer a digital zoom function. This simply crops from the center of the image and scales the image up using processing algorithms (the same effect can be achieved in an image editor later). Unlike a zoom lens, or optical zoom, the effective resolution is reduced as the zoom level increases; 2× digital zoom uses ¼ of the image sensor area, 3× uses 1/9, and so on.

download Sending a data file from the computer to another device, such as a printer. More commonly, this has come to mean taking a file from the Internet or remote server and putting it onto the desktop computer. See also *upload*

dpi (dots-per-inch) A measure of resolution in halftone printing. See also ppi.

drag Moving an icon or a selected image across the screen, normally by moving the mouse while keeping its button pressed.

drag-and-drop Moving an icon from one file to another by means of dragging and then dropping it at its destination by releasing the mouse button. See also drag.

dynamic range The range of tones that an imaging device can distinguish, measured as the difference between its dmin and dmax. It is affected by the sensitivity of the hardware and by the bit depth.

edge lighting Light that hits the subject from behind and slightly to one side, creating flare or a bright "rim lighting" effect around the edges of the subject.

Ev Exposure Value, how the brightness of a scene is measured.

exposure How much light reaches a camera's sensor.

fade-out The extent of any graduated effect, such as blur or feather. With an airbrush tool, for example, the fade-out is the softness of the edges as you spray.

fast A term used to describe a lens with a large maximum aperture, usually f2.8 or wider.

feathering In image-processing, the fading of the edge of an image or selection.

file format The method of writing and storing a digital image. Formats commonly used for photographs include TIFF, PICT, BMP, and JPEG (the latter is also a means of compression).

fill flash A technique that uses the on-camera flash or an external flash in combination with natural or ambient light to reveal detail in shadows.

fill light An additional light used to supplement the main light source. Fill can be provided by a separate unit or a reflector.

filter (1) A thin sheet of transparent material placed over a camera lens or light source to modify the quality or color of the light passing through. **(2)** A feature in an image-processing application that alters or transforms selected pixels for some kind of visual effect. Some filters, such as Diffuse, produce the same effect as the optical filters used in photography after which they are named; others create effects unique to electronic imaging.

flash meter A light meter especially designed to verify exposure in flash photography. It does this by recording values from the moment of a test flash, rather than simply measuring the "live" light level.

fluorescent light Domestic lighting that doesn't get hot, but gives blue/green color casts.

flag Something used to partially block a light source to control the amount of light that falls on the subject.

focal length The distance between the mid-point of the plane of the lens and the sensor or film in a camera.

focal point The center of interest in a photograph, the area where you focus your camera.

focal range The range over which a camera or lens is able to focus on a subject (for example, 0.5m to Infinity).

focus (1) The optical state where the light rays converge on the film or imaging sensor to produce the sharpest possible image. **(2)** When you adjust the lens or camera to ensure that your image is as sharp as possible.

foreground The part of the scene between the camera and the subject.

fringe In image-processing, an unwanted border effect to a selection, where the pixels combine some of the colors inside the selection and some from the background.

frontal light Light that hits the subject from behind the camera, creating bright, high-contrast images, but with flat shadows and less relief.

f-stop The measurement of the variable opening in a lens (the aperture) that allows light to pass through it and reach the sensor or film. f1.4 is a large, or "fast" aperture; f22 is a small aperture.

gamma A measure of the contrast of an image, expressed as the steepness of the characteristic curve of an image.

GB (GigaByte) Approximately one billion bytes (actually 1,073,741,824).

global correction Color correction applied to the entire image.

gobo Anything used to block or partially block light, particularly when it contributes a shape or texture to the light as it falls on the scene—much like a stencil.

golden hour The period after dawn and before dusk that offers a soft, golden light ideal for dramatic photography.

gradation The smooth blending of one tone or color into another, or from transparent to colored in a tint. A graduated lens filter, for instance, might be dark on one side, fading to clear on the other.

grayscale An image made up of a sequential series of 256 gray tones, covering the entire gamut between black and white.

GUI (Graphic User Interface) Screen display that uses icons and other graphic means to simplify using a computer. The Macintosh GUI was one of the reasons for Apple's original success in desktop computing.

halogen bulb Common in modern spotlighting, halogen lights use a tungsten filament surrounded by halogen gas, allowing it to burn hotter, longer and brighter.

haze The scattering of light by particles in the atmosphere, usually caused by fine dust, high humidity, or pollution. Haze makes a scene paler with distance, and softens the hard edges of sunlight.

hard disk, hard drive A sealed storage unit composed of one or more rigid disks that are coated with a magnetically sensitive surface, with the heads needed to read them. This can be installed inside the computer's housing (internal), or in a separate unit linked by a bus (external).

HDRI (High Dynamic Range Imaging) A method of combining digital images taken at different exposures to draw detail from areas which would traditionally have been over or under exposed. This effect is typically achieved using a Photoshop plugin, and HDRI images can contain significantly more information than can be rendered on screen or even percieved by the human eye.

high-key Low-contrast images that have a feeling of light airiness and positivity.

highlights Technically, the pure white parts of an image, but often it refers to the lightest areas of an image.

histogram A map of the distribution of tones in an image, arranged as a graph. The horizontal axis goes from the darkest tones to the lightest, while the vertical axis shows the number of pixels in that range.

HMI (Hydrargyrum Medium-arc Iodide) A lighting technology known as "daylight" since it provides light with a color temperature of around 5600 K.

honeycomb grid In lighting, a grid can be placed over a light to prevent light straying. The light can either travel through the grid in the correct direction, or will be absorbed by the walls of each cell in the honeycomb.

hot shoe An accessory fitting found on most digital and film SLR cameras and some high-end compact models, normally used to control an external flash unit. Depending on the model of camera, information to lighting attachments might be passed via the metal contacts of the shoe.

HSB (Hue, Saturation, Brightness) The three dimensions of color, and the standard color model used to adjust color in many image-processing applications.

hue The pure color defined by position on the color spectrum; what is generally meant by "color" in lay terms.

icon A symbol that appears on-screen to represent a tool, file, or some other unit of software.

image compression A digital procedure in which the file size of an image is reduced by discarding less important data.

image-processing program Software that makes it possible to enhance and alter a scanned image.

image file format The form in which an image is handled and stored electronically. There are many such formats, each developed by different manufacturers and with different advantages according to the type of image and how it is intended to be used. Some are more suitable than others for high-resolution images, or for object-oriented images, and so on.

incandescent lighting This strictly means light created by burning, referring to traditional filament bulbs. They are also know as hotlights, since they remain on and become very hot.

incident meter A standalone light-measuring instrument, distinct from the metering systems built into many cameras. These are used by hand to measure the light falling at a particular place, rather than (as the camera does) the light reflected off of a particular subject.

interface Circuit that enables two hardware devices to communicate. Also used for the screen display that allows the user to communicate with the computer. See also GUIinterpolation Bitmapping procedure used in resizing an image to maintain resolution. When the number of pixels is increased, interpolation fills in the gaps by comparing the values of adjacent pixels.

ISO An international standard rating for film speed and imaging sensor sensitivity, with the sensitivity increasing as the rating increases ISO 400 is twice as sensitive as ISO 200, and will produce a correct exposure with less light and/or a shorter exposure. However, higher ISOs tend to produce more grain and noise in the exposure, too.

JPEG (Joint Photographic Experts Group)
Pronounced "jay-peg," a system for compressing images, developed as an industry standard by the International Standards Organization. Compression ratios are typically between 10:1 and 20:1, although lossy (but not necessarily noticeable to the eye).

KB (KiloByte) Approximately one thousand bytes (actually 1,024).

kelvin Scientific measure of temperature based on absolute zero (simply take 273.15 from any temperature in Celsius to convert to kelvin). In photography measurements in kelvin refer to color temperature. Unlike other measures of temperature, the degrees symbol in not used.

landscape A photograph of a vista; the orientation of the frame so that the longer edges form the horizontal borders.

lasso A selection tool used to draw an outline around an area of the image.

layer One level of an image file, separate from the rest, allowing different elements to be edited separately.

LCD (Liquid Crystal Display) Flat screen display used in digital cameras and some monitors. A liquid-crystal solution held between two clear polarizing sheets is subject to an electrical current, which alters the alignment of the crystals so that they either pass or block the light.

leading line A line in an image that draws the eye to the subject.

lens A piece of glass with curved sides that allows you to focus and direct rays of light.

light pipe A clear plastic material that transmits like, like a prism or optical fiber.

light tent A tent-like structure, varying in size and material, used to diffuse light over a wider area for close-up shots.

lossless (lossy) Type of image compression in which no information is lost, and so most effective in images that have consistent areas of color and tone. For this reason, not so useful with a typical photograph.

Low-key High-contrast photographs, usually very dark in tone, that have a feeling of brooding.

lumens A measure of the light emitted by a lightsource, derived from candela.

luminaires A complete light unit, comprising an internal focusing mechanism and a fresnel lens. An example would be a focusing spot light. The name luminaires derives from the French, but is used by professional photographers across the world.

luminosity The brightness of a color, independent of the hue or saturation.

lux A scale for measuring illumination, derived from lumens. It is defined as one lumen per square meter, or the amount of light falling from a light source of one candela one metre from the subject.

macro (1) A photograph taken in extreme close-up, often of small things, for example insects. **(2)** A mode offered by some lenses and cameras that enables the lens or camera to focus in extreme close-up.

Manual An exposure mode that allows you to directly determine aperture and shutter speed to create the exposure that you want.

mask A grayscale template that hides part of an image. One of the most important tools in processing an image, it is used to make changes to a limited area. A mask is created by using one of the several selection tools in an image-processing program; these isolate a picture element from its surroundings, and this selection can then be moved or altered independently.

MB (MegaByte) Approximately one million bytes (actually 1,048,576).

megapixel (1) About one million pixels, also the term used to express the resolution of your camera's sensors. **(2)** A rating of resolution for a digital camera, directly related to the number of pixels forming or output by the CMOS or CCD sensor. The higher the megapixel rating, the higher the resolution of images created by the camera.

mid-tone The parts of an image that are approximately average in tone, falling midway between the highlights and shadows.

mode One of a number of alternative operating conditions for a program. For instance, in an image-processing program, color and grayscale are two possible modes.

modeling light A small light built into studio flash units which remains on continuously. It can be used to position the flash, approximating the light that will be cast by the flash.

monobloc An all-in-one flash unit with the controls and power supply built-in. Monoblocs can be synchronized together to create more elaborate lighting setups.

negative space Areas of a photograph that do not contain any subject matter.

neutral density filter A neutral color filter that absorbs light from different wavelengths without altering the overall color of an image, permitting longer exposures or wider apertures when there is too much available light.

noise (1) The graininess in images that appears as you increase the sensitivity of your sensor to light. **(2)** Random pattern of small spots on a digital image that are generally unwanted, caused by non-image-forming electrical signals.

normal lens A lens with a focal length between 40mm and 60mm.

object-oriented (image, program) Software technology using mathematical equations rather than pixels to describe an image element. Scalable, in contrast to bitmapped elements.

open flash The technique of leaving the shutter open and triggering the flash one or more times, perhaps from different positions in the scene.

orientation Vertical, horizontal, or somewhere in between: How you hold your camera.

Overexposure What happens when too much light reaches the sensor or film and a photograph is too bright with too many pure-white areas in the frame.

P Program mode, an autoexposure mode in which the camera chooses both the aperture and shutter speed, but you can manually change the relationship between these variables, and all other camera settings remain adjustable.

panning A photographic technique in which you move the camera in time with a subject in motion to create a image where the subject is sharp and the background is blurred.

panorama A wide view of a scene, usually a landscape.

PDF (Portable Document Format) An industry standard file type for page layouts including images. Can be compressed for Internet viewing or retain full press quality; in either case the software to view the files—Adobe Reader—is free.

peripheral An additional hardware device connected to and operated by the computer, such as a drive or printer.

perspective The phenomenon that allows images rendered in only two dimension, for example on paper, to appear as if they have depth.

photo-composition The traditional, non-electronic method of combining different picture elements into a single, new image, generally using physical film masks.

pixel The smallest units of a digital image, pixels are the square screen dots that make up a bitmapped picture. Each pixel carries a specific tone and color.

plugin In image-processing, software produced by a third party and intended to supplement a program's features or performance.

portrait A photograph of a person; the orientation of the frame so that the shorter edges form the horizontal borders.

post-production The adjustment of images after they have been recorded by the camera.

power pack The separate unit in flash lighting systems (other than monoblocks) which provides power to the lights.

ppi (pixels-per-inch) A measure of resolution for a bitmapped image. See also dpi.

prime lens A lens with a fixed focal length.

processor A silicon chip containing millions of micro-switches, designed for performing specific functions in a computer or digital camera (in which it converts the information captured by the sensor into an editable, viewable image file).

program A list of coded instructions that makes the computer perform a specific task. See also software.

RAID (Redundant Array of Independent Disks) A stack of hard disks that function as one, but with greater capacity.

RAM (Random Access Memory) The working memory of a computer, to which the central processing unit (cpu) has direct, immediate access.

Raw files A digital image format, known sometimes as the "digital negative," which preserves higher levels of color depth than traditional 8 bits per channel images. The image can then be adjusted in software—potentially by three f-stops—without loss of quality. The file also stores camera data including meter readings, aperture settings and more. In fact, most camera models create their own kind of proprietary Raw file format, though leading models are supported by software like Adobe Photoshop.

real-time The appearance of instant reaction on the screen to the commands that the user makes—that is, no appreciable time-lag in operations. This is particularly important when carrying out bitmap image-processing, such as when using a paint or clone tool.

reflector An object or material used to bounce light onto the subject, often softening and dispersing the light for a more attractive result.

resampling Changing the resolution of an image either by removing pixels (lowering resolution) or adding them by interpolation (increasing resolution).

resolution The level of detail in an image, measured in pixels (e.g. 1024 by 768 pixels), lines-per-inch (on a monitor) or dots-per-inch (in the halftone pattern produced by a printer, e.g. 1200 dpi).

RFS (Radio Frequency System) A technology used to control lights where control signals are passed by radio rather than cable. It has the advantage of not requiring line-of-sight between the transceiver and device.

RGB (Red, Green, Blue) The primary colors of the additive model, used in monitors and image-processing programs.

rim-lighting Light from the side and behind a subject which falls on the edge (hence rim) of the subject.

ring-flash A lighting device with a hole in the center so that the lens can be placed through it, resulting in shadow-free images.

rubber-stamp A paint tool in an image-processing program that is used to clone one selected area of the picture onto another. It allows painting with a texture rather than a single tone/color, and is particularly useful for extending complex textures such as vegetation, stone, and brickwork.

satellite In lighting, this is a parabolic dish designed to reflect and diffuse light.

saturation The intensity of a color or hue.

scrim A light, open-weave fabric, used to cover softboxes.

selection In image-processing, a part of an on-screen image that is chosen and defined by a border in preparation for manipulation or movement.

sensitivity How reactive a sensor, or film, is to light (see ISO).

sharp In focus, clear.

shutter The device inside a conventional camera that controls the length of time during which the recording medium (sensor) is exposed to light. Many digital cameras don't have a shutter, but the term is still used as shorthand to describe the electronic mechanism that controls the length of exposure for the imaging sensor.

Shutter priority A camera setting that allows you to control shutter speed, while the camera determines aperture to ensure a good exposure.

shutter speed The period of time for which the shutter remains open and allows light to reach the sensor or film.

side-lighting Light that hits the subject from the side, as opposed to the front or back.

silhouette The outline of a subject against a brighter background.

slow sync The technique of firing the flash in conjunction with a slow shutter speed (as in rear-curtain sync).

SLR (Single Lens Reflex) A camera that transmits the same image via a mirror to the film and viewfinder, ensuring that you get exactly what you see in terms of focus and composition.

snoot A tapered barrel attached to a lamp in order to concentrate the light emitted into a spotlight.

soft-box A studio lighting accessory consisting of a flexible box that attaches to a light source at one end and has an adjustable diffusion screen at the other, softening the light and any shadows cast by the subject.

software Programs that enable a computer to perform tasks, from its operating system to job-specific applications such as image-processing programs and third-party filters.

spot meter A specialized light meter, or function of the camera light meter, that takes an exposure reading for a precise area of a scene.

stop An increment of the measurement of aperture.

stop down When you reduce the size of the aperture, and increase depth of field.

stylus Penlike device used for drawing and selecting, instead of a mouse. Used with a graphics tablet.

subject The main focus of a photograph sync cord. The electronic cable used to connect camera and flash.

telephoto A photographic lens with a long focal length in excess of 70mm that enables distant objects to be enlarged. The drawbacks include a limited depth of field and angle of view. thumbnail Miniature on-screen representation of an image file.

TIFF (Tagged Image File Format) A file format for bitmapped images. It supports CMYK, RGB, and grayscale files with alpha channels, and lab, indexed-color, and it can use LZW lossless compression. It is now the most widely used standard for good-resolution digital photographic images.

tool A program specifically designed to produce a particular effect on-screen, activated by choosing an icon and using it as the cursor. In image-processing, many tools are the equivalents of traditional graphic ones, such as a paintbrush, pencil, or airbrush.

toolbox A set of programs available for the computer user, called tools, each of which creates a particular on-screen effect. See also tool

top lighting Lighting from above, useful in product photography since it removes reflections.

trackball An alternative input device to a mouse, used to move the cursor on-screen. Mechanically, it works as an upside-down mouse, with a ball embedded in a case or the keyboard.

tripod A three-legged device to stabilize a camera during a longer exposure, preventing camera shake.

TTL (Through The Lens) Describes metering systems that use the light passing through the lens to evaluate exposure details.

tungsten light Incandescent light, light from normal ceiling bulbs and standard lamps; it's usually warm in color.

Tv "Time value," the term used to indicate shutter priority mode on some cameras.

umbrella In photographic lighting umbrellas with reflective surfaces are used in conjunction with a light to diffuse the beam.

underexposure When too little light reaches the sensor or film and a photograph is too dark.

upgrade Either a new version of a program or an enhancement of hardware by addition.

upload To send computer files, images, etc. to another computer. See also download

USB (Universal Serial Bus) In recent years this has become the standard interface for attaching devices to the computer, from mice and keyboards to printers and cameras. It allows "hot-swapping," in that devices can be plugged and unplugged while the computer is still switched on.

USM (Unsharp Mask) A sharpening technique achieved by combining a slightly blurred negative version of an image with its original positive.

vapor discharge light A lighting technology common in stores and street lighting. It tends to produce color casts, especially the orange sodium vapor lights.

virtual memory The use of free space on a hard drive to act as temporary (but slow-to-access) memory.

White balance (1) The color balance of light that ensures white always looks white. **(2)** A digital camera control used to balance exposure and color settings for artificial lighting types.

wide-angle lens A lens with a focal length under 35mm.

WiFi A wireless connectivity standard, commonly used to connect computers to the Internet via a wireless modem or router.

window light A softbox, typically rectangular and suitably diffused.

workstation A computer, monitor, and its peripherals dedicated to a single use.

zoom A camera lens with an adjustable focal length, giving, in effect, a range of lenses in one. Drawbacks include a smaller maximum aperture and increased distortion over a prime lens (one with a fixed focal length).

zoom lens A lens with a range of variable focal lengths.

Index